Journey of a Starfish

My life across two continents

BABU RAMABADRAN

CO-AUTHOR: XIAOYU DUAN

INDIA • SINGAPORE • MALAYSIA

ISBN
Paperback 979-8-89415-955-3
Hardcase 979-8-89475-962-3

Dedication

I dedicate this book to the victims of COVID-19
all around the world.

Contents

Introduction

The year was 2014, and I was preoccupied with the idea of writing my story. It had been on my mind for some time. My colleague at the Federal Reserve, Xiaoyu Duan, encouraged me to write my story. Although I didn't know where or how to begin, Xiaoyu promised to help me. Together, we brainstormed an outline, starting with one-sentence ideas for each chapter, like my village, my family, and my friends. With these ideas in place, I could elaborate and develop each into readable chapters.

Xiaoyu and I met weekly during lunch hours to discuss the content in detail. I often came up short, writing only two to three pages, while Xiaoyu insisted on four to five. I went back to provide more details, but after several months, progress halted. Xiaoyu became a father and was pursuing his master's in screenwriting. Without his accountability, I became lazy and stopped writing. Nothing happened for another six to seven years.

My writing gained traction again during the COVID-19 pandemic when I had plenty of time at home. I met someone named Steve who promised to help me. Over the next three months, we met via Zoom, where I explained everything, and he took notes and asked questions. We set a date for Steve to deliver an introduction and a couple of chapters, but he never showed up. Despite my attempts to contact him, he vanished, taking the $1500 I had paid him as an initial payment. I was more upset about the book's lack of progress than the lost money.

Determined to bring Steve to justice, I filed a case in small claims court. Although the judge awarded the case to me, the court did not assist in collecting the funds. Frustrated and unwilling to spend more money and energy, I gave up and looked for other ways to finish the book.

When I ran into Xiaoyu and explained what had happened, he felt sorry for me and promised to help finish the book, despite being busy with his own screenwriting projects. We met regularly for over a year and finally completed the book by the end of 2023. It wasn't easy, but we persisted and worked tirelessly. Xiaoyu often had to beg, threaten, and yell at me to get me to work and finish the book. His persistence and dedication were commendable, and I am immensely proud of our accomplishment. I thank Xiaoyu deeply for helping me with the book.

I also want to thank my friend Kalirajan from my engineering school for recommending Notion Press. I was very impressed with their professionalism and quick responses. I appreciate their great work ethic and efficient turnaround time.

Lastly, I extend my heartfelt thanks to my friends and family for their immense support and encouragement throughout this writing process.

If you need to contact the author please use one of the following.

LinkedIn : https://www.linkedin.com/in/babu-ramabadran/

Email: baburam99@gmail.com

Prologue

It was March 4th, 2020. 8:29 am. I was about to enter a 1-on-1 video call with my boss.

I was a Senior Business Analyst at the Federal Reserve Bank of San Francisco—a position I had held for 11 years. Our group, known as STAR, which stands for Statistics and Reserves, was responsible for gathering information from financial institutions, creating reports, and sending them to the Board of Governors for making major financial decisions, such as interest rates. My duties included collecting data from requirements, creating test plans, and qualifying software applications.

However, my involvement at the bank extended well beyond my job responsibilities. I was a Fed Ambassador, responsible for educating the public, including high school students, about the bank and helping them gain financial literacy by providing tours of our office in the heart of San Francisco's financial district. Additionally, I served as the Area Director of a nonprofit educational organization called Toastmasters, which operates clubs worldwide to promote communication, public speaking, and leadership. As a Communications Coordinator at the Bank Club, I also assisted with promoting and marketing bank events. The list of my contributions could go on and on. In summary, I enthusiastically participated in activities that promoted the bank as a public service organization and contributed to various good causes. My colleagues appreciated my work, and my manager was pleased with my performance and encouraged my involvement with bank-related activities.

My boss, Andrew Adamick, was an exemplary manager. He consistently provided unwavering support and encouragement, empowering me to explore new avenues and make a meaningful impact. Andrew was a rare breed of leaders who did not need to be the loudest person in the room to have a profound influence on others.

When the pandemic hit, we were all compelled to work from home. So usually for our regular 1-on-1 meetings, Andrew would call me on my cell phone in the afternoon. During our conversations, besides work-related topics, we often discussed our personal lives, including his baby daughter and my son's schooling.

But this time, it was different. Not only did Andrew schedule a Microsoft Teams Video call, but also it was at 8:30 in the morning, which is unusually early for both of us. I messaged him asking if he could call me on my cell phone instead, but he insisted I join the video conference. So, at 8:29 am, on March 4th, 2020, I called into a video conference for my routine 1-on-1 meeting.

When Andrew appeared on the screen, he looked a little different. Though he seemed normal, he was not sporting his trademark smile and appeared a bit stressed. Nevertheless, it was good to see him again, as we had not met face-to-face in two months. While we were exchanging some small talk, I noticed that Betty Wong from the HR department had also joined the call.

Betty was a dear friend of mine for a long time. We crossed paths through Toastmasters and later teamed up to participate in the United Way Campaign to raise funds. I was surprised to see her, but when David Moore, the director of our group, joined the call, I sensed that something was seriously awry.

To gauge the nature of the call, I observed Betty Wong and David Moore's facial expressions closely. Despite feeling unsettled, Betty appeared content and always maintained a cheerful demeanor. David Moore typically wore a solemn expression, but I did not detect any visible cause for concern from him either.

Andrew addressed me, "Babu, you have been an indispensable member of the STAR ITS team for the past five years. Your contributions to the team have been tremendous, and you have always played an integral role." As he continued to shower me with praise, my heart sank. David Moore added, "Your involvement in numerous activities at the bank has made you well-liked by everyone in the department and the team. Thank you for your excellent work."

Without prolonging the situation, Andrew got straight to the point, "However, STAR ITS is now heading in a new direction with automation, cloud, and a few other advanced technologies. Unfortunately, we regret to inform you that your position has been eliminated."

I was shell-shocked.

What did I do wrong? Why me? What was to become of me? Numerous questions raced through my mind, but I could not grasp any of them. As each person on the screen spoke, it felt

like watching a tasteless movie where the dialogue bounced off me. All I could think of was my future and what it held for me.

Being a part of the Federal Reserve Bank was my life, and I planned to retire there in a few years. I could not imagine a life without it. For eleven years, I had formed close friendships and professional relationships that meant more to me than anywhere else I had worked. Recently, I even started a Fed Green Club to combat global warming by planting trees, cleaning up beaches, and educating the public about its dangers. The Fed (Federal Reserve Bank) has allowed me to fulfill my lifelong passion for travel, and I have great memories and experiences that I will cherish all my life. I have collected countless souvenirs and photos from the places I have visited that I hardly have room in my house to display.

Now, I was left with thoughts that plagued me. What would happen to me? How could I survive without my Fed family? Would I be alone once again at this stage in my life?

Chapter 1:
My Village

It was the year 1964. The crowd gathered in the village of Dondireddy Pallayam to celebrate my cousin Malliga's puberty. My mother was among the guests in my aunt's house, waiting for her turn to bless Malliga.

Malliga, dressed in a silk half-saree and adorned with jewelry, was seated in the center of the stage, surrounded by women who were offering their blessings by placing a red dot on her forehead, sprinkling flowers, yellow rice, and holy water on her.

While waiting for her turn to give her blessing, my mother suddenly clutched her stomach and winced in pain, causing a commotion in the crowd. A neighboring woman inquired in Telugu, our native language, if she was okay, but my mother did not respond. She was holding her belly, breathing heavily. "She's going into labor!" the woman yelled. The nearest hospital was two hours away by bullock cart, the only mode of transportation available in the village then. My mother could not wait that long and was already screaming in agony. The joyous celebration turned into anxiety and drama in an instant. Meanwhile, my cousin Malliga remained seated at the center of the stage, dressed in silk and jewelry, perplexed about what to do.

After some time, a few villagers helped relocate my mother to a private room, and a midwife came from the village. After several hours of arduous labor, a baby was delivered - a boy! Everyone was overjoyed, especially my family, as it was highly significant in Indian culture to have a male heir to continue the family's legacy. My aunts and uncles extended their congratulations to my mother. After consecutively giving birth to four girls, she finally had a boy, and in the most unusual way.

Yup, that was how I was born.

However, the reality of my birth was not as pleasant as it may seem. Many years later, my mother revealed that it nearly never happened. When she became pregnant, she had already given birth to four girls. She was certain that she did not want to have another girl, as girls in India are still viewed as a financial burden due to the practice of dowry, which I will elaborate on in Chapter 3. She attempted to obtain an abortion, but the doctor informed her that it was too late and dangerous at that point. Despite her reservations, she ultimately agreed to continue with the pregnancy. I suppose I just lucked out.

When I reflect on the past, I strive not to dwell on the negativity but instead to focus on the positives—that I am here, flourishing and being a good son, which brings my mother immense happiness. I have been a steadfast pillar of support for our family, providing financial assistance to my mother and sisters and mentoring my nieces and nephews. Well, I am getting ahead of myself. Let us just say that not a single day goes by when I do not contemplate how my fortunes shifted, not only because of my birth but also because of the various pivotal moments that ensued.

Growing up in my native village of Kothambakam, surrounded by farmers, taught me the importance of simplicity and hard work. I learned firsthand how humbling it was to lead a simple life in a rural setting.

There was a boy named Segar who was three years older than me. Even at eight, he was already working and taking care of the cows in our house, earning him the nickname "the Cowboy." Segar would arrive at our home at 6 am every day and make hot water in a large container by burning dry sugar cane leaves to boil it. I often spent my free time talking to him while watching the leaves spark in the fire. Segar would share stories about his simple life, and I was amazed to learn about someone's life outside my family. It was the first time that a thought crossed my mind about what my life would be like if I had to feed myself at such a young age instead of attending school. Later, Segar would take our three cows to pastures to graze all day. He would sit in the shade and make sure they did not stray into the fields and bring them back home at dusk. It was the same routine day in and day out.

Life in the village meant hard intense labor work, particularly for the farmers. Both men and women had to toil in the scorching sun all day, planting seedlings, pulling weeds, and harvesting sugarcane, rice, millets, and other crops. There were no hats or shoes, or machinery to ease the burden. The farmers walked around barefooted and had to endure the hot sun scorching their heads and feet.

My village lacked a nearby river, so we relied on underground water as our primary source of irrigation. Each field had a motor house and a watchman whose duty was to start the motor once a day. The Electricity Board supplied power for the village, which was rationed to only six hours a day. The water flowed from the engine to a huge tank and spilled into a small canal encircling the field. A watchman would walk around the field, guiding the water to the crops until they were fully irrigated, after which he would stop the flow. This manual and laborious process had to be repeated daily. On hot summer days, I would play in the water tank, asking the watchman to join me, but he would politely decline.

Various crops were grown and harvested in different seasons of the year, such as sugarcane, rice, savukku tree (a tropical pine), tapioca, sweet yam, peanuts, cotton, sesame, and other local grains. Sugarcane was and still is one of the main crops that thrive in our region.

Sugar mills or cane factories usually supported the sugarcane farms. A cane inspector would visit the farmers and negotiate the amount they should plant each season. Once they agreed on the number of acres, the farmers would plant sugarcane seedlings, usually six inches tall, in rows. Over the next six months, the sugarcane would grow quickly, and the farm workers would pick weeds and remove the leaves from the bottom of the canes to promote healthy growth. The canes could reach a height of ten feet, and their leaves had small thorns. If anyone were to cross the field or weed the area, they would undoubtedly experience scrapes and persistent itchiness caused by the thorns until they showered. However, the workers could only take a shower at the end of the day, so they had to suffer through the itching and scratching all day, every day.

Most farms in the region primarily cultivated rice and sugarcane. These farms, typically ranging from 5 to 20 acres, were owned by members of the landlord community in the village. The farm workers, comprising entire families, would work for a single landlord for their whole lives and remain loyal to them. The head of the family would serve as the watchman, while the wife would assist with household and gardening tasks. If a child helped with chores, the boy would act as a cowboy, while the girl would serve as a helper for the landlords.

My family was one such landlord. We owned two sets of 20-acre land in different parts of the village and had two farming families who had been loyal to us for more than 50 years. I adored these families and enjoyed giving them snacks, money, or whatever I could get my hands on. I recall my mother shouting at them when they disobeyed orders, and I could not understand why she would treat them so harshly. I felt sorry for them.

Despite being landlords, we faced financial difficulties. We did not have a consistent monthly income, and expenses accumulated during the season. To plant sugarcane, we had to take out a loan from the bank with the understanding that we would repay the loan once we sold the crop to the sugar mill. The bank established an account with the sugar mill on our behalf as a security measure. Once the crop was harvested, the bank would receive loan repayment directly from the sugar mill, and we would receive the remaining funds. This meant we were already behind. We had to spend a significant sum of money before the crop was harvested on maintaining the crop, paying farm workers, covering family expenses, and so on. Life was a continual struggle to make ends meet.

The prospect of drought would bring about significant hardships for the entire family. It would cause the water level in the wells to drop, making it exceedingly difficult to pump water for irrigation purposes. The crops relied heavily on either rainfall or water sourced from neighboring farms; without it, they would wilt and perish. This would result in reduced juice yield in the sugar cane, translating into lesser tonnage for the sugar mill and a decline in our income.

I remained unaware of the difficulties faced by my family and other families in the region until I reached high school. Growing up, my family provided me with a comfortable and nurturing environment, shielding me from these struggles. My sole focus was on my education. However, I became aware of one thing—I had no desire to continue my family's farming business. I wanted to pursue higher education and establish a career outside of agriculture.

Figure 1 Two farm worker families that worked for my family (man in blue and the old couple in the middle) and an independent worker (the lady in yellow) in 2003.

Figure 2 Me standing in the sugar cane field (2003)

Chapter 2:
My Childhood

Reflecting on my childhood spent in the village half a century ago, most of the memories feel pretty hazy. Nevertheless, a few vivid recollections still stand out in my mind.

I attended the village's local elementary/middle school for my first year. The school was basic, with only roofs and classrooms for different grades. Each room was equipped with benches, chairs, and a blackboard with chalk. The teachers were primarily Christian families. I have fond memories of learning the basics of the alphabet in school, and the headmaster was especially kind to me. These are the only memories I have of my early education at the local village school.

As for the neighbors, the family to the right had an Alsatian dog that was always tied up with a chain. Whenever someone crossed the road, the dog would bark and try to jump at them. People, especially kids like me, were afraid of the dog. Maybe that is why I have never owned a dog in my life. However, research has shown that having a dog can boost one's mood and alleviate stress, so I may give it a try one day.

The neighbors to the left of our house were an older couple who never had children, and no one knew why. They were very kind to me, and I loved spending time with them. Whenever I ran to their house to play, they would treat me to snacks or drinks. At the time, I did not know why I enjoyed being with them so much, but I felt inexplicably drawn to them.

Each morning at 5 am, a milkman would arrive at our home to milk our cows. He would skillfully place a large jug between his knees and begin the rhythmic process of milking. The soothing sound of the milk hitting the bottom of the jug became a familiar morning alarm for me. I would awaken to the sound and listen to it in bed. The jug would gradually fill with foam, emitting the enticing aroma of fresh milk.

Whenever I detected the delightful scent, I would eagerly make my way over to the milkman. I would dip my finger into the jug and savor the freshness before he even brought it inside our home.

We had a skilled cook, an elderly woman who resided with us and prepared outstanding meals. She would boil fresh milk and prepare Indian coffee using a silver coffee filter composed of two parts. She would pour hot water over fresh coffee powder in the top part, which would percolate into the bottom container. Next, she would pour hot milk into stainless steel tumblers, known as "Eversilver," and add coffee and sugar. One of my fondest childhood memories was drinking hot coffee made with fresh cow milk.

During my childhood, I cherished spending time in the field. When the farm manager visited the field, I sometimes followed him around. The houses where the farmers resided were basic huts, the roof of which was made of sugarcane and rice straws, and mud walls supporting them. It was such an exhilarating experience that I desired to enter and observe their way of life. Unfortunately, the supervisor always forbade me from doing so, explaining that we were not allowed to visit their homes. I later learned the reason behind this prohibition, which I will discuss later in this chapter.

It was a delight to witness the actions unfold in the field. During the sowing period, the female workers would gather the rice seedlings in bundles and walk in muddy water up to their ankles. They would then bend down and plant the seedlings individually with remarkable speed. Within a short period, the workers would have planted a few rows of seedlings. Once planted, the rice field resembled an army of soldiers, uniform and ready for battle. In three months, the seedlings would grow into thick grass, sporting budding paddies at the top.

The female workers returned to the field every fifteen days to weed the rice field. As a hyper kid, I would mimic them and join in the mud to plant seedlings or pull weeds myself. My silliness amused the workers, and we enjoyed the laughter that ensued.

At home, I was an energetic kid who ran around in the house, raising hell and causing a headache for everyone. We had a 30-foot-deep well at the back of the house, and my favorite pastime was to pick up items around the house and throw them in the well. My mom had to hire a worker to retrieve everything I threw in the well every month. The worker would climb down the well using a rope and retrieve all the items. Although the well was deep, it had no water in it.

As time passed, the summers grew increasingly warmer, and despite drilling deeper wells, the water levels continued to decline until all the wells dried-up. As a child, I recall using a rope and bucket to fetch water from the well in the backyard for showering, dishwashing, and watering the plants. However, the well dried-up after several years and was ultimately sealed with mud and stones. I wondered if the water would ever return, but at that time, we did not realize that it was the beginning of global warming.

At the tender age of four, I had a traumatic incident. In Southern Indian villages, traditional homes have an opening in the center, and my ancestral 170-year-old house was constructed in the same style. The water would pour directly into the house whenever it rained, splattering and soaking everything. As a result, our family built a small wall about a foot high to prevent the rain from splashing in. As a youngster, I could easily climb on top of the wall, and it became one of my favorite pastimes.

One day, I was climbing on the wall, imagining myself as Arjun fighting Kauravas at the battle of Kurukshetra. I kept jumping on and off the wall, disregarding my mother's warnings. Unfortunately, on one of my jumps, I slipped and fell.

My mother and sisters heard me crying and rushed to see me with a bloody mouth and a piece of my tongue hanging out. They quickly brought me to a nearby hospital, where the tongue was stitched back together. It was a terrifying experience for them and an agonizing one for me. To this day, the stitches are still visible on my tongue, serving as a testament to how energetic I was as a youngster.

In Indian villages, a brutal practice known as untouchability originated thousands of years ago as a social divide between the wealthy and the poor. The rich had the luxury of living in comfortable brick houses equipped with running water and toilets, while the poor lived in straw huts with mud walls and had to share a communal tap for their daily water needs. They had to use the fields when they needed to go to the restroom, which was not only inconvenient but also a source of shame, particularly for women.

As a child, I was always perplexed as to why the farmer's houses were situated half a kilometer away from ours and why the farm supervisor advised against visiting them. Whenever they visited our house, they were not allowed to enter but instead had to remain outside the door while speaking to us. If they came into contact with any of our dishes, we had to rinse them before using them, and if they touched our bodies, we had to take a shower. Furthermore, we were forbidden from consuming their food under any circumstances. All of these rules felt odd and wrong to me. Therefore, I secretly broke them by interacting with the farmers, visiting their huts, and eating their food. At first, they were taken aback, but they eventually grew to enjoy our interactions.

Fortunately, the situation has improved significantly in my village nowadays. The farm workers are permitted to come into our house to clean and wash dishes, but my family still maintains some distance from them. When I retire and return to India, I want to shift people's mindsets and educate them about the importance of treating everyone with respect and kindness. This objective has been firmly embedded in my mind for a long time. The more I contemplate it, the more restless I become. I believe we are on this planet to assist and support one another, not harm one another.

Figure 3 Me at one year

Figure 4 With parents in Pondicherry when I went back to attend my 2008 High school reunion

suburbs are attempting to distance themselves from this practice, but it remains a major social issue in rural areas.

One of the reasons why I hold my mother in such high regard is because of the challenges and struggles she faced while raising our family and caring for my ailing father. I send her money every month to cover her medical and daily expenses. Additionally, I am in the process of restoring our family home, which is over 170 years old. It was constructed around the 1850s and is in dire need of repairs. Very few houses as old as ours still have people living in them. I want to restore it not only for its historical significance and to capture my childhood memories but also, more importantly, to bring a smile to my mother's face.

I have four sisters. My eldest sister, Vijaya, married Ramasamy, whom I normally referred to as "my brother-in-law" when she was only fourteen. She did not finish high school because it was customary at that time to marry off girls once they reached puberty. Vijaya was a very obedient and submissive wife who always served Ramasamy well. She cooked for him, washed his clothes, and never talked back. These were the typical traits of a married woman in India from the 60s to the 80s. If a woman spoke out or disrespected her husband, she would be seen as a rebel who was unsuitable for married life. Women were pressured to conform to these societal expectations. Although there have been some improvements, these basic expectations have largely remained the same.

My brother-in-law, Ramasamy, never finished college and had an opportunity to work as a coal mine supervisor. However, his mother talked him out of it, fearing that he might die on the job. He never had any proper jobs after that. Vijaya and Ramasamy have three children, and my favorite among them is Sathi, who worked full-time as a software engineer with IBM in Bengaluru. I advised him to quit his job and pursue a career in the USA, and he listened. He overcame all the difficulties and eventually settled in Chicago, where he has been working for the past 13 years and recently obtained his green card.

My second sister, Subashini, got married at an even younger age of thirteen. She was always caring and showed me a lot of love when I was a child. Even now, she talks to me fondly and always prepares my favorite dishes whenever I visit her house. Her husband, Bhaskar, was adopted by our neighbors and never finished high school. He managed his family's agricultural properties before moving to Chennai with my sister. They have two children: Kumar, their elder son, and Parimala, their daughter.

Parimala serves as a compelling illustration of the significance of education in India. Neither she nor her husband Ruban pursued education and instead worked blue-collar jobs for approximately two decades. The onset of the COVID-19 pandemic plunged them into severe financial challenges, making it difficult to meet their basic needs. Subsequently, they have successfully overcome these hardships. Now, Parimala holds a stable job, while Ruban manages a tourist resort in his hometown of Munnar, a picturesque hill station in the south. Their son, Prakash, has recently completed his degree in Computer Science.

My third sister, Samitha, is married to Vijayaraghavan, my only brother-in-law, who is educated and has a job. I hold Vijayaraghavan in high regard for his humility, respect for women, and equal treatment of all. I learned a lot from him about humility and the importance of not speaking your mind when it is not appropriate. After being childless for over a decade, they resorted to artificial insemination, which resulted in the birth of their twin daughters. Their arrival coincided with my departure to the United States.

My fourth sister, Hema, is the most educated of all my siblings. She completed eleventh grade but had to leave school to marry our distant relative, Santhanam. She attended boarding school in Villupuram and later a Catholic school in Pondicherry, where she became fluent in English. Her husband did not complete high school and managed agricultural properties. They have a son who completed an engineering degree and now operates an organic farming business.

Evidently, all my sisters have entered into matrimony through arranged marriages—a time-honored tradition in India spanning millennia. Parental control of marriage may have originated during 500 BC to prevent the intermixing of ethnic groups and castes. Women were deprived of their traditional independence and placed under male custodianship, first of their fathers during childhood, then of their husbands in married life, and finally of their sons in old age.

Despite the fact that romantic love is "wholly celebrated" in both Indian mass media, such as Bollywood, and folklore, the tradition of arranged marriage has remained "surprisingly robust" and has adapted to changing social circumstances, defying predictions of decline as India modernized. In fact, my own marriage was arranged, which I will discuss in a later chapter.

Although there is much controversy surrounding arranged marriage, it is challenging to simply label it as good or bad. On one hand, there is little romance in marriage, and there is no guarantee that the family will not fall apart. On the other hand, the divorce rate in India is only 1%, compared to 41% in the USA in 2021. Of course, one may argue that unbroken marriages do not necessarily equate to happy families, but the same argument applies to the 59% of families that stayed together in the US. Moreover, a broken family can adversely affect all aspects of a child's development and significantly impact their future as an adult and parents. Therefore, for now, I am undecided on the matter.

Figure 5 Reunion with my sisters in Samitha's house in 2022. From left to right: me, Hema, Samitha, Subashini, and Vijaya

Figure 6 Our village house in (2008)

Interlude 1: Vijaya

My eldest sister, Vijaya, has been an unwavering source of support in our household ever since her family relocated to Pondicherry for the better education of my three nephews—Nithi, Sathi, and Lokesh. She would work tirelessly in the kitchen from 5 am to 9 pm with only a few hours of rest in the afternoon, standing and cooking in front of the hot stove every day. She could not afford to fall sick even for a day, except during her menstrual cycle when, according to Indian tradition, women were not allowed to enter the kitchen or any sacred area of the house as they were deemed impure during that time. One might wonder if this is a blessing in disguise for her as it provides her with a natural two-day respite from her duties.

On a typical day, Vijaya would begin at 5 am by making coffee for the whole family, followed by breakfast. She would then prepare an early lunch for my brother-in-law, who usually skipped breakfast and had his meal around 11 am. Between 12-1 pm, she would serve lunch to everyone else. After a rest of about two hours, she would start preparing the second round of coffee in the afternoon, followed by dinner. If the dinner consisted of dosa or chapati, she would first have to make the curry or chutney and then the dosa/chapati, which usually took a couple of hours. With 10 to 12 people living in the house at any given time, she not only had to tend to her daily chores but also entertain any guests that arrived, cooking for them and meeting their needs. Sometimes, I would become upset with her and complain about the repetitive and unsatisfying meals.

I recall an instance where she once attempted suicide by swallowing a diamond. Thankfully, she received timely medical attention. At that time, I was in high school and did not have much knowledge about her situation. Last year, when I visited my nephew's house, my mother and sister were also present, and it was then that I realized the extent of her struggles and the difficulties she faced in her life. I was overwhelmed with a sense of guilt and shame and tried to assist her by purchasing whatever she needed to make her happy. Although it might be too little too late, she found contentment in having stocked grocery racks and kitchen utensils in order.

During my visit this time, her husband still mistreated her and forced her to cook, clean, serve food, do laundry, and wash dishes. Considering that she had grandchildren of her own, it was not appropriate for her to work so hard at her age. This situation arises from the male-dominated Indian society, where men control the family, and women remain in the background. Men typically do not engage in kitchen activities, leaving women to toil in the heat and carry out other household chores. Unfortunately, the situation remains unchanged even today.

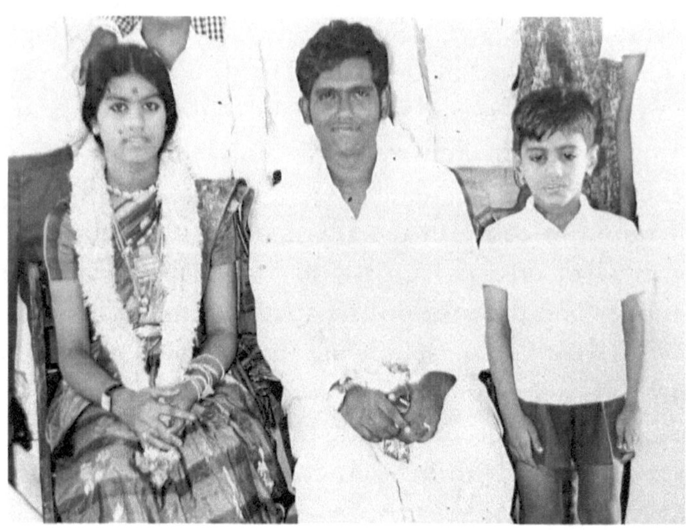

Figure 7 From left to right, my oldest sister Vijaya, Brother-in-law Ramasamy and me at their wedding in 1970

Figure 8 Front row from left to right: me, my oldest sister Vijaya, and her husband, Ramasamy. Back row from left to right: my mother and my father

Chapter 4:
Moving to Pondicherry

My grandmother had a distant relative named Kamala who lived in Pondicherry, a city about 20 kilometers away from my village. My mother wanted to send me to a better school there, but we could not afford the boarding and living expenses since we were already paying for my sister Hema's expenses in Villupuram. The only way I could study in Pondicherry was to live with Kamala's family, so my mother talked to her about the possibility, and Kamala agreed to host me. In exchange, my family would periodically provide them with rice, grains, and vegetables.

Pondicherry, presently known as Puducherry, is located on the southeast coast of India and is the capital and most populous city of the Union Territory of Puducherry. In 1674, the French East India Company established a trading center there, eventually becoming India's primary French settlement. Over the next hundred years or so, Pondicherry became a subject of a power struggle between the French, Dutch, and British as ownership transferred back and forth until it joined the Indian family in 1962. The city's colonial past has left a distinct imprint on its architecture, religion, cuisine, and culture. Even today, there is a significant French influence on the lives of the people in Puducherry.

Going to school in Pondicherry was a once-in-a-lifetime opportunity for me to learn and grow. Otherwise, I would have been stuck in a ramshackle village school like all my sisters, with no prospects for a decent education. The thought of leaving my family, the love and care of my sisters, and my familiar surroundings behind to stay with total strangers as a guest made me feel very sad. As a five-year-old, I did not know how to handle that.

Kamala's family lived in a prominent area of town called Ranga Pillai Street, which was named after a famous 16th-century resident of Pondicherry. Kamala's husband owned a bakery called the New Biscuit

Factory, and they had five children: Rani, Rajeswari, Viveganandan, Sundaram, and Saroja. Despite being considered middle-class, the family already had five children, so adding one more mouth to feed was a financial burden. To address this issue, my accommodation was paid for with rice, grains, and vegetables instead of cash–a clever solution to a difficult situation.

When my mother left me at Kamala's house, I cried. However, like any normal child, I soon became distracted by my new surroundings. The hustle and bustle of the big city fascinated me, as I had never experienced such traffic, chaos, and sheer volume of people before. This was a stark contrast to my previous life, surrounded by blue skies, nature, paddy fields, and cow dung. Every day, I would walk to school with Sundaram, who was a couple of years older than me.

The day after my arrival, my mother took me to the Immaculate School of Convent, but I was not admitted due to my age not meeting the minimum requirement. To remedy the situation, my mother altered my age by three months, changing my birthday from September to June. At that time, there were no birth certificates, so schools relied on the information provided by parents. Eventually, I was admitted to a public school named Ecole Anglais, which meant "English School," where all subjects were taught in English. On a side note, June remains my birth month in all my official documents to this day.

School at Ecole Anglais was a unique experience for me, and I struggled at first. The consequences for not completing homework or behaving in class were severe: kneeling outside the classroom for twenty minutes, enduring painful knees, and disapproving looks from passersby. Sometimes, the teacher would come out and beat unruly students with a ruler on their legs. Fortunately, I managed to stay afloat and avoid this ordeal.

Compared with the school in my village which was more laid-back with obedient students, the school in Pondicherry was more chaotic, with more vocal and mischievous students despite the punishments. Additionally, the complexity and workload of the class subjects were significantly greater than what I had experienced in the village school.

Mathematics was excruciatingly complex, and the English class came with endless grammar and propositions. Nevertheless, I found everything to be different, new, and exciting.

One of my most vivid memories is of my very first teacher, Murugan, and his patient and methodical teaching approaches. He taught me the basics of English, Math, and Science. Unlike other teachers, he preferred to guide the students instead of forcing them, and I fell in love with his sincere and enlightening teaching methods.

During my time in Pondicherry, I stayed with Kamala and her family, who were all kind to me, especially her husband. I would find excuses to walk to his bakery, which was located near their house. He would always allow me to choose a treat of my choice from the bakery, and I would often pick a cream biscuit or a cupcake to savor later. This experience is one of my favorite childhood memories.

Upon returning home, I would be greeted by Rani, the eldest sister, who would inquire about my schoolwork with strict yet helpful attention. I appreciated her interest in my learning and was grateful for her tough love approach in teaching me the basics of the English language.

Rajeshwari, the second sister, treated me like a little brother and showered me with affection. She would always take an interest in my life and provide me with comforting hugs whenever I was not feeling well. Rajeshwari was the one who truly connected with me, which was especially meaningful given that I was living under someone else's roof.

Vivekananda (also known as Babu), the older brother, was a serious individual who excelled in both academics and sports. However, he did not have much time for me as he was preoccupied with his life.

Sundaram, the middle son, was the odd one out whom I despised at the time. He relentlessly bullied me by hitting me on the head, chasing me, calling me names, and so on. When I reported this to his parents, they disregarded my concerns, leaving me perplexed by their negligence. Consequently, I stopped complaining and instead tried evading him, which only intensified his bullying. He was my biggest challenge at the time, and his actions left a lasting impression on me. I saw my son Arjun experience similar bullying during his high school years due to his quiet and geeky nature. The bullies would taunt him, pull his bag, and ridicule him constantly. Although I attempted to assist, the school systems made intervening difficult for parents. Thankfully, due to COVID-19, the majority of his last year of high school was conducted virtually, allowing him to complete it peacefully at home. However, I was uncertain whether keeping students home was the best solution to bullying. Nevertheless, in my case, I was much younger and had to endure bullying from a fellow resident in the same house.

Saro, the youngest of us, was just one year my junior and became my constant playmate. Our bond was much stronger than that with anyone else in the household. I spent most of my time with Saro and the other girls in the neighborhood, learning all their games. I found their games less intimidating and less challenging than the boys'. During our playtime, I even picked up a few French songs.

My childhood was a mixture of enjoyable moments and harrowing experiences. I always longed for a friend and a helpful hand to guide me as a lost child in a vast city.

Figure 9 Ranga Pillai Street in 2023 (picture from internet)

Chapter 5:
School Life in Pondicherry

As time passed, I found myself in fourth grade and struggling in school. The subjects were difficult, and I received little to no help from anyone. The same went for my friends Saro and Sundaram. Our families came together and decided to send us to a notorious tutor known for his strict teaching methods and tendency to hit students who failed to write or read properly.

The tutor was nicknamed "Kulla Vathiar," which translated to "short teacher" because he was only four feet five inches. He carried a thick ruler and would strike students' knuckles, palms, and fingers with it, causing many to cry from the pain. It was a terrifying prospect for us.

On a fine weekday evening after school, Saro, Sundaram, and I made our way to the tutor's house, dreading what was to come. We were aware of his reputation and feared for our safety. Upon entering the house, I was filled with such fear that I almost fainted. I sat in a corner, trying to do my homework while feeling a knot in my stomach.

Soon enough, the teacher approached me and looked at my notebook. With one quick glance, he declared my handwriting to be ugly and demanded that I extend my palm. Reluctantly, I complied, and he began striking my hand with his ruler—bam, bam! He then asked me to turn my hand over and struck my knuckles with the same force. The pain was excruciating, and I clenched my hands and cried. The teacher's message was clear: I needed to write more neatly or face the consequences.

He had been using this approach since the beginning of his tutoring career, and there were no laws in place to protect children from physical punishment, nor did parents intervene. It was generally accepted that teachers could physically discipline children without any justification.

Teachers held complete authority, and parents or guardians expected students to comply with the teacher's expectations on their terms. It has left a lasting impact on me.

Although India has progressed since then, this was the reality of my upbringing. Children were expected to learn through fear and intimidation. While some children were able to move on from this experience quickly and forget about it, others, like myself, carried the trauma for a long time. In my case, it was a mix of both. I was terrified of my teacher for years, but eventually, it became a distant memory.

On the day that my thumb became swollen and looked like a baseball due to the beating, I cried and complained to others about the teacher's actions. However, people just told me to tough it out and that things would get better with time, but they never did. The beatings continued, and I would sometimes get lucky when the teacher was busy with other students or not in the mood to beat me. However, most of the time, luck was not my best friend. My classmates Saro and Sundaram went through a similar ordeal, but Saro's situation was somewhat better as she was a young girl.

After enduring repeated beatings from the tutor, a miracle happened: I had the most beautiful handwriting in the family. Everyone, including myself, was amazed. However, the price I paid was substantial. I had to endure physical pain and tremendous trauma. I struggled to sleep at night and was constantly anxious about being hit.

As a 10-year-old, it was a difficult experience to endure both physically and mentally. I needed someone to confide in and alleviate my anxiety. I first turned to Rajeshwari, who sympathetically listened to me, but being only a few years older than myself, she could not offer any assistance. I could not find an adult to assist me, as my family was far away in the village. Saro and Sundaram, on the other hand, managed to excuse themselves from the tutoring. I endured the torture on my own for a few more months until I finally had an opportunity to escape.

During my mom and uncle's visit, I saw an opportunity to avoid my tutoring lesson. I pretended to have a stomach ache and refused to go despite my family's attempts to convince me otherwise. Unfortunately, telling the truth was not an option, as I knew the educational system would ignore teachers' mistreatment of students. Therefore, lying was my only escape.

But the relief was only temporary. The following week, I was summoned to see Kulla Vathiyar during recess, and I was frightened. He questioned me about why I missed my tutoring lesson, and I replied with my stomach pain excuse. He then asked me to lie down on the table so he could examine me. He asked a student to bring a knife to operate on my stomach. I panicked and screamed. As a 10-year-old, I could not discern whether he was joking or being serious. Eventually, he let me go, and that was our final interaction. My handwriting worsened, but I couldn't care less. I left after the seventh grade for a private school.

The academic year at Ecole Anglais was divided into three periods: quarterly, half-yearly, and annual. At the end of each season, we would have exams followed by breaks. The quarterly break would last a week, the half-yearly break would be about three weeks, and the annual break would be the longest, typically lasting for two months during the summer. Those were some of the best moments of my life, and I eagerly anticipated those holidays throughout the year. During those breaks, an elderly gentleman who supervised our lands would travel to Pondicherry to accompany me back to the village on the train.

One of my fondest memories was the train ride. I would sit by the window, savoring the scenic views of fields, rivers, houses, and people whizzing by. When the wind caressed my face, I would close my eyes and daydream about all the delightful things I would do with my family. I would even extend my hand out of the window and feel the wind on my skin. The train would stop approximately a kilometer away from our house, and we would walk the rest of the way.

Once I arrived home, I would rush to embrace my sisters and share my tales of school, friends, and plays. They would treat me to some of my favorite foods. I would savor tender coconuts picked from the trees in our backyard, vegetables grown in our garden, and fruits gathered from the locals. Jackfruit was one of my favorite fruits. A worker would bring a large fruit to our house, and he would coat his hands with oil before slicing it open. The fruit was incredibly sticky inside, but the oil helped alleviate the stickiness, making peeling and eating the slices easier. They were exceedingly sweet, and I would devour them until I had a stomach ache.

To the left of my house lived an elderly woman who resided alone, and people feared her. As a child, I did not share the same apprehensions. I would greet her, and she would invite me inside, often offering me a snack. One day, she announced that her grandson, Ravi, was going to visit her during the holidays. I was thrilled by the news. Ravi's parents lived in Villupuram, which was closer to my village than Pondicherry.

On the day of his arrival, I eagerly ran to their house, and there he was. Ravi and I were the same age, and I was ecstatic to have someone to play with in the village. Ravi taught me many games, and we would venture into the fields, swim in the water tank, climb mango trees, and pick mangoes. We even watched our favorite heroes' matinee at the nearby movie theater. Ravi continued to visit his grandmother during his school breaks, and I would go back home during mine. It worked out perfectly, and we eventually became close friends.

Figure 10 My favorite fruit, Jackfruit, in my village garden (2018)

Interlude 2: Learning to Ride a Bike

Back in the day, learning to ride a bike in India was such a torment because there were no training wheels or balance bikes. One approach was to have someone run behind you while holding the bike, then let go at a certain point. This often led to panic and falls. Another method involved someone pushing the bike as fast as possible before letting you ride on your own. I attempted both of these harsh methods but eventually gave up because of the pain and fear from the fall.

In contrast, Saro learned to ride a bike when she was only seven years old, making me feel ashamed. Every time I returned to the village during the holidays, I sought someone's help to learn. I sat on the bike and had them push me from behind, hoping to maintain my balance. However, I would fail and experience excruciating pain, causing me to give up again. This went on until I was in the eighth grade.

One of the reasons I looked forward to visiting my village during the holidays was my friend Ravi. We would often go to the village at the same time, spending time together playing, chatting, and wandering the streets. Ravi saw my struggle with the bike and promised to assist me.

Ravi took me to a field one day and proposed that we try something different. We proceeded to an open space with a large haystack on one side. Ravi instructed me to get on the bike, and as usual, I was scared. However, he assured me that I would not get hurt, and because he was true to his word, I trusted him and mounted the bike. When I gathered some speed, Ravi pushed me as hard as he could toward the haystack. Filled with fear, I shut my eyes, let the bike go, and crashed into the haystack at a breakneck pace. When I opened my eyes, I anticipated blood all over my body, but much to my surprise, I didn't even have a single scratch.

Same approach, different outcomes. We started visiting the field every day, and in just a few days, I became proficient in balancing and could actually ride the bike without falling. I still needed to learn how to turn and stop, but I was no longer scared. I realized that the key to riding a bike was not to fall. I continued practicing, and after a couple of weeks, I was thrilled to announce that I had become a skilled bike rider.

Life is not solely about achieving success; it's also about failing and learning from it. Failing quickly and falling forward and getting up are the keys to success. Once you learn to fall and are no longer intimidated by failure, there can be only one outcome.

Figure 11 Me and Ravi (2022)

Chapter 6:
The Dictator

As mentioned earlier, my oldest sister Vijaya's family moved to Pondicherry for better schooling for my three nephews. In the seventh grade, I joined them, leaving Kamala's house on Ranga Pillai Street. At the time, I was overjoyed, but I had no idea what awaited me.

Vijaya's husband, Ramasamy, married Vijaya when I was only six years old. Vijaya was fourteen, and Ramasamy was twenty. It was commonplace for people to get married at that age. A mutual relative arranged their marriage, and Ramasamy, who had completed vocational training but lacked a job, was eligible to marry as long as his family-owned some agricultural property.

Ramasamy was raised by his mother, along with his younger brother, following his parents' separation. Even after getting married, he continued to live with his family. His mother, a woman of great mental fortitude, defied societal norms in India at that time, where divorce or separation was considered taboo. She took her sons and left the family system, while Ramasamy's father remained in the village to manage their farm alone. Ramasamy's formative years must have left an indelible impression on his personality, instilling in him two important values: mental strength and the belief that education was the key to escaping poverty.

Ramasamy had a tumultuous relationship with my mother, with plenty of love and hate. As a single mother, my mother raised four daughters and me independently. Her brother, my maternal uncle, was responsible for managing the family's agriculture and finances. He mismanaged the funds and did not supervise properly and so my mother had told him not to look after our lands anymore. We needed someone new immediately and so Ramasamy, my brother-in-law, came into the picture. As a woman in our community, my mother had limited options and was not allowed to oversee the family's fields. She needed a man to handle this task on her behalf. Ramasamy volunteered and pledged to supervise farming and family finances. He also expressed an interest in my education. With no other choices, my mother accepted his offer. She held Ramasamy in high regard for his involvement and hard work.

However, Ramasamy was not particularly skilled in management or finance himself. He made a mess of even his own family's properties, eventually selling everything after his mother passed away. The proceeds from the sale were distributed between his brother's outstanding debts and his reckless spending. All the agricultural properties inherited from his father were sold, and his brother received the majority of the proceeds.

But when it came to my family, Ramasamy deserves recognition for accomplishing more work than my uncle did. However, he did it in a manner that involved complete domination, leaving no room for anyone else's input. He controlled everyone's life, including my mother's. Even when it came to deciding where she could go, she had to listen to him. My mother relished the opportunity to travel to different relatives' homes to attend weddings and other ceremonies. She would provide guidance on how to conduct those events. Sometimes, Ramasamy would disagree with her, which upset my mother, but she ultimately acquiesced to his decision.

When I moved to my sister's house, Ramasamy wasted no time in exerting his authority over me. His children were too young to run errands, so he dispatched me to the store at all hours to buy whatever he needed, whether it be groceries, magazines, or other odds and ends. Even when I had important exams to study for, he showed no concern and expected everything to be done his way. I vividly remember one instance when I was studying late at night, and he insisted that I turn off the lights, I had to secretly use a candle to continue my studies.

Ramasamy was especially persistent about me memorizing multiplication tables up to 20, frequently testing me on them. I struggled with the tables between 12 and 19, and he would harass me whenever he had nothing else to do. My aversion to those tables became particularly strong. In addition, he made me eat greens that I detested and berated me whenever I wanted to go to the movies. If I did manage to go, he would become furious.

As I matured, I realized that Ramasamy was old-fashioned and set in his ways. But at thirteen years old, I was unaware of people's intentions and methods, taking life as it came, resulting in significant setbacks that left a lasting impact. Even to this day, when I see Ramasamy, memories of those days and the torment I endured persist in the back of my mind.

During those trying times, my sister Vijaya was my beacon of hope. She comforted me whenever my brother-in-law was harsh and secretly gave me money to attend movies with my friends. The movies were a sanctuary where I could forget about my chores and Math tables and immerse myself in another world.

When Vijaya visited me in the United States in 2020, I noticed her calloused palms and worn-out nails from washing dishes with chemicals using her bare hands. Seeing her hands brought me to tears, and I held them against my face. Vijaya's eyes grew misty as we shared a rare moment of emotional connection.

In the eighth grade, my life changed forever when Ramasamy did something unexpected. I attended Ecole Anglais, a government-run school that offered education up to the eigth standard. As with most government-run schools, the standards were mediocre, and without a mentor to guide me, I was an average student. Ramasamy discovered that Petit Séminaire was the best school in Pondicherry at the time, where 60% to 70% of students earned high marks and moved on to secure medical and engineering seats for college. He utilized his contacts with the principal to transfer me there. I did not dare to object.

At Petit Seminaire, I excelled in my studies and achieved exceptional results in my Tenth grade Matriculation exams, securing the coveted first group in Science, Math, and Biology. I continued my education at the same institution, completing my twelfth grade before pursuing engineering, which ultimately changed the course of my future. Ramasamy's own children could not handle the rigorous standards at Petit Séminaire and moved on to other schools in Pondicherry.

Transferring to Petit Séminaire proved to be a crucial moment in my early life. Had I stayed at Ecole Anglais, I would probably still be living in Pondicherry, working in a dead-end job, and unable to travel the world or meet a diverse range of people. Life in the United States has opened up numerous opportunities for me. I have been able to assist my family out of financial difficulties and indulge my passion for travel by visiting various countries and having new experiences. However, this was not the only time Ramasamy had a pivotal role in my life. We will come to that later.

Reflecting on my past and the emotional wounds I endured, I must admit his methods were successful. I am grateful for what he has done for me, and he continues to take pride in my accomplishments to this day.

Figure 12 Vijaya and Ramasamy at Lake Michigan in 2010 when they were in Chicago to take care of their newborn grandson

Chapter 7:
Life in Petit Séminaire

The history of Petit Séminaire dates back to 1844, when it was a seminary attended by 89 students, 25 of whom were seminarians. In 1873, it became a public college. In July 1978, Petit Séminaire was renamed Petit Séminaire Higher Secondary School, and it began offering two courses of study at the higher secondary level. This is when I enrolled in the school for my eighth grade.

The school's motto is "Nil Magnum Nisi Bonum," which means "Nothing is great unless it is good." The graduates from the school became doctors, engineers, lawyers, and other professionals who significantly impacted Pondicherry and its surroundings. Out of a total of 120 students from our grade, at least ten students went on to medical school, about 40 became engineers, and the rest pursued other fields. Today, some of those doctors have become major surgeons and medical experts, playing a crucial role in the health system of Pondicherry and Tamil Nadu, the neighboring state. Some of the civil, mechanical, and electrical engineers have contributed to the construction industry, established major factories, and provided utility and job opportunities to the state and the country.

However, my transition from a public to a private school was never easy. The subjects were difficult to follow, and I did not have the discipline or work ethic to meet the high standards. As a result, I did not perform well in the quarterly, half-yearly, and annual exams. In the end, I failed my eighth grade, which was the most humiliating thing for a student in India. It was an awful feeling to sit through the first few months of repeating my eighth grade while sharing the classroom with my juniors.

As the year progressed, I became more proficient in my studies and was able to comprehend the concepts better. During my ninth grade,

Father Peter, the principal, imparted grammar lessons in a unique and simplistic manner. He initiated by using uncomplicated sentences to teach the present, past, and future tenses. We relied on the book Wren and Martin, which was considered the English grammar bible. While many students struggled to construct sentences, I had a natural talent for English and found grammar easy to follow. Consequently, my comprehension abilities excelled, and English swiftly became my favorite subject, strengthening my academic performance and making my schooling experience pleasurable.

At the same time, I developed lasting friendships that provided me with solace and support, some of which continue to endure. Without the friendships I formed, I am uncertain where I would be today. My close friends would gather in front of my house during lunch or after school and engage in long conversations. I became particularly close among them to Sebastian, Sundar, Albert Ravi, Sathian, Sai, Pattabi, Dass, Uma, Alphonse, and Thulasi. Our bond was strengthened by our shared passion for sports, and I grew closer to Sundar, Adiaman, Pattabi, Dass, and others. More about them will be discussed in the next chapter.

After spending three years at Petit Séminaire, I fully embraced the school's culture, established numerous friendships, and was excelling academically. As I entered the tenth grade, also referred to as Matriculation in private schools across India, I was fully aware of the significance of this year. Matriculation marks the final year of the tenth class and culminates in the national or state board exams, commonly known as "matriculation exams," which are pivotal in determining a student's eligibility for higher education. Every student aspires to perform well in these exams and achieve excellent grades.

Matriculation marks a significant milestone in a student's academic career. Those who earn high grades gain automatic admission into Math, Science, and Biology programs, thereby paving the way for their medical or engineering aspirations. Securing admission into medical or engineering schools is crucial for male students, as failure to do so may put an end to their careers or even their lives. It is their only shot at a brighter future. Traditionally, college graduates majoring in arts, commerce, and other disciplines struggled to find decent-paying jobs that could support themselves or their families. However, the advent of the computer age in the 90s changed the game. Nowadays, students can pursue any degree or learn programming and related computer skills to excel in their chosen field.

During my Matriculation year for the tenth grade, there were six subjects: English, Tamil (as a second language), Mathematics, Science, History, and Geography. The exams were held at my school, which made me feel comfortable and at ease. Upon arriving at school, I exchanged last-minute tips with my friends as we were all anxious and excited about the exams. As soon as I received my paper, I began writing and requested extra blank sheets as my thoughts were flowing nonstop. In some cases, I was able to complete the exams well before time and even revisited my answers a couple of times. After finishing my exams, I felt a great relief as I stepped out of the examination hall.

When the results were announced, I had scored high enough to be admitted to the Math and Science section, which was the top tier. I was overjoyed, as were my family and friends. Every member of our gang had scored high grades, and we had all ranked in the top fifty of the entire school.

However, I was surprised to find myself struggling to understand the subjects when I started eleventh grade, also known as the first year of higher secondary school. Most students were facing the same challenge, so we opted for tutoring. Viswakumar, our Chemistry teacher, was the most popular tutor among the students, and I also joined his sessions. He taught Chemistry, Physics, and Mathematics; each class had at least 30 students. While Chemistry is often considered an esoteric subject, he transformed it into an animation story, drawing chemical elements like characters and resolving compound equations in a fun and easy way for us to understand.

My performance in Math and Science significantly improved, but English remained my favorite subject. Teacher Thomas seamlessly continued where Father Peter had left off, making English an enjoyable experience. We read captivating works by Charles Dickens, including

"Pickwick Papers" and "Tale of Two Cities," as well as the thrilling "The Scarlet Pimpernel," set during the French Revolution.

However, my school life was not entirely smooth sailing. During that time, every student had a nickname. One of my ninth grade Math teachers even gave me the nickname "Phossy Jaw" due to my long, pointed jaw. Phossy Jaw refers to an occupational disease affecting workers in the matchstick industry during the 19th and early 20th centuries, caused by exposure to white phosphorus without proper precautions. Later, my peers took it a step further and started calling me "goat," frequently mocking me by pointing their fingers like horns. Thanks to my insensitive nature, I laughed it off and even enjoyed the attention I received from my fellow students.

Looking back, I now realize that I was a victim of bullying during my school days. Unfortunately, back then, the school system did not have any mechanism to address bullying or raise awareness about it. As a result, students had to endure it as a part of their daily life. Fortunately, I was insensitive and attention-seeking, which helped me cope with the situation. However, I often wonder about other students who were not as lucky as I was. I wish I had access to the support and awareness that is available now, especially in the Western world, where bullying continues to be a prevalent social issue.

When I started twelfth grade, I suddenly felt under immense pressure. The twelfth grade, just like the tenth grade, has public exams that are primarily used for admission into professional courses such as medicine, engineering, and agriculture Science. Despite warnings from my friend Sebastian to focus on my studies, I was confident that I would pass the exams with flying colors, just like I had done in the Matriculation exams.

After the exams, I realized straight away that I had underestimated the difficulty of the subjects and had not put in enough effort. As a result, I barely scored enough to gain admission into the local arts and Science college, which were considered the lowest of the lows in terms of a student's future prospects.

With limited options, I applied for a bachelor's degree in Science at Tagore Arts College in Pondicherry. This was my last resort to gain admission into any college. Although there were occasional exceptions, finishing a bachelor's degree at the art college was not a promising career path at that time. But I had no other alternatives. I decided to pursue a major in botany and later transferred to a Mathematics major.

Figure 13 Petit Séminaire Higher Secondary School in (2008)

Chapter 8:
The Gang

Friends can be compared to fellow passengers on a train, as some may join you at the beginning of the journey and bid farewell after a few stops, while others may board the train later but stay with you for a long time. The timing of departures is uncertain, but we are grateful to fate for bringing us together for this fleeting moment in life. And in my case, I feel blessed to have had the pleasure of the company of certain fellow travelers for an enjoyable, extended period of time.

Marie Joseph Sebastian St. Jean

Sebastian relocated from Karaikal, a town situated eight hours away from Pondicherry, after one of his sisters got employed as a nurse there. We both joined Petit Séminaire in the same year, and our friendship developed while repeating the eighth grade in the same class. Sebastian used to be a bit chubby, so he was constantly bullied in school. He was an easy target; other kids made fun of his weight, pronunciation, and anything else they could think of.

Sebastian's father was a lawyer who worked in Paris and passed away when Sebastian was seven years old, and he was buried in Paris. Due to financial and visa difficulties, the family could not attend the funeral. Consequently, Sebastian grew up without a father figure, just like me. Nevertheless, his mother and three sisters showered him immense love as my family did.

Sebastian was a gifted poet. He wrote modern poems and shared them with me for my feedback, which he valued highly. His mother, also a poet, was fond of Tamil. Sebastian also appreciated good music. It was Sebastian who introduced me to the world of music at a time when the prevalent Indian movie songs were most commonly enjoyed. Among these, the works of Ilayaraja, a celebrated musician in Tamil films, stood the test of time. Sebastian often played these songs loudly in his home, but I regularly lowered the volume. This resulted in a constant squabble between us.

He also introduced me to the latest movies by Bharathi Raja, a revolutionary director who portrayed rural issues brilliantly with Ilayaraja's music, resulting in instant hits. Sebastian and I watched all of them together.

Sebastian and I used to go to the botanical garden, where we studied for exams, chatted freely, and appreciated nature. Sebastian would write poems and recite them to me.

Sebastian hated Petit Séminaire and despised Father Peter, who frequently picked on him. Therefore, he left the school during his ninth grade and joined Fatima Higher Secondary School, another Catholic school that was less strict. Sebastian finished high school at Fatima and enrolled in Loyola College in Chennai, which was a prestigious private college. He pursued a bachelor's degree in commerce.

Sebastian was always clear about what he wanted to do. He completed his master's in Social work. He was passionate about human resources work and rapidly climbed the ranks to become a director at several multinational companies. Later, he started his own training company for human resources personnel and achieved great success.

Sebastian has been a role model to me in numerous ways. He wedded his beloved and has raised two accomplished sons. He rescued his family from a dire financial crisis by paying off their exorbitant debts. I hold him in high esteem when it comes to life-altering decisions. Even now, we frequently converse and recollect our past experiences. In 2019, Sebastian came to the USA, and we spent a delightful week together exploring California and relishing each other's company.

Sundar

Sundar and I started off on the wrong foot. I first met him in eighth grade and immediately noticed his prestigious Hero fountain pen. In our school days, other kids did not even have a ballpoint pen until ninth grade.

The Hero pen was worth ten rupees, a significant sum of money at the time that could cover a couple of meals or a train ticket to an overnight destination. I admired its shiny golden cap and exquisite craftsmanship. He agreed to let me try it. However, when I was removing the cap, I accidentally dropped the pen on the cement floor and broke the tip.

Sundar was furious and threatened to tell his dad unless I paid him for a new pen. Having never experienced such a situation before, I was scared and feared getting into trouble. I shuddered at the thought of my brother-in-law's anger when he found out. I confided in my sister Vijaya, who gave me ten rupees from her secret savings to appease Sundar's anger. Despite his frustration with me, I still wanted to befriend him out of curiosity, and I continued to talk to him after that episode. Eventually, we became best friends.

Sundar was ahead of his time. He read Science fiction novels by famous American authors such as Isaac Asimov and vividly retold the stories to us, leaving us in awe. He transported us to a future world we never knew existed.

When other kids were watching Indian movies, Sundar was already a big Hollywood movie buff. In Pondicherry, a theater named Ratna exclusively screened English movies, and Sundar eagerly watched every new release. Sundar was obsessed with Bruce Lee, watched his movies repeatedly, and even became skilled in using the Nunchaku. He would act out the action scenes in front of his friends.

Sundar's passion for self-improvement extended beyond movies. He practiced yoga and meditation and inspired his friends to read English novels. I began my reading journey with James Hadley Chase, a pulp fiction writer whose detective novels had a simplistic yet engaging style. However, my preferred author was James A. Michener, an American writer who specialized in vividly describing the history and culture of a particular state in the US or a country from its inception to the present day. Hawaii, Alaska, and Chesapeake were my favorites among his outstanding works.

After high school, Sundar was thrilled to receive admission to an engineering school in a different state, but his joy was short-lived. His father, an alcoholic, refused to pay for his education. Despite being financially capable of doing so, he was more concerned with maintaining his drinking budget. Sundar had no choice but to give up his engineering dreams and join a local arts college. He fell into a self-destructive mode and made no positive moves in his career. He continues to hold a grudge to this day.

Upon completing his Bachelor of Science degree, specializing in Mathematics, he found himself working a dead-end job as an office secretary. One day, his grandmother called him and asked if he would be interested in going to France. Although Sundar was initially disinterested, he reluctantly agreed just to please her. His grandmother proposed to sponsor his French passport as she was a citizen of France through Sundar's grandfather, who had worked for the French Government when they ruled Pondicherry. During that time, many people in Pondicherry had the opportunity to work for the French Government. As a tribute, the French Government granted them French citizenship, which extended to their children, grandchildren, and great-grandchildren. Sundar reluctantly completed the necessary paperwork.

Soon, Sundar was summoned to the French Consulate. After a few regular questions, the immigration officer enquired about his plans to travel to France. Although caught off guard, Sundar managed to answer the questions satisfactorily and eventually received his French passport. The following day, he joined us at our regular meeting spot on the beach and shared the good news. He also confided in us that he had made a promise to the consulate to travel to France within two months. Unfortunately, he lacked the financial resources to cover the cost of airfare and expenses. Of course, his father was not going to foot the bill.

Sebastian, Umachandran, Alphonse, a few other friends, and I had recently started earning some money from work. We collectively decided to pool our resources together to fund his trip to Paris. We were able to purchase a plane ticket, some clothing, and travel necessities, and we still had some leftovers for his living expenses. We saw him off with a joyful heart at the airport, unaware that we would not see him again for more than twenty years (details in a future chapter). Sundar never returned to India and remained abroad to this day.

Selvan

In high school, Selvan was known for his humorous, outgoing, and friendly nature, but his playful behavior sometimes landed him in trouble. Henry Muthappa was our Physics teacher, who had a reputation for being strict, and students often made fun of him behind his back. One Friday afternoon, during his lecture on quantum Physics, a chalk piece accidentally fell near his foot from the back of the classroom.

As he slowly turned around, brewing anger, the classroom fell silent. Henry Muthappa demanded to know who threw the chalk. However, no one came forward, and he refused to continue the class and left.

The students were perplexed and scared. While some witnessed the incident, the vast majority had no idea who did it. Soon after, Father M. Peter entered the classroom and requested the students to anonymously write down the name of the student they thought threw the chalk. While most students took part, I chose not to name anyone and wrote that I had not witnessed the event.

Ramesh Selvaraj, the student with the most votes, was asked to visit the principal's office. He was later suspended and sent home. Selvan received the second-highest votes and was called next. The principal requested Selvan to acknowledge the incident, write a detailed report about it, and then sign it. The principal assured him that he would not be punished if he admitted to it. However, as soon as Selvan signed the report, the principal suspended him and sent him home.

Feeling devastated and cheated, Selvan retrieved his bike (students typically commuted by bike back then) and disappeared. During lunchtime, his close friend, Sathya Sai, found a note from Selvan on his bike, which he always parked next to Selvan's. The note revealed that Selvan was going to Chennai, a big city two hours away, to join the Air Force there.

Sai brought the note to Selvan's mother, who was the principal of a nearby school. Selvan's mother calmly read the note and assured Sai that she would take care of the situation. After aimlessly wandering for a while, Selvan became tired and hungry and decided to return home.

Upon arrival, his mother hugged and fed him before listening to what he had to say. She consoled him and promised to help him through the situation, recognizing that this was a critical moment when a teenager needed emotional support from their parents, friends, and teachers.

Later, Selvan's father returned home and learned of the incident. He became furious and started beating Selvan, but Selvan's mother intervened. Elizabeth, a neighbor of Selvan's, heard the commotion and went to the school to vouch for Selvan's character, having known him since the first grade. Selvan's parents then pleaded with the principal for Selvan to be reinstated in school, writing a letter promising that one more incident would result in Selvan's removal from the school. Ultimately, Selvan was reinstated on the first day of the half-yearly exam under the condition that he would be removed if another incident occurred.

After three months, Selvan's classmate made fun of Father Paul's name. As a result, the principal called that student into his office, and Selvan's name was somehow mentioned. Subsequently, Selvan was also summoned and interrogated. Enraged by this unjust treatment, Selvan later confronted the student who had dragged him into the situation and pulled his shirt, resulting in all the buttons ripped off. The student then reported the incident to the principal, who took action against Selvan. Fearing the worst, Selvan approached the vice-principal, Regis, and explained the entire situation. In the end, Selvan was cleared of the charges but was given a final warning.

When writing this chapter, I spoke to Selvan to obtain more information about the chalk incident, and he eventually revealed the truth. Selvan, Ramesh Selvaraj, and others were playfully tossing the chalk around and hitting each other with it. One of Selvan's chalks accidentally fell near the teacher. However, one can imagine being a sixteen year old and admitting to something so serious could tarnish the reputation and put one in deep trouble and have serious consequences.

However, the incident with the chalk and the fight were not the end of Selvan's troubles. After the Matriculation results were posted on the bulletin board, students gathered around to view their scores. Selvan received a 72 percent grade, which was considered very good. Father

Paul walked by and congratulated the students, attributing their success to their teachers. Selvan interjected, stating that they had worked hard as well. Father Paul glared at him but remained silent. Several months later, when all the students received their admission cards for eleventh grade, Selvan did not receive his. Selvan's father had to plead with the principal for admission. After several days of tense pleading, Selvan was ultimately accepted into the school.

Despite his eventful adolescence, Selvan persevered, largely due to the immense support he received from his parents, neighbors, and friends. Today, he works in the software industry in San Antonio, Texas, and is happily married with a daughter pursuing a career in medicine.

Besides the core gang members, there were other friends with whom I cherished my time.

Murugadass (Dass for short) and I became close friends during my time at Tagore Arts College. He contracted polio at a young age when there was little awareness about the disease in India. Many people simply believed it to be a common fever. Dass was eventually taken to emergency care as his condition worsened, and as a result, his left hand was deformed. Despite this physical disability, he remained a diligent student and became very knowledgeable about world affairs and politics. Currently, he holds a senior manager position at a major bank in India and has two children who are attending college.

Murugan and I went to school together until the tenth grade, but then he moved to Calve College in Pondicherry. We lost touch until he later joined me at Tagore Arts College. In 2008, he played a crucial role in reuniting our high school group "Meendum 16," which means "16 Again." Thanks to his efforts, we held a grand 25th-anniversary alumni celebration in Pondicherry. Murugan is an exceptionally kind-hearted person who works tirelessly to keep our group together and to expand our membership. Whenever one of us returns, he organizes gatherings to bring us all together. Currently, he is facing some health challenges, and I pray for his swift and complete recovery.

Alphonse Ligouri Raj Joseph, or Alphonse, resided behind our house in Pondicherry. He has four sisters and two brothers; his father was employed at a bank. When he was younger, he was thin and small. However, after his father passed away from cancer during his college years, Alphonse, as the eldest son, shouldered the responsibility of ensuring that all his siblings received a proper education, graduated from college, and found employment despite the family's financial constraints.

Umachandran was a close friend of mine in my high school days. He surprised us all by taking up commerce in higher secondary school. Back in the late seventies, high school was divided into two sections, the eleventh and twelfth grades, which were referred to as higher secondary. After completing the public exam in the tenth grade, students were allowed to select their path from Science, medicine, engineering, commerce, or accounting. The higher secondary focused on these areas of study and paved the way for further education and career advancement. Although no one understood Unachandran's choice, he was confident in his decision. He excelled in commerce, obtained his MBA, and became a major corporation's chief financial officer. He is part of Art of Living, an organization in India that assists financially, physically, and spiritually disadvantaged individuals. He is my role model for giving back to the community.

Albert Ravi and I became close friends in eighth grade and often hung out in front of his house with our other friends. He came from a family of two sisters and a brother, and his father was an accountant at a clothing mill in Pondicherry. Albert Ravi was an outgoing, bubbly, and fun-loving guy. Along with our friend Sundar, we used to go to the movies and took our first outing to Auroville, which I will discuss in the next chapter. After becoming a Chemical Engineer, Albert Ravi currently works as a technical officer in Malaysia. His daughter is an engineer in Melbourne, Australia. In 2010, Albert Ravi visited me in San Ramon, California; in 2019, I visited him in Kuala Lumpur. We reminisced about our old memories and found it amusing how our lives have twisted and turned.

I became friends with **Pattabiraman**, who went by Pattabi, in the ninth grade after he joined our school due to his father's transfer. Pattabi's father was a police commissioner, and his family lived in a police quarter, where we found a ping pong table. Sundar, Adiaman, Sainath, Pattabi, and I would compete against each other in the evenings after school, and it quickly became our favorite pastime.

Pattabi's mother became very close to me and treated me like her own son. She prayed for my health and future at several temples and even fasted several days a month for me. She was always kind and caring toward me and my family. She was a pious woman who held her family dear. However, Pattabi's father passed away from a heart attack at a rather young age. His mother was heartbroken and passed away soon after. This saddened me deeply because she was a kind soul who genuinely cared about me and my wellbeing. I wish I could have spent more time getting to know her and being there for her.

Adiaman became a part of my circle during the eleventh grade. After Pattabi's family moved away from the police headquarters and built their own house, we lost access to the ping pong table and felt restricted. Adiaman found a table in a community center that we could use. So, we started going there after school every day and became close friends. Adiaman had two brothers and a sister, and both of his parents were high school teachers. His parents had fallen in love during their college days, which was a rare occurrence in the 50s. They had high expectations for their children. Adiaman's older brother went on to become an agricultural engineer and later moved to the USA. He is currently a professor at a university in Nebraska and has two children.

Selvan, Sai, Dass, Murugan, Alphonse, Umachandran, Albert Ravi, Pattabi, and Adiaman are my closest friends, and I admire and have learned a great deal from them. Each of them has helped me in one way or another. Recently, when my mother had a stroke, Murugan contacted Dr. Ramesh, another friend of ours who was the head of COVID operations in Pondicherry. Dr. Ramesh assisted me in obtaining an emergency visa to India by providing me with a letter. He also recommended the head of the Pondicherry Institute of Medical Sciences, where my mother was transferred and well taken care of. Dr. Ramesh even visited my sister's home in the village of Pillayarkuppam, where my mother was recuperating, to check on her. My friends are my support system and beacon, both in my personal and professional development, and our friendship will endure for a lifetime.

Figure 14 Sebastian and me (2003)

Figure 15 Me (first from left, front row), Sai (third from left, front row), Adiaman (in black), Sundar (back row, second from left), Alphonse (back row, third from left), Sundar standing second from left, Anand(extreme right sitting) and Pattabi (back row, fourth from left), in 1987

Interlude 3: Major Challenges India Faced in the 1970s Fighting Polio

As mentioned in the previous chapter, Murugadass contracted polio, which was mistaken as a common cold and resulted in his deformity. Poliomyelitis, commonly called polio, is a severe and life-threatening illness caused by the poliovirus. The virus spreads from one person to another and can infect the spinal cord, resulting in paralysis. Fortunately, the polio vaccine can easily prevent this fatal disease, particularly the enhanced-potency IPV that was licensed in the United States in November 1987. Consequently, by the late 1990s and early 2000s, all American, European, and Western Pacific countries, including China and Australia, declared themselves polio-free. However, it was not until the 2010s that the last case of polio was finally eradicated in India.

During my childhood in the 1970s, India encountered significant challenges in combating polio due to six major reasons:

- Population: The primary obstacle is the project's vast scale, which involves vaccinating 172 million children twice a year. It is worth noting that at the time, there were only seven countries worldwide with a total population exceeding 172 million.

- Population Density: In Shantis, there were, on average, 107 people living within a 30-square-yard plot of land. A shanti, or shed, typically measured about 10 feet by 10 feet and housed a family of six. Due to the limited space, family members had to alternate sleeping on the floor. This brought to mind the story of a Vietnamese colleague of mine at the Federal Reserve Bank who was imprisoned in Vietnam for attempting to flee the communist regime. Along with others trying to escape, he was captured at sea and detained in a small cell measuring only 8 feet by 8 feet with three other individuals. The other three were forced to stand when one person needed to sleep. Fortunately, he eventually made it to the United States, where he pursued a successful career as an engineer.

- Insanitary Conditions: The living sanitation conditions in many areas, particularly in the states of Uttar Pradesh and Bihar, were appalling. Open sewers were filled with refuse, and humans defecated in plain view. Plants and crops were contaminated, among other issues.

- Contaminated drinking water: Currently, millions of people continue to suffer from a lack of access to safe and clean drinking water. Many are forced to rely on shallow wells that lack proper sanitation infrastructure, resulting in a dangerous mix of sewage and drinking water.

- Malnourishment: It appears that malnourished children do not develop the same level of immunity from the vaccine as healthy children, which is not unexpected. In developed countries, children typically receive three doses of the vaccine to achieve adequate immunity. However, in India, even after receiving 18 documented doses, some children still became infected.

- Enteric diseases: Several Indian communities suffer from the highest incidence of enteric diseases worldwide. Consequently, children receiving oral vaccine doses would not acquire immunity due to diarrhea, as the vaccine cannot stay in the body long enough to provide any benefits.

During the 1980s, the number of polio cases worldwide was estimated to be around 350,000 per year, with 150,000 of them being in India alone. However, in a WHO report released in 2013, it was revealed that only 403 cases of polio were reported globally, and none of them were in India. This is a significant reduction from the numbers reported in the 1980s.

Chapter 9:
Walk to Auroville

During my eighth grade year, my friends Ravi, Sundar, Sebastian, and I convened as usual after school to discuss our plans for the upcoming holidays. Our conversation turned to a unique town known as Auroville.

This town, located in South India, was established as a universal city devoted to the ideal of human unity. The town was inspired by the philosophy of the famous philosopher, yoga guru, and nationalist Sri Aurobindo, as well as The Mother (Mirra Alfassa, a spiritual guru and occultist who worked alongside Sri Aurobindo). Together, they envisioned a place where people of all nations could live in peace and harmony, free from the constraints of creeds, politics, and nationalities. Their goal was to achieve human unity.

Though we had heard much about Auroville, we had little information about it. All we knew was that the town was somewhere in the north and was still under construction, but we were uncertain about the exact distance. Someone said it was several kilometers away, but it sounded more like guesswork. What did we kids know about kilometers? However, our lack of knowledge only intensified our curiosity, and we became determined to explore this new land and discover all its hidden treasures. The only problem was that we lacked transportation. We were like little Columbus and Magellan, eager to explore new lands but without a means of getting there.

So, we decided to walk.

On a Saturday morning, we gathered in front of my house at the crack of dawn. With our limited funds, we bought some snacks from a nearby bakery. Instead of informing our parents about our first escapade, we simply told them that we were headed to the beach, less than a kilometer from our house.

After walking for an hour, we reached the outskirts of Pondicherry, and our legs were already feeling a bit weary. We took a quick break to have some snacks and water, and then we resumed our journey. During the trip, we shared stories about ourselves. Sundar was full of jokes and tricks that kept us entertained and prevented boredom from setting in.

Suddenly, we found ourselves walking through a fishing village, with the beach on our right and an open expanse of palm trees on our left. On the beach, we saw the fishermen's boats, with the fishermen sitting on them and repairing their nets, getting ready to begin their day on the water. The sun had already risen, and the reflection cast thousands of gold pieces on the water. We were having the time of our lives.

As we walked along the coast, some of the fishermen we passed gave us friendly smiles, and their children began to follow us. We reciprocated their gestures, exchanging high-fives with them, and continued on our way. The sun shone brightly, and its heat was intensifying. We asked the fishermen where Auroville was. They pointed us in a direction and informed us that it was a few kilometers ahead.

We walked and walked but saw no signs of Auroville. We were now in serious trouble as we had no clue where our destination was or how much further we had to go. Even if we did eventually find Auroville, it could be late in the day, and we would not have enough time to make it back before dark. However, we were already too far to turn back. The group made the decision to press on. Only later did we learn that Auroville was actually 10 kilometers away from Pondicherry.

Around midday, we passed through a mango orchard and a few more villages, feeling exhausted and hungry. The villagers told us that we were only twenty minutes away from our destination. This news immediately lifted our spirits, and we picked up our pace. Soon, we spotted a round structure looming in the distance, beckoning us to hope. We hastened toward it, almost running. When we finally arrived, we were astounded by what we saw: an open structure with several cylindrical domes that stood at our height, and a massive cement ball loomed in the background. It was unlike anything we had ever seen before and was truly unique and admirable. The only issue was that it provided very little shade, and the sun was scorching hot.

We approached the enormous cement globe situated at the center, with terracotta-colored extensions radiating outwards like pedals, and studied it closely. However, we could not discern its purpose since there were no signs or people around to ask. After wandering around for a few minutes, we decided to head back.

Later I learned that the giant globe was known as Matrimandir, which translated to "Temple of the Mother," and that it was a meditation hall that served as the heart of the spiritual community of Auroville. The concept of Auroville had been conceived in the 1960s, and construction began in the 1970s, taking 25 years to complete before being opened to the international community. Hence, when we visited, the city was still in its infancy and had yet to gain much attention.

When I returned to Auroville 30 years later in the early 2010s, it had become a vastly different place. What was once barren land had been transformed into a thriving village where approximately 2500 people worldwide lived together in harmony. Each person worked in their preferred occupation, earning the same wage, and children pursued their interests in education. The entire community lived peacefully, and I found it to be an inspiring example of human cooperation and coexistence.

Regarding Matrimandir, it had emerged as the busiest attraction in the city, drawing thousands of visitors who gathered outside the cordoned-off area. The cement sphere was now adorned with numerous shiny golden disks, imparting an aura of elegance and solemnity to the structure. We had to wait in stages at several checkpoints before being allowed to enter in small groups.

Quietly, we made our way across the overpass inside the structure. As I ascended to the meditation hall, also known as the inner chamber, located in the center, I noticed sunlight streaming in through a small window at the top. There was a colossal crystal ball, which happened to be the largest optically-perfect glass orb globally. The sun reflected on the crystal ball, casting rays in every direction. We all took our seats and faced the crystal globe to meditate. The sight resembled a scene straight out of a Star Wars movie.

With my eyes closed, I meditated in a peaceful, serene environment for ten minutes. Flashbacks of our stroll nearly three decades ago raced through my mind. I envisioned those exhausted and thirsty youngsters frantically searching for shade and water, almost collapsing but still pleased and proud of themselves. Only now, they had all grown up and moved on.

Returning to our story, as the sun gracefully descended below the horizon, the arduously extended voyage homeward appeared never-ending. We were quite anxious that our parents might dispatch a search party. Since we lacked the funds for the bus, we had no alternative but to walk and bolster each other's spirits. Ravi was despondent at the prospect of his parents being upset with him for not telling them his whereabouts. I comforted him and pledged to shoulder the blame, stating that I would tell them it was my idea. Meanwhile, Sundar was concerned about something else, and we had to reassure each other while maintaining a steady pace.

This was a new experience for us. At thirteen or fourteen, we had never spent an entire day without informing our parents of our location. At that time, there was no mobile phone or internet. We had nothing but weary legs and empty stomachs. The only thing that supported us was each other. Eventually, we arrived at my place, which was the first stop on our route, around 8 pm.

At the time, I was living at my sister's place. My mother frequently visited me and brought rice, grains, and vegetables from the village to support my sister's family. On that particular night, she was there when I arrived, and as soon as she saw me, she began shouting at me, expressing her concern and her intention to call the police. It took the efforts of Ravi and Sundar to calm her down. It was ironic that they had to explain it to my mother instead of me comforting Ravi's mother as I had promised. The gang then departed for their respective homes, leaving me at my sister's house. I was starving and hastily gobbled down the food that my sister had served.

Despite the stress and worry it brought to the families, the walk was one of the most profound experiences of our lives. We were self-reliant in our conceptualization, exploration, and achievement of our goal. We accomplished it without an incident and returned unscathed.

This experience provided us with confidence and forged a lifelong bond among us.

Figure 16 Fishermen starting the day (2023)

Figure 17 Matrimandir (2016)

Chapter 10:
Sholingur Trip for Father

During my eleventh grade summer break, my family decided to take my father on a 48-day religious retreat to a temple recommended by a priest to restore my father's physical and mental state. The temple, located in Sholingur, is one of the most famous sites of Narasimha and was also the site of a battle between the British and Hyder Ali in July, 1781, which the British won.

The temple we visited was called Thirukadigai, and it was believed to offer blessings to devotees whose worship lasted for a Kadigai (24 minutes). There were two hills, each with a temple on top. The larger hill housed the Narasimha temple, which is dedicated to the Hindu deity Narasimha, an avatar of Vishnu and his consort Lakshmi in Hindu mythology. The smaller hill had a temple dedicated to Hanuman, the monkey god who aided Lord Rama in finding Sita.

According to the priest, every morning, the entire family had to climb the smaller hill and circumambulate the outer walls of the Hanuman temple 108 times before breaking our fast. On Fridays, we had to climb the bigger hill, which was much more challenging, and circumambulate the walls of the Narasimha temple another 108 times. By the time we completed our worship, we were exhausted and sore, ready to collapse at any moment.

The retreat was extremely demanding, particularly when the sun was out during summer, and the temperature could easily reach 100 degrees Fahrenheit, which felt much hotter due to the humidity. As a 17-year-old, I preferred spending my summer break with my friends, watching Hollywood movies, or playing ping pong, but this was something I had to do for my father. Compared to my nephews (Nithi was 11, Sathi was 9, and Lokesh was seven at that time), who was my father's grandkids, I felt more obligated to be there as a son.

Every day, we adhered strictly to the routine to please the gods and cure my father's dementia. My brother-in-law, Ramasamy, was in charge of ensuring that every family member, including my nephews, completed their religious practices before eating. Since he controlled everyone, no one dared to question him, and most of us trusted in our traditions and customs. We complied with what was expected of us without asking any questions.

During the retreat, my other sisters joined us for part of the time due to their family obligations. Even my father was asked to climb hills and circle the temple 108 times with us. Although he had no idea what he was doing and would occasionally resist, my brother-in-law would yell at him and drag him along. My father's dementia made it easier for my brother-in-law to manipulate him, as he occasionally forgot what was happening and wandered off.

During the challenging and exhausting period, I needed a distraction from the physical suffering. I wrote letters detailing my experiences and daily struggles to my friend Sebastian. He sympathized with me and reminded me that enduring this hardship was necessary for my father's wellbeing. Since we did not have a landline at home until the late 90s, postal mail was the only way we could communicate. By the time we finally got a landline, I had already moved to the US.

As the saying goes, "Every cloud has a silver lining," and I learned this at 17. About halfway through the retreat, I befriended our cook/helper named Ramu, who prepared our meals and assisted with household chores like laundry and cleaning. Ramu had lost his left eye in an accident, leaving a hole with a blue eyelid in its place that scared children but did not deter me. Once we started talking, I discovered that he was a kind and wise person who shared funny stories and insights from his life experiences.

In front of the temple at ground level was a large pond, a typical feature of every Hindu temple in South India. These ponds, also known as temple tanks or Pushkarinis/Kalyanis, are built as part of the temple complex and serve as venues for social and cultural interactions among local residents.

When I saw the pond filled with water, I instantly realized that it was an opportunity for me. I had always yearned to learn how to swim but never got a chance. Now, the day has come. I asked Ramu if he could assist me, and he willingly obliged. I trusted that he might know a way to teach me, and he did. He brought a towel, tied it around my waist, and had me jump into the water. As I flapped about, Ramu held onto the towel to keep me from sinking. We practiced this routine around the same time every day, and after a week, I was able to swim on my own. I was ecstatic because swimming was an important skill that could save lives.

During that time, several kids were in the group: my nephews and nieces, aged between seven and ten. One afternoon, I proposed that we all climb a nearby hill. Although the hill was not very steep, it was a gradual climb. I challenged everyone to reach the top and return. The kids were initially enthusiastic, but as time passed, they became exhausted and wanted to turn back. I encouraged them to keep going, and eventually, everyone made it to the top.

It was already getting dark when we reached the house. My brother-in-law cornered me and demanded to know where we had been. I replied that we had gone for a hike at a nearby hill. He began shouting at me, accusing me of being irresponsible for taking the children on a hike without their parents' permission. While I did not think it was necessary, I learned a valuable lesson from his scolding.

For the remainder of the days, we repeated the same ritual over and over again. We completed the 48-day challenge successfully and returned home safely. Only my father was never cured. However, the hope that fueled these offerings was incredibly powerful and unyielding. Even though I did not believe in the ritual, I was determined to endure it to support my family's faith.

Hindus have such strong religious beliefs that they make offerings to their gods that may seem unconventional to followers of other religions. One such example is offering their hair to a specific God at a temple. If their wish is granted, they may visit the temple and shave their heads as a sign of gratitude. I myself have participated in a practice that may seem peculiar to foreigners. After successfully graduating from college, I went to the temple of my college in Melmaruvathur and offered to roll in the sand around the temple as a token of my gratitude to the gods. Although I cannot say how the gods received my offering, I can attest to the discomfort of rolling in a wet dhoti around my waist. The dhoti kept slipping, making it difficult to stay on track, and I even ended up bumping into walls and people.

There are other types of offerings that are much more agonizing than what I did. For instance, some individuals had hooks pierced through their flesh in the back and were then pulled into a chariot through ropes tied to the hooks. Others walked on a row of firebricks that stretched about ten feet long on the floor. Additionally, some individuals pierced their tongues with an arrow as a sacrifice to Lord Muruga, and it is common to witness people piercing their bodies with hooks, skewers, or small lances (Vels) during Thaipusam at Murugan Temples. Thaipusam is a festival celebrated by the Hindu Tamil community on the full moon in the Tamil month of Thai. The tradition is also festively celebrated in Malaysia and Singapore among the Tamil community there.

Finally, after forty-eight days of toil, it all came to an end. I was exhausted and eager to return home. When we arrived, I celebrated by watching a Hollywood movie with Sundar. Unfortunately, I cannot recall the name of the movie or its plot now. I suppose any movie would have sufficed.

Figure 18 Father, me, and mom (2008)

Figure 19 Sholingur in 2023 (picture from internet)

Chapter 11:
Tagore Arts College

Upon completing high school, I was admitted to Tagore Arts College to pursue a Bachelor of Science degree at the age of 18. Though disappointed about not being accepted into an engineering program, I had to come to terms with the reality and move on. The campus was situated on a hill roughly five kilometers from Pondicherry, and commuting felt like a daily excursion. I decided to skip the first month of college because of senior students' ritualistic bullying of first-year students, commonly known as "ragging" in India.

Ragging is a customary "initiation ritual" that is prevalent in higher education institutions throughout the Indian subcontinent, encompassing India, Pakistan, Bangladesh, and Sri Lanka. This practice is comparable to hazing in North America, bizutage in France, praxe in Portugal, and comparable practices in academic institutions globally. Ragging involves the abuse, humiliation, or harassment of new entrants or junior students by senior students. Seniors may intimidate or threaten juniors to complete their assignments, skip classes, refrain from participating in activities or clubs, etc. Sometimes, freshmen are not permitted to engage in any academic-related tasks other than attending lectures during university hours. It frequently takes a malicious form, with newcomers being subjected to psychological or physical torture or both. In 2009, the University Grants Commission of India implemented regulations in Indian universities to curb ragging and established a toll-free "anti-ragging helpline."

In 1996, the dismembered body of Pon Navarasu, a 19-year-old student at Rajah Muthiah Medical College in Chidambaram, Tamil Nadu, was found scattered across different parts of the state. It was alleged that his senior, John David, had physically assaulted him when he refused to strip and lick David's footwear. David was subsequently found guilty and sentenced to two consecutive life sentences.

Another incident occurred in 2009 at Dr. Rajendra Prasad Medical College in Himachal Pradesh, where a freshman named Aman Satya Kachroo was ragged to death by four seniors, Ajay Verma, Naveen Verma, Mukul Sharma, and Abhinav Verma, who were all under the influence of alcohol. The four accused students gathered around several 13 first-year students and ordered them to slap and hit each other, which continued until 4 am the following day. Kachroo sustained fatal head injuries and passed away that night. The four accused were granted early release based on their "good conduct" in 2013 and were subsequently re-enrolled in a government college.

The problem of ragging is widespread in India, and even esteemed institutions such as medical colleges have a history of it. It is sometimes viewed as a college tradition, but in recent years, it has come under increasing scrutiny due to the rising number of cases resulting in severe injuries or deaths being reported and exposed.

At the national level, ragging is currently defined as any act of physical or mental abuse, including bullying and exclusion, that targets a student, whether a freshman or not, based on their color, race, religion, caste, ethnicity, gender (including transgender), sexual orientation, appearance, nationality, regional origins, linguistic identity, place of birth, place of residence, or economic background. In compliance with Supreme Court orders, the Indian government launched a National Anti-Ragging Helpline in 2009. Additionally, the Anti-Ragging NGO Society Against Violence in Education (SAVE) has reported that ragging is prevalent in medical schools, engineering, and other institutions.

Although ragging is now illegal, it still continues to occur in secret, and victims are often too afraid to report it to authorities. As a result, I decided to skip the first month of college entirely, as ragging was supposed to stop officially after that period. Attendance was not a problem because it was not closely monitored by the school. Instead, it was largely controlled by students, and the lecturers and professors often left after teaching their classes.

When I finally started college, I attended botany and Biology classes initially, but after a few weeks, I was able to transfer to Mathematics, which was a highly sought-after subject, second only to Physics and Chemistry. Fortunately, Sundar was also in my Mathematics class, and I was relieved to have someone to attend classes and share notes with. Alphonse was also a student at Tagore Arts but studied in the commerce department. Alphonse lived right behind my house, and we rode to college together on one bike. Since I had to give up my bike to my cousin, who needed it for school during the day, Alphonse often gave me a ride on his bike, which was quite heavy and made the journey to college even more arduous.

One day, feeling sorry for Alphonse, I offered to ride the bike, and to my surprise, it was not as bad as I expected until we hit the hilly road that we had to pass through each time. Climbing uphill was challenging, but I managed to overcome it. After arriving at college and going to our respective classes, I began to feel a strange sensation in my throat, as if something was blocking it, making it difficult to breathe. Despite drinking water to relieve the blockage, the sensation persisted. At lunch, I told Sundar and Alphonse something was wrong with me.

Immediately, they offered to give me a ride home. As soon as I arrived, Sebastian's second sister, Vasanthi, who happened to be a nurse, rushed over to check on me. She thoroughly examined my breathing and heartbeat and advised that I be taken to the hospital right away. Once at the hospital, an X-ray was taken, and the doctor recommended that I be transferred to JIPMER, a larger hospital with more medical equipment and specialists.

Without delay, I was taken to JIPMER, and a lung specialist examined my X-ray and promptly admitted me. After further examination, it was discovered that I had a condition known as "Emphysematous Bullae," or "Bullous Emphysema," which literally means "a bubble in the lung" but is better known as the "vanishing lung syndrome." This condition is characterized by damage to the inner walls of the air sacs (alveoli) in the lungs, eventually leading to their rupture.

Consequently, a larger air space is created, reducing the available surface area for gas exchange. In the United States, the condition ranks as the third leading cause of death, and individuals living with it are at higher risk of developing a collapsed lung, which can be fatal if their lung function is already compromised. Unfortunately, there is currently no cure for this condition, and patients are advised to rest and alter their lifestyles, such as quitting smoking.

During my hospitalization, I spent a week alone, and my family brought me food every day. Although Sebastian, Sundar, Alphonse, and other friends visited me, I felt lonely when nobody was around. During the Pongal festival, my sister was supposed to bring me special food, but she arrived very late, and I became angry because I was starving. Looking back now, I realize that my reaction was unreasonable, and I feel guilty about it.

After my condition stabilized, I was discharged from the hospital. It was the closest I had ever come to death.

Aside from my scare of Bullous Emphysema, my college experience was marked by a dearth of activities and tedium. There simply was not a whole lot to do: Ping Pong was the most popular sport, but the seniors often occupied the tables, and the juniors were hesitant to challenge them. Despite the presence of girls in the college, they tended to socialize separately from the boys. Although the boys attempted to initiate conversations with the girls, they generally kept their distance. While occasionally, boys and girls formed relationships, religious and caste disparities often created obstacles.

In college, I struggled with Mathematics and earned poor grades. Trigonometry and equations proved too challenging for me, and I did not devote enough time to studying. Yet this college was already the lowest tier of all colleges—the pecking order went from arts, Science, law, agriculture, and engineering to medicine, with medicine at the top and arts at the bottom. I lacked motivation and passion for my studies and had no career aspirations or direction. I attended classes merely for the sake of attendance. My friends were the same. None of us knew what the future held.

Figure 20 Tagore Arts College in 2023 (picture from internet)

Interlude 4: My First Bike

Until ninth grade, I did not own a bicycle. In the 70s and 80s, before motorcycles and scooters became prevalent in India, bikes were a crucial mode of transportation. In a small town like Pondicherry, owning a bike was essential for daily activities like going to school, the market, or meeting friends. However, for a long time, I had to get around on foot.

In contrast, all my friends had the latest bicycles, which made me feel ashamed of relying on them to hang out and move around town. One day, my third brother-in-law, Vijayaraghavan, the only brother-in-law who was educated and held a job, showed up at my door with a bike. He said it was for me.

Vijayaraghavan was a kind, straightforward, and calm person. Unlike my other three brother-in-laws, he had a bachelor's degree and treated my sister gently. At the time, he was in his twenties and working in the administration office of a sugarcane factory. I had immense respect for him for living within his means.

Vijayaraghavan noticed my struggle to travel and my dependency on my friends for mobility. Despite having limited savings, he made a compassionate decision to purchase a used bike and rode 30 kilometers to deliver it to me at my sister's house. The generosity and care he displayed for my wellbeing left me incredulous. I had always held Vijayaraghavan in high regard, but this act of kindness raised my respect for him even further.

After that day, I relished the freedom of riding the bike and the pleasure of the wind caressing my hair as I cruised around town.

Fast forward to 2018, when Vijayaraghavan's daughter Deva was getting married, I was able to return the favor. By then, he had retired and was struggling to make ends meet. The cost of the wedding was overwhelming for him, and I stepped in to share the expenses with him. We successfully organized a beautiful wedding, and Deva was happily married. I felt grateful for the opportunity to repay Vijayaraghavan's kindness and glad to be of help. The image of him arriving at my door on a bike during my school days would never fade away.

Figure 21 Vijayaraghavan and my third sister Samitha celebrating Vijayaraghavan's 70th birthday (2022)

Chapter 12:
Engineering at APEC

When I was in my second year at Tagore Arts College with my career plan in limbo, Ramasamy, my brother-in-law, one day told me that I was admitted to an engineering college. I could not believe my ears. He had used his connections to secure me a spot at a newly established college called Adhiparasakthi Engineering College (APEC). The campus was situated in Melmaruvathur, a town located approximately two and a half hours away from Pondicherry, but it was close enough that I could return home on weekends.

Without hesitation, I decided to leave Tagore Arts College and join APEC. Although I was apprehensive about pursuing engineering after struggling at the art college, I was determined to succeed. APEC offered three streams of study: Civil, Mechanical, and Electronics and Communication Engineering. I dismissed Civil Engineering due to the prevailing notion at the time that civil engineers had difficulty finding jobs. Mechanical Engineering seemed too complex, involving lathe, machine drawing, and various machinery. Electronics and Communication Engineering was a relatively unknown field, but I was always intrigued by the unknown and motivated by mysteries. Later, I discovered that many of my classmates shared my confusion when it came to selecting a major—they were equally clueless.

As the college was new, the classrooms were makeshift and resembled huts with thatched roofs. Despite the modest accommodations, no one complained since we were content to be studying engineering. I resided in the dormitory, which was called a "hostel" in India, with approximately twenty other students, where we shared a large hall and slept on mats and pillows placed on the floor. Each of us had only one box to hold our clothes and possessions. Life was uncomplicated for college students, and our daily routine consisted of waking up in the morning, attending classes, returning to the hostel, having our meals, completing homework, and going to bed. Although it was tedious, I was delighted to do all the mundane tasks and establish friendships that would last a lifetime.

Occasionally, we deviated from our routine and took a stroll around the neighboring fields. Since the college was constructed on farmland, some enormous wells were nearby. The wells were massive, with clear water and steps leading down to it. I had not gone swimming since I was in eleventh grade at Sholingur in the temple pond, and the water appeared inviting.

I persuaded a couple of my classmates to join me, and we ventured down the steps to explore the water. We noticed another student in the water who seemed to be an experienced swimmer. I asked him if he could assist me in swimming across to the other side of the well, which was roughly 20 feet long, and he agreed.

I began confidently, but as I reached the center of the water, I was suddenly gripped by panic. I waved my hands frantically, trying to signal the other student for help, but he was nowhere to be seen. As I flailed about in terror, I felt someone grab me by the stomach and carry me to the other side of the well.

The incident kept me away from the water for a few days; then, I was tempted to go swimming again. I convinced a friend named Saravanan to accompany me to the well. When we arrived, memories of the previous incident flooded my mind, and I became hesitant to proceed. Saravanan shared my apprehension. However, after a brief moment, we mustered the courage to descend the stairs. I jumped into the water and began swimming near the steps, inspiring Saravanan to follow suit. He stepped onto what he thought was a stair, but it turned out to be just a void covered in dead leaves, causing him to plunge straight into the water. He bobbed up and down, gasping for air and swallowing water. I quickly swam over, grabbed his arm, and pulled him ashore.

Our little adventure was over. We dried ourselves off, dressed, and returned to the hostel. From that day forward, we never ventured into the water without assistance again.

On weekends, I would occasionally visit Sebastian in Chennai. During one such visit, my second sister Subhashini and her husband happened to be passing by Maduranthakam. They somehow discovered my address and decided to pay me a visit. When they knocked on the door, my roommates and some friends were watching, let us just say, a movie for mature people. My friends panicked and shouted from inside that Babu was not home and would not return soon. Subhashini was curious and wanted to come in and see where I lived, but my roommates would only allow them to enter over their dead bodies. As a result, Subha had no choice but to leave.

Later, when Subhashini saw me, she expressed her disappointment and asked what my roommates were doing that was so important they could not let her in. I told her they were preparing for an exam and could not be disturbed, but she did not seem entirely convinced.

As mentioned earlier, I was content with the mundane routine, but not everyone felt the same. During my first year, some students were bored on weekends and always seemed to be looking for trouble. On one occasion, they decided to shave their mustaches and thought it would be a good idea to give everyone else a free shave, too.

Mustaches were a big part of a man's feature back then in India. It was a symbol of masculinity, maturity, and authority. The news circulated around my hostel, causing us to panic. However, one of my roommates, Giri, who believed himself to be strong and fast, decided to challenge the group responsible for taking students' mustaches.

Upon hearing the challenge, the group quickly captured Giri, pinned him to the ground, and shaved off his mustache using a razor despite Giri's pleas for mercy. Later on, he walked around attempting to persuade others that he looked even cooler without his mustache.

As for myself, I considered my mustache to be a source of pride, and I refused to part with it at any cost. Consequently, I devised a "brilliant plan" to seek refuge in the warden's room. After learning about the situation, the warden summoned the group responsible and issued them a warning. As a result, the students abandoned their behavior, and I was perceived as a traitor for a significant period. However, I was unconcerned as long as my mustache remained on my face. In retrospect,

I am uncertain if informing the group was the best solution to the matter, but the entire situation was undoubtedly comical.

Apart from the incidents mentioned above, my college life was plain sailing, or was supposed to be, until a specific event occurred one day.

Figure 22 APEC class reunion in 2013

Figure 23 Most wanted men in India... just kidding... my student headshot in 1984

Chapter 13:
Off the Campus

August marked monsoon's arrival in Tamil Nadu, where our college was located. Despite being known for mild rainfall, the region had been facing drought for several consecutive years. However, this year was unlike any other; the rain was unrelenting and led to devastating floods.

The college was situated on the dried-up base of a lake that had remained barren for over two decades. The heavy rainfall caused the entire area to flood, and the hostel was submerged in knee-deep water. We managed to salvage our belongings from the muddy water and were eventually sent back home.

After a few weeks, the water receded, and the college resumed operations. However, the toilets were still filled with water, making them unusable. As a result, we were forced to relieve ourselves in the nearby fields behind the bushes, which was humiliating and hazardous. Furthermore, the flood-enriched mud became a breeding ground for insects and diseases, risking our health. To address the issue, ten students, including myself, formed a representative body to negotiate with the administration.

The representatives conveyed our living conditions to the administration and requested an alternative living arrangement until the situation improved. The administration listened to our concerns and agreed to our demands, promising to find a solution within two weeks. However, the deadline came and went without any progress. Another week passed, yet nothing changed, leaving us with no choice but to protest. We took to the highway, stopping passenger buses and chanting our slogan, "Down, down, APEC!" We simply wanted to live in normal conditions and not like animals in the woods.

After a couple of months, the floods finally subsided, and everything was back to normal in the hostel. The hostel had been cleaned, and we no longer had to use the bushes as bathrooms. All the problems we had encountered were forgotten.

When summer break ended, I arrived at the hostel with my luggage, eager to begin my second year of classes. However, an administrator stopped me at the entrance and informed me that I was not registered to live there. He suggested I go to the administration office to sort things out. I went to the office and spoke with one of the accountants, a short, fair, and plump man in his thirties. I explained that there must have been a mistake, but he checked the records and confirmed that there was no mistake. He told me in no uncertain terms that students responsible for the protest the previous year were not allowed to stay in the hostel. Sadly, I had no choice but to leave in disappointment.

I spoke to my friends Ramesh, Rajendran, and Sudhakar, and they all faced the same fate. We decided to search for a room in Maduranthakam, and luckily, we found a spacious one we liked on the first floor of a landlord's house (equivalent to the second floor in the US). The rent was only 200 rupees then, which was quite affordable. We ate at nearby restaurants, which were dingy and served tasteless food, but it was all we could afford. Most of the students, including myself, went home for the weekend on Friday evening. I was happy to be reunited with my family and friends.

Despite the cheap rent, my financial situation was dire. In addition to paying for tuition and my apartment, I required an average of fifty rupees per week for bus fare and food expenses. Although it was not much, my family struggled to come up with the money, forcing me to borrow from other students. At the end of the year, I would receive a summons from the administration and be compelled to visit the accountant's office with shame. They would then caution me that unless I paid my college fees for the year, I would be unable to take the final exams, and there would be a significant penalty for late payment. My brother-in-law had to acquire another loan on top of the ones we had already taken out to pay the tuition and the penalty. Looking back, I am astounded by how I managed to survive those difficult financial times year after year.

My brother-in-law employed a cook to allow us to enjoy home-cooked meals in college. We shared the cost of groceries as well as the cook's salary. The cook prepared delectable meals and brought them to campus during lunch hour, and we were extremely pleased with the food and the cook's services. Unfortunately, the cook had family obligations and could only work for one month. As a result, we were once again forced to eat subpar food at low-quality eateries.

As mentioned before, my first brother-in-law, Ramasamy, was handling the finances of the family. But he had no clue how finances worked. His motto was, as I understood it, "Just borrow it." This included lending money out, often resulting in the funds not being returned. Ramasamy would borrow money from friends, relatives, and acquaintances at a high-interest rate. When it came time to pay back the debt, he would simply borrow from someone else, continuing a vicious cycle. Sometimes, I wondered if he was a finance amateur or a Pyramid scheme mastermind. Lenders frequently visited our home, and it was not uncommon for them to create a scene outside, embarrassing our family.

We had a wise, elderly gentleman who visited our home every week, attempting to collect the money we owed him. Despite not receiving any payments, he would patiently spend hours talking to Ramasamy and then leave empty-handed. Unfortunately, he never saw his money returned in his lifetime. Years later, after I started working in the US, I discussed the numerous pending loans with my mother and Ramasamy, many of which had astronomical compound interest. We created a list of all the debts, and I started paying them off one by one.

Due to my lack of trust in Ramasamy regarding financial matters, I decided to send the loan repayment to Vijayaraghavan, my third brother-in-law, who had a reputation for being proficient in handling finances. Despite Ramasamy's objection, I remained resolute in my decision. I was sure that if I sent the money to him, he would allocate it toward other expenses and neglect repaying the loans. Eventually, after several years, I managed to repay all the loans with interest.

Living in the village shielded me from the allure of Pondicherry, which allowed me to concentrate on my studies despite experiencing financial difficulties. Unlike many other students who could not resist the temptation of social events and entertainment in Pondicherry, I used my study holidays to travel to Kothambakkam and focus on my studies. Except for my fourth semester, I passed all my exams on the first attempt, which was a significant accomplishment. I felt proud of myself for achieving this feat.

On some weekends, when we had classes, we had to stay in Melmaruvathur. A Professor from Anna University, a renowned university in Tamil Nadu, came to teach us Statistics and Probability Theory, a rather tricky subject. Although the topic was abstruse, I managed to pass the exam, while many students did not.

During our third year of college, we had our first computer. It was kept in an air-conditioned room, and to enter, we had to remove our shoes, similar to how we show respect to a shrine in a sacred temple. Only a few privileged individuals who knew about computers were allowed to touch them. Unfortunately, I never had the opportunity to use it myself. Even after starting my first job as an associate lecturer, I could not access a computer. It was not until I began my master's program in the US that I finally laid my hands on computers. The first computer I used was a mainframe terminal that was not easy to operate and was already outdated. Nonetheless, I always knew that my strength was not in technology, so I did not miss much.

Figure 24 Monsoon season in Chennai (picture from internet)

Chapter 14:

Rajan

During my final year in college, I came across the principal in the hallway on my way to my class. I greeted him, expecting him to walk by, but instead, he came over and said, "Babu, can you come to my office after the classes, please? I have to talk to you."

It filled me with fear. I considered all the possibilities that could have led to the request, including poor grades or saying something negative about the college. As a less-than-exemplary student, especially following the protest incident, the thought of failing to graduate in my final year caused me to shudder at the potential implications for my future.

Throughout the day, I could not focus on my coursework, with a massive cloud of fear hanging over me. Eventually, I walked into his office, consumed by a sense of impending doom. The principal told me to sit down and asked if I was from Pondicherry. I replied yes. He then told me that a freshman named Rajan was also from Pondicherry but had not attended classes in several weeks. He asked if I could check on him when I went home on the weekend. I had a big sigh of relief followed by a responsibilit that I could actually help someone.

The following weekend, before heading home, I went directly to Rajan's house. Upon knocking on the door, a middle-aged woman answered and seemed perplexed when I inquired about Rajan's whereabouts. She told me that she was waiting for him to return from college. I asked if I could speak with her for a few minutes. She invited me inside and offered me a cup of coffee. I explained the reason why I was there.

Rajan's mother's expression conveyed a mixture of shock, horror, and sadness. Immediately, tears streamed down her face. She told me that Rajan's father worked in Chennai, which was a three-hour drive from

Pondicherry. Consequently, he could only visit on weekends and had neither the time nor resources to monitor Rajan's college attendance. Rajan's mother felt powerless and uncertain about what to do. She was too afraid to tell her husband about the situation.

Although my mission was complete, I felt compelled to offer assistance. Perhaps it was because I understood Rajan's confusion and pain, having also lacked guidance from my father. I promised his mother that I would uncover the root cause of the issue and persuade Rajan to return to college. She expressed relief and gratitude and told me that Rajan typically returned home at 7 pm, which was in one hour.

I waited in the house until a fair, slim young man of average height arrived at precisely 7 o'clock. Rajan was taken aback when he saw me. I introduced myself and requested a private conversation, so we took a short walk. Rajan lit a cigarette and offered me one. I politely declined and told him I did not smoke. Then, I broached the topic and inquired why he was not attending classes. That was when he opened up.

Rajan did not like anything about the college. He thought the college did not have proper infrastructure, lacked laboratories, and the instructors were incompetent. When I inquired about his alternative plan, he expressed an interest in studying something in the field of art. However, when I asked him about his specific area of passion, he revealed that he had none. I then questioned why he could not complete his current studies to establish a secure financial foundation for future endeavors, given that he had no immediate plans.

It is important to note that a bachelor's degree in the arts did not guarantee a promising career back then, and many graduates struggled to find employment with a decent pay. Financial support from parents was often necessary, but was challenging for those from low-income families, such as myself. I shared my personal financial struggles with Rajan, and he considered my words carefully.

After some contemplation, Rajan asked about the possibility of returning to college despite having missed significant amounts of school. He expressed concerns that the principal and lecturers might not allow him to catch up on missed coursework. However, I assured him I would speak to them and that he could make up for missed classes and laboratory work through hard work and determination.

On Monday, I picked up Rajan from his house, and we took the bus together to school, which took ninety minutes. We chatted about his interests during the ride and discovered our shared love for Bollywood movies and music. Our conversation led to a strong bond, and by the end of the ride, Rajan was much friendlier toward me. He realized that I had his best interests at heart, and I was happy to have made a positive impact on someone's life.

Upon arrival at college, we went to the principal's office, where Rajan was warmly welcomed. The principal expressed gratitude toward me and assured me that he would take care of Rajan. I left, curious about what would happen to Rajan. Later, I learned that he had not faced any repercussions for his prior absence from school and had fulfilled his commitment to attending classes regularly. He focused on his studies and turned his academic life around. While I saw him several times on-campus, I never heard from him after graduation.

Several years later, during my visit to India from the USA, I was in Pondicherry and recalled Rajan. I wondered how he was doing, so I asked my nephew to drive around the area and look for Rajan's house. Finding his house was an easy task as I vividly remembered the place.

I knocked on the door, and like the last time, his mother opened it. She recognized me right away and was so happy to see me. She invited us inside and made us coffee just like the last time. I asked about Rajan. She said he worked as a software engineer in the Netherlands and was happily married with a child. I was so excited to hear this news. It felt like I was just given an adrenaline shot. I had no idea he could have gone this far, and maybe the little talk we had back then had something to do with it.

It was fulfilling and heartfelt that I could make some impact and play a role in someone else's life. Since then, mentorship has become one of my passions. There is no greater satisfaction in life than making an impact on someone else's life and changing it for the better, especially in a country like India, where millions, if not billions, of people still live in poverty without much education. Sometimes, a nudge in the right direction can turn their fortunes around. The discovery of mentorship opened a new horizon for me.

Figure 25 APEC in early 2020s (picture from internet)

Interlude 5: Sports

I began playing sports much later than my peers of the same generation. It was not until the ninth grade that I tried my hand at ball badminton.

Ball badminton is different from regular badminton in that instead of a shuttlecock; you play with a softball larger than a ping pong ball but smaller than a tennis ball. My friends Pattabi, Adiaman, Sundar, and I would gather at Pattabi's house before heading to the court to play.

Through playing ball badminton, I discovered that I was a slow learner, with a longer reaction time than most kids. To help me improve, my friends positioned me next to the net and instructed me to keep my bat upright and smash the ball when it came my way. This strategy worked wonders, and I was able to do a decent job.

Later in high school, we moved on to playing ping pong. We stumbled upon a table inside the police headquarters, where Pattabi's father worked as a police commissioner. The table was in a storage unit, surrounded by furniture, police gear, and miscellaneous items. Despite the dust, the ping pong table beckoned us to play, and we quickly became hooked.

After school, we gathered at the quarters to play every day. I developed a defensive playing style while Sundar became more offensive. We even started a little competition among ourselves. We learned that to produce good spin on serves and shots, we needed a good paddle, which cost 100 rupees at the time. However, this was a luxury for me, given my family's financial situation—the rent for the four-bedroom house I lived in with my older sister Vijaya was 200 rupees. So, while Pattabi and Adiaman were able to obtain good paddles right away, I had to come up with a solution on my own.

I began to save money diligently and opportunistically, collecting one rupee here and another rupee there. My fixation at the time was a high-quality ping pong paddle, which I desired more than anything else in the world. Whenever my mother visited, I would request a few rupees and set them aside. Similarly, when Vijaya gave me an allowance, I stashed it beneath a book in my suitcase. If a family member requested that I purchase an item from the store, I would ask if I could keep the change. After six months of frugal saving, I amassed one hundred rupees and gave the money to Pattabi's cousin, who lives in New Delhi. Only stores in that city carried the high-end paddles that I craved.

I had to wait until the summer when Pattabi's cousin visited Pondicherry with the paddle I had coveted. I was overjoyed when I finally held the paddle; it was made from a special type of rubber that produced better spin. I began to play immediately and quickly discovered it was an ideal fit for my playing style. I could now defeat players who had previously beaten me, thanks to the paddle's exceptional quality. Additionally, I developed a powerful spin that none of my friends could handle. For a time, ping pong became my main preoccupation.

After happily playing for a few years at the quarters, things changed one day when Pattabi's family built their own house and moved away. Consequently, we lost access to the ping pong table. Although we managed to find another table in a different part of town, it lasted only a short time.

Later on, everyone moved away for college, and our ping pong dreams were crushed. I did not get a chance to play again until thirty years later when I went to South Dakota in the 90s. After I joined the Federal Reserve Bank of San Francisco, we had a ping pong tournament, and I won the intermediate level. I was glad I still had the touch after over a quarter of a century.

Upon arriving in the United States, I was astounded to find public tennis courts in every school and park in Oklahoma. In India, tennis was considered an even greater luxury than ping pong, and most children could not afford a racket, nor were there any public tennis courts. Membership in a tennis club was necessary to play the sport.

Although I was curious about tennis in Oklahoma, I had limited time to explore as I was only there for a single summer. Once I began attending school in Brookings, South Dakota, I purchased a tennis racket from Walmart for a mere $10 and started playing with friends. I was eager to invite anyone and everyone to play, which some people found a bit manic. Despite this, I became quite skilled in a short amount of time. I even played in frigid temperatures with a friend named Bob. We had to clear the snow from the court with a broom and play while wearing gloves, a scarf, and a thick jacket.

From sports, I gained resilience and a fighting spirit that has proven essential in navigating life's challenging game. It's impossible to win without these qualities, and by enduring the sweat and pain, we grow into better versions of ourselves.

Years later, while I was writing this, my passion for sports waned. It has been over a year since I last stepped on the field, court, or pitch. However, my enthusiasm for sports has led me to watch some of the most significant events in the world of athletics, including the 2011 London Wimbledon, the 2012 London Olympics, the 2014 Brazil Soccer World Cup, the 2018 Australian Open, the 2018 Sydney 7 rugby, the Bashers cricket game in Melbourne in 2018, and the 2019 US Open. I'll discuss these experiences in more detail in later chapters.

Figure 26 Me at a Ping Pong tournament in Chinatown in San Francisco (2014)

Figure 27 Winners of a Fed Ping Pong tournament (2015)

Chapter 15:
First Professional Job

After completing my college education, I was filled with energy and enthusiasm, eager to conquer the world. I began my job search with great hope, submitting many applications and interviewing with numerous companies, and received zero offers.

Despondent but not deterred, I applied for public service and military positions, such as the Air Force, and had to travel to the city of Mysore for an overnight bus ride to take the exam. I also attempted an engineering position at Bhabha Atomic Research Center in Bombay, but once again, no luck. Without any prior work experience, finding a job proved to be incredibly challenging, leading to frustration and distress on a daily basis. The financial situation at home did not make things any easier, and after six months of searching, nothing had changed.

One day, while perusing the classified ads in the national newspaper of India, Indian Express, an advertisement caught my eye. The ad was for "Associate Lecturers" at a private college in Bangalore named "Dr. Ambedkar Institute of Technology." Something about the name struck a chord with me, and I soon realized that it was the same college where my high school friend Rosario Anand had been going.

Although I knew the odds were slim, I felt a sense of karma and decided to apply anyway. Little did I know, it was the best decision I ever made, and looking back years later, it was the decision that led me to embark on an adventure to a faraway land thousands of miles away from home.

A week after submitting my application, I received a call on a Friday night from the college inviting me for an interview. Without hesitation, I traveled overnight to Bangalore and arrived at the college early Monday morning. I was greeted by the head of the Electrical and Electronics

Department in a conference room, where he quickly scanned my Bio Data, which is the equivalent of a resume in the US, and proceeded to discuss job duties and salary. He asked if I could start as soon as possible, to which I replied yes without hesitation. The entire interview lasted less than five minutes, and I was immediately led to his office for the paperwork.

I was overjoyed at the prospect of my first job in my career. Finally, someone was actually willing to pay me for my skills. The contract offered a salary of one thousand rupees per month, with two hundred and fifty rupees withheld until I had completed a certain number of years with the school. Though this was significantly lower than the typical starting salary of five thousand rupees for an engineering position, I was thrilled to have the opportunity to kickstart my career and begin earning a living.

After the initial excitement faded, I realized that the one thousand rupees would barely cover my expenses, let alone provide any relief to my financially strained family. I stayed with my friend Anand for the first three months in Malleshwaram, a major town in Bangalore. The daily commute to college was unbearable, involving two crowded buses. Students were flocking to nearby villages like Malathahalli, where new buildings were springing up to cater to their accommodation needs. The late 80s and early 90s saw a significant influx of students from all over India, particularly from Andhra Pradesh (Pradesh means state or province) and Jammu/Kashmir region, to engineering colleges in Bangalore.

After three months, I moved in with my college friend Saravanan, who was also struggling to find a job. I suggested that he apply to my school, and he was offered a position, leading him to join me in Bangalore. Despite the distance, I would make a monthly trip back to Pondicherry, where I met my friend Danabalou Ramachandran (also known as DR). Although he had graduated from a prestigious college in the town of Kakinada in Andhra Pradesh a year before me, he was still unemployed. I referred him to my school, and he was offered a position, much to his mother's relief, who personally thanked me. DR moved into my room, and we later welcomed Sivakumar, another friend from

Pondicherry who had joined the college as an associate lecturer, making our room a foursome accommodation.

Life in Mallathalli was uncomplicated and enjoyable. At one point, our room housed five people, four of whom came from Pondy (short for Pondicherry). On weekdays, I would attend college, teach, grade papers, and then return home. Afterward, my friends and I usually headed to an open field and played cricket until it got dark. Despite my inability to bowl or field, I developed a keen interest in cricket and could at least bat a little. I had the opportunity to watch two cricket matches in Bangalore: India vs Australia, a one-day international game, and India vs New Zealand, a five-day test match, where the legendary Sir Richard Hadlee was playing.

On weekends, I would visit Mahatma Gandhi Road located downtown, where I could watch two to three Hollywood movies back-to-back. During the break after the first movie, I would treat myself to a buffet lunch at a good restaurant before returning to the theater for the second movie. Later, I would have dinner and end the day with the third movie in the evening. I would then catch the last bus home and usually return quite late. Regrettably, I spent many weekends just watching movies without being productive. Looking back now, I could have achieved so much more in my life. I could have pursued further studies, worked part-time, acquired new skills, and so on. But at that time, I was not thinking about my future or considering my options; I was simply living in the moment.

Although it may have sounded carefree, I was quite anxious initially. As someone without a teaching background, public speaking was a daunting task. In eighth grade, when I first joined Petit Séminaire High School, the school hosted a speaking competition in the Tamil language. Although I had never spoken in public before, for some reason, I was excited and signed up immediately. I memorized the speech word-for-word and thought I was ready. However, when my name was called and I went up on stage, I suddenly began sweating profusely, my mouth became dry, and my tongue was stuck. I managed to stutter the first sentence, but then I froze. Nothing came out of my mouth after that, and I stood there for five minutes before returning to my seat dejected. To this day, I still vividly remember the feeling.

Before beginning my lecturer job at Dr. Ambedkar Institute of Technology, I was worried about what might happen during my classes. Would I embarrass myself and become a laughingstock for the school and students? Would I be fired if they found out I could not speak in front of a class? Losing this job would be devastating for my career. However, when I stepped up to the podium, I was surprised to find that I was able to speak comfortably in front of a room of 30 students. I had no idea why, but it came naturally to me. I was amazed that I was able to survive the situation. I had thought I was terrible at public speaking, but I proved myself wrong and discovered a hidden talent instead.

After that, things began to move more smoothly. One aspect of this job that I particularly enjoyed was the opportunity to positively impact my students' lives. I encouraged them to be courageous and confident, sometimes even asking them to stand at the front of the classroom and teach their peers using the blackboard. This exercise helped many students overcome their fear of public speaking. My unconventional teaching methods were well-liked by the students; some even sought my advice and assistance.

As I gained experience, I continued to refine my skills. I even started tutoring Mathematics, a subject that was not part of my college education. To prepare for the role, I studied the subject in advance and ensured that I was well-equipped to answer any questions that came my way. My proficiency in English, on the other hand, proved helpful for students who needed assistance in this area.

My responsibilities expanded rapidly. The college administration assigned me to host college events and later to supervise and grade papers for the annual exams. The final exams were a significant undertaking, but I was able to handle my responsibilities effectively. The icing on the cake was that I was paid for my work.

I endeavored to excel in my role there, using every possible means to succeed. Unfortunately, the meager income could not sustain my family, who were burdened with debts. I had to take drastic measures to put myself in a position to survive and repay the loans and support them. Changes were imperative.

Dr. Ambedkar Institute of Technology was my first professional job, and it provided me with the means to survive. I was grateful and did my best for the school. However, I regretted the manner in which I left. When a better opportunity presented itself, I resigned without notifying the school, fearing that they might not approve it. Some of my colleagues did the same thing. By leaving in this way, I left money on the table. I had been with the school for almost four years and was eligible for the withheld salary, which amounted to about 10,000 rupees. Additionally, I did not give the school an opportunity to arrange a smooth transition or bid farewell to my students. In retrospect, I could have and should have planned my exit better.

*Figure 28 Dr. Ambedkar Institute of Technology in 2023
(picture from the internet)*

Chapter 16:
Kullu Manali Hiking Trip

During my stay in Bangalore, I stumbled upon the Bangalore Youth Hostel and its activities. I was familiar with the concept of youth hostels because I had lived close to one in Pondicherry. I found the idea of young people traveling and staying in hostels, exchanging ideas, and meeting people from different parts of the world fascinating. This experience laid the foundation for my later passion for travel.

During that year, the Bangalore Youth Hostel had planned a summer hiking trip in the Himalayas. One of my college peers mentioned it to me, and I was immediately interested. The two-week hiking trip was to be held in the state of Himachal Pradesh along the banks of the Beas River in the Kullu Manali Valley. Attending the information session at the youth hostel got me instantly hooked, and I signed up right away. The cost was a meager five hundred rupees, which was roughly equivalent to 30 US dollars at the time. This fee included food, lodging, and training for the hiking trip.

I informed my mother of my plan to travel to Delhi, which would take two days by train, followed by a bus journey to Himachal Pradesh. At that time, I had only traveled within the state and to Bangalore. My mother was concerned, but I reassured her that everything would be fine. A few days later, to my astonishment, I found her and my cousin Selaguru at the entrance of Bangalore University, where they were waiting to take the transit bus to Dr. Ambedkar Institute of Technology. Selaguru was the younger brother of my brother-in-law Ramasamy and was studying in Pondicherry.

I took them to my small room, which I shared with three other roommates. It had limited space, including a tiny kitchen, one bathroom, and a small living room. Despite feeling ashamed, I had no choice but to accommodate my mother in the same room. However, she did not mind and was pleased to see me.

The next day, I took my mother and cousin to visit tourist attractions in Bangalore, such as Lal Bagh, Cubbon Bagh, MG Road, and Vidhana Soudha. My mother was happy to see that I could take care of myself. She knew that I was adventurous and prone to doing crazy things to get my adrenaline flowing, so she simply asked me to be careful and gave me her blessing.

The agenda for the hiking trip started with training as the top priority, which was planned in Hassan, a town located a few hours away from Bangalore. Upon arriving in Hassan by bus, we were greeted by rocky terrain with a breathtaking view. The training focused on rock climbing using ropes tied around our waist, crossing rivers on a semi-zip line, and acquiring skills to survive in emergencies. As someone who had never done anything like this before, I was thrilled but struggled with the training. Later, I learned that hiking in the Himalayas with snow would be ten times more fun yet difficult than what I had experienced in Hassan.

The long-awaited day finally arrived, and I boarded the train to Delhi, settling into my seat. Across from me sat two young travelers from Ulsoor Lake, a popular area in Bangalore, who were also going on the same hiking trip. We struck up a conversation, and for the remainder of the two-day journey, we played cards and shared our life stories. These days, trains are much faster, and the same ride takes less than a day. Additionally, frequent flights are affordable for the average person, unlike 30 years ago.

Upon arriving in Delhi, I was immediately hit by a wave of scorching heat, as dry as the climate in Nevada in the US. I checked into a youth hostel, where I was surprised to find hot water spurting out from the shower despite the shower only having cold water. Fortunately, we only stayed for a day before embarking on a 14-hour bus journey to Kullu in Himachal Pradesh. However, the journey was grueling, with hard and uncomfortable seats not meant for overnight sleep. We arrived at the base camp in Kullu feeling exhausted and sore.

At the base camp, tents were set up right beside the Beas River for us to stay in. The toilets were merely holes in the ground with no flushing system, reminding me of my APEC days. We found it more convenient to use the bushes and wash ourselves off in the river, although I wondered if other tourists did the same upstream. Due to the high elevation, temperatures dropped significantly at night, becoming extremely cold in the small hours of the morning. Thankfully, we had thick woolen blankets to keep us warm while we slept.

The following day was packed with more training, including rock climbing and river crossings, under the guidance of expert campers. We were warned not to venture into the local villages and their temples, which struck me as strange because, despite being Hindu temples, even Hindus from other parts of the country were not allowed entry as it was believed that outsiders would bring impurity to the sacred temples. This custom within our own country left me bewildered.

Our group was ready to embark on our adventure, and we were divided into groups of 10 to 15 hikers. Each group was led by an experienced leader responsible for ensuring the group's safety. We did not have any local guides to assist us, but we relied on the red arrow markings on rocks to navigate.

Our daily routine was straightforward: hike to the next campsite, rest for the night, and then continue our journey. For dinner, we were served freshly prepared meals by a cook, who was the only staff member at the campsite. We enjoyed our meals around a campfire and spent the evening singing, telling stories, and having fun.

The next morning, we performed our morning duties in nature near the river before gathering our belongings and the packed lunch provided for us. We started our daily hike from one tent, stopped for lunch along the way, and continued to the next tent.

However, some days proved to be a challenge for me. Physically, I wasn't prepared for the demanding hikes. As a vegetarian, I also did not have a suitable diet for the trek. The steep uphill and downhill hikes were especially difficult, and the heat and humidity in the Himalayas made it worse. My knees were aching, and a fellow hiker suggested that I walk backward to lessen the strain on my knees. It was challenging at first, and

I was afraid of falling and injuring myself. But as I continued, I became better at it. For the remainder of the hike, I walked backward during downhill treks to alleviate the pressure on my knees.

While ascending in elevation, I had the opportunity to witness snow on the ground for the very first time in my life. Although the snow was already a few days old, I was elated and began to throw snowballs at other hikers. This was a unique and unfamiliar phenomenon for most of us, as it was uncommon to see snow near the Tropic of Cancer.

An hour into our hike in the morning, we encountered a colossal downward slope covered in a large patch of snow. It was nearly impossible to traverse, but there was no alternative route. Our leader instructed us to wait while he assessed the situation.

Then he came up with a crazy plan—we would slide down the hill on the snow. This way, we would not have to worry about losing our foothold, assuming no one collided with a rock or obstacle. We were exhilarated at the thought of sliding down on the snow like a kid. Well, at least I was. Only I did not want to be the first to go.

An athletic young man volunteered to go first. He was given a push and slid down the slope with elegance, maintaining his balance, and reached the foot of the hill unscathed. This boosted the morale of everyone. A couple of hikers followed suit and replicated his achievement. Next, a heavy-set lady was sent down the slope. She made it two-thirds of the way but lost her balance and tumbled down. When she reached the end, she was uninjured but covered in snow from head to toe and was shaken up like a featherless hen. She slowly got back to her feet in silence and did not speak a word to anyone.

Now, it was my turn. Having witnessed what happened to the lady, my heart raced, and I blanked out. I sat on top of the slope, reluctant to go. Suddenly, someone gave me a hard shove on my back. Everything became a blur as I zoomed downwards, similar to going down a slide in a playground, but this ride was not designed for kids aged 5-14. Various objects seemed to jump at me at an unimaginable speed that my eyes could not keep up with. When I was two-thirds down the slope, the same spot where the lady lost her balance, I began tumbling as well. However, somehow, I managed to regain my composure and made it to the bottom of the slope in one piece. It was an exhilarating experience that I would never forget.

On the final day of our hike, as usual, we split into small groups of two or three individuals. I was leading the way with a fellow hiker who had become a close friend. Shortly after, we found ourselves far ahead of the rest of the hikers as we turned a corner and came across a road, indicating that we were very close to the base camp. Suddenly, a truck carrying a load of cement approached us. Since nobody else had seen us, we decided to hitchhike the remainder of our journey on the truck, which was only about one kilometer.

As we arrived at the base camp, the organizing committee welcomed us with fruits and snacks that were much better than the sliced bread we had been eating. Moreover, we were all exhausted and starved. We had dinner in front of the campfire, sharing our experiences and reminiscing about the fantastic hike we had on one of the world's most beautiful mountains. The next morning, I boarded a bus to Jammu, capping off fourteen days of pure fun and adventure. Although the Kullu Manali hiking trip was not the most comfortable, it was undoubtedly the most memorable. Needless to say, this adventure sparked my lifelong pursuit of exploring new challenges.

Figure 29 Me doing what I do...

Chapter 17:

Kashmir

Jammu and Kashmir, located in the southwestern part of the Kashmir region, is administered by India as a Union Territory. During the winter, when heavy snow and rock slides block the mountainous roads, Jammu serves as the capital city, while Srinagar is the summer capital. Despite ongoing political issues, Kashmir remains one of the most breathtaking places in the world.

Due to the political unrest in the region, there was a large influx of Muslim and Hindu students from Kashmir to Bangalore. The youth had to flee the area to avoid being forced to join the militants, where they would likely kill or get killed by people they did not even know. Going to school offered a much better prospect, motivating them to work hard on their studies.

On my first sightseeing trip to Kashmir, I traveled alone and stayed with my student, Ashok Kumar Ganjoo, who offered me his place in Srinagar. When I arrived in Kashmir around 10 pm, I could not find a bus to Ganjoo's house, and I did not want to disturb his family so late at night, so I decided to stay in a youth hostel. The taxi driver circled around the city to put more mileage on the clock, knowing I was not familiar with the area, but I remained patient until we finally arrived. When it was time to pay, I told the driver I would only pay 5 rupees as the actual distance was not far. He tried to argue but eventually conceded. It was a common practice for taxi drivers to cheat, and I refused to fall for it.

The next morning, I was awakened by a loud commotion outside. When I peeped through the window, I saw a large group of people protesting and shouting slogans outside. They were using the recent death of Ayatollah Khomeini, the Iranian leader, as an excuse to protest against the Indian government. The protesters targeted the downtown and prime business areas, and unfortunately, I found myself at the epicenter of the intense activities.

The territorial dispute over Jammu and Kashmir has been ongoing between India and Pakistan since India gained independence from British rule in 1947. Although the initial disaffection stemmed from failures in Indian governance and democracy, Pakistan significantly escalated it into a full-fledged armed insurgency. Some insurgent groups in Kashmir seek total independence, while others aim for the region's accession to Pakistan.

Moreover, the roots of the insurgency are tied to a dispute over local autonomy. Until the late 1970s, democratic development in Kashmir was limited. By 1988, many of the democratic reforms provided by the Indian government had been rolled back, and non-violent channels for expressing discontent were limited. This caused a dramatic increase in support for insurgents advocating violent secession from India.

I quietly prepared myself and slipped out into the crowd. As the people were preoccupied with the protesters, no one paid any heed to me. Though it might not have made a difference, even if they did, I preferred not to take any chances. Fortunately, I reached the bus station and caught a local bus to Ganjoo's house.

Ganjoo was delighted to see me. His father was a high school teacher who had just spent his life savings to construct the house they were living in. Ganjoo was their only son. They were a simple, humble Pandit family. His mother prepared delicious Kashmiri cuisine for us.

Later that day, we visited the Vaishno Devi Temple, a well-known Hindu shrine, and another temple located atop a hill. The next day, we went to Dal Lake, which was the most stunning lake I had ever seen in my life. The clouds and mountains were reflected in the water's mirror-like surface, and the lake was renowned for its houseboats. I had a habit of jumping into any body of water that I saw, and this time was no different. I took off my clothes and splashed into the water, surprising Ganjoo. The water was silky and refreshing.

During our visit to Srinagar, we explored the Shalimar Bagh Mughal Gardens, which were constructed during the Mughal era and have been impeccably maintained to this day. Situated in Jammu and Kashmir, India, the garden is connected to Dal Lake via a channel. Later, we went for a hike on a nearby hill, where I saw numerous cable cars parked in close proximity. Ganjoo told me that a cable car line was being constructed to connect the hill to the roads leading to Srinagar. Upon climbing the hill, I was thrilled to see snow on the ground and had a snowball fight with my companions. This was the first time I had seen so much snow.

That evening, I spoke to Ganjoo's father about the recent protest downtown. He expressed concern about the ongoing developments in Srinagar and Kashmir. The Hindu Pandits were a minority group, accounting for only 5% of the total population in Kashmir, while the remaining 95% were Muslims. They had coexisted peacefully until the 1970s, when conflicts began to arise, escalating in the 1990s. Ganjoo's father was apprehensive that the Pandits would one day be forced out of Kashmir. I wished them luck and bid them farewell the following morning.

After ten years, Ganjoo's father's worst nightmare became a reality when a Muslim insurgent entered their neighbor's home and killed the entire family because they were Hindus. Fearing for their lives, the Ganjoo family made the difficult decision to abandon their home and leave Kashmir. Sadly, in doing so, they lost their life savings and livelihood overnight.

It is tragic that a beautiful place like Kashmir has been plagued by controversy and violence. As a result, it has become unsafe for travelers. Hopefully, one day, Kashmir will regain its former glory and become a peaceful and tranquil state once again, attracting tourists from all corners of the world.

Figure 30 Me and Ganjoo's family in their house in Kashmir

Interlude 6: Taj Mahal

After bidding farewell to Ganjoo's family, I embarked on a 14-hour bus journey to New Delhi to see the Taj Mahal, the renowned ivory-white marble mausoleum on the right bank of the Yamuna River in the city of Agra.

I registered for a guided tour that included a visit to the Mathra temple on the way to Agra Fort and, eventually, the Taj Mahal. Mathura was believed to be the city governed by Lord Krishna, the incarnation of Vishnu and the savior of Hindu gods. The primary pilgrimage destination in Mathura is the Krishna Janmabhoomi temple, which is thought to have been erected around the prison cell where Lord Krishna was born. It is regarded as the most significant place in the celebrated tales of Lord Krishna.

Subsequently, we traveled for another hour and arrived at the city of Agra. The city was one of the filthiest places I had ever witnessed, with monkeys, donkeys, dogs, cats, pigs, and cows wandering the streets. The flow of traffic was frequently disrupted or halted when a large cow was sitting in the middle of the road, contentedly munching on grass. Since many animals were deemed sacred in India, people could do nothing but wait until the creatures moved on by themselves.

The city of Agra is situated in the northern part of India, and the Yamuna River, also spelled Jamuna, flows through it. The Yamuna River is not only the longest tributary in India but also the second-largest tributary of the Ganges by discharge. Hinduism considers the Yamuna River as highly venerated and worshipped as the goddess Yamuna, like the Ganges. According to Hindu mythology, Yamuna is the daughter of the sun god, Surya, and the sister of Yama, the god of death. Therefore, she is also known as Yami. Legend has it that bathing in the sacred waters of Yamuna can free one from the torments of death.

The Taj Mahal, which stands on the banks of the Yamuna River, is a monument commissioned by the Mughal emperor Shah Jahan in 1632 as a testament to his love for his favorite wife, Mumtaz Mahal. It was named "Crown of the Palace" and is a symbol of love and devotion. It houses the tomb of Shah Jahan himself and is the centerpiece of a 42-acre complex that includes a mosque and a guest house. The Taj Mahal is set in formal gardens enclosed by a crenelated wall on three sides.

The construction of a black Taj Mahal was planned to be built across the Yamuna River, creating a mirrored effect with the white Taj Mahal as a monument for Shah Jahan himself. However, his son Aurangzeb seized the throne by killing his brothers and took power. Upon seeing the empty treasury, Aurangzeb immediately halted the construction of the black Taj Mahal.

The Taj Mahal has been designated as a UNESCO World Heritage Site since 1983, recognized for being "the jewel of Muslim art in India" and a masterpiece of the world's heritage. It is widely regarded as the finest example of Mughal architecture and an iconic symbol of India's rich history. Furthermore, it was declared a winner of the New 7 Wonders of the World initiative.

The stunning beauty of the Taj Mahal was said to be reflected in the Yamuna River's sparkling blue waters, which had been holding a clear image of the Monument of Love for centuries. However, during my visit, the river was almost dry and contaminated with sewage, which posed a significant threat to the foundation of the white marble mausoleum. Pollution had already started to show a yellowish tint on the monument. Conservationists were worried that a dry Yamuna River would weaken the wooden foundation of the Taj Mahal. During the summer, the river had very little water, and people used it to dump trash, wash clothes, and defecate on the banks, further polluting the already contaminated river. Now, the Yamuna River is considered to be the most polluted river in the world, covered in toxic foams, making it look like a giant bubble bath.

The pollution of the Yamuna River in the city of Delhi and Agra is caused by four primary factors: the poor quality of water discharged by effluent treatment factories, municipal and household disposal sites, deforestation due to agricultural development, which involves cutting down vast areas of trees, and the chemicals from fertilizers and pesticide runoff from commercial and industrial sites.

Having witnessed the 400-year-old building's resilience over time, I could not help but ponder its future. The preservation of the Taj Mahal, the river's need for clean water, and the locals' dire need for assistance were pressing concerns.

As I stood outside the mausoleum, I observed construction workers toiling under the scorching sun, carrying bricks and cement on their heads for a nearby project. Curiosity piqued, I inquired about their origin, and they revealed that they had traveled 200 kilometers from a village outside of Agra to earn a paltry 200 rupees, equivalent to approximately $3 per day. Their living conditions were abysmal, with a dilapidated hut for shelter, no running water or electricity, and a kilometer walk to access potable water. They resorted to using bushes as makeshift toilets. They would have preferred farming in their village, but the unrelenting drought forced them to search for employment elsewhere.

Upon returning home, I conducted some research on the Taj Mahal's construction workers, who numbered over 20,000 and labored for 22 years to erect the stunning modern wonder of the world. The workers were paid a meager 15 rupees per month, with equally wretched living conditions. Many of them had traveled far from their homes and perished in the process. Beyond the Taj Mahal's grandeur lay the stories of countless unnamed families who made immense sacrifices for its creation.

Figure 31 Revisiting Taj Mahal in 2018

Chapter 18:
The Cauvery Issue

Life in Mallathalli was enjoyable. I had plenty of free time once work was done. I socialized with other lecturers and students in the village, and we would often play cricket at a nearby dried-up lake. I also followed cricket matches on TV and in the stadium.

For meals, we frequented a family-owned canteen that served a standard meal of dal, chapati, and curry. Although the food was satisfactory at first, we eventually grew tired of it. We learned of a new canteen that had recently opened, attracting students with its diverse menu, and decided to give it a try.

Upon arrival, we ordered our food and were served one glass of water for each of the four of us. As I was about to take a sip, I caught sight of something moving in my glass, and to my horror, it was a live mouse. I immediately called out to the server, who seemed unfazed by my distress. He poured the contaminated water outside and refilled my glass with water from the same container as before. We silently left the canteen and never returned. Unsurprisingly, the place shut down within six months.

Commuting back then was much more challenging compared to the present day. The most common means of travel between cities was by coach, which was often a tiring and uncomfortable experience. Local buses were also overcrowded and unclean. I recall standing in the back of a crowded bus once and noticing a passenger who appeared unwell and was holding his stomach. I kept a close eye on him and eventually decided to move away. In no time, he could not hold it any longer and ended up throwing up his entire breakfast inside the packed bus, drenching at least ten people in vomit. People began swearing at him and gestured for the driver to stop the bus. Those affected had to quickly get off the bus. This was a common occurrence in major cities during that time.

There is a river called Cauvery that originates in the state of Karnataka and flows into the neighboring state of Tamil Nadu. During the summer season, the river shrinks and becomes trapped between the dams in Karnataka. By the time it reaches Tamil Nadu, it has reduced to a trickle. Unfortunately, farmers in Tamil Nadu rely heavily on the waters of Cauvery during the summer. Consequently, with the central government's intervention, several treaties have been signed between the two state governments to ensure that Karnataka allows sufficient water to flow into Tamil Nadu. However, more often than not, this does not happen. Consequently, every year, the issue turns into political conflicts, and farmers in Tamil Nadu suffer. In 1991, the issue escalated, and riots erupted everywhere. The Tamil people in Karnataka, especially in Bangalore, were attacked by the locals and lived in constant fear.

During the middle of the semester, an incident occurred that forced everyone to go home. I managed to return to Pondy just before the bus services between the two states ceased. After a month, things started to go back to normal even though I had not received any news from the school. Not knowing whether classes were starting or not, I made the decision to go back to Mallathahalli.

During that time, there were many Tamil Nadu students residing in Mallathahalli. Giri, a lecturer from Kancheepuram, a city in Tamil Nadu, was also there. One day, while eating at a canteen with Sathish and Venkateswaran's brother, who was visiting from the south of Tamil Nadu, the canteen owner's son approached us and informed us that some villagers were targeting to attack the Tamils living in the village.

After assessing the situation, we concluded that we needed to leave Mallathahalli immediately. We had to wait until dark to leave unnoticed. We quickly packed our bags, laid low until dusk, and cautiously left our apartment. In order to reach the road, we had to cross a shop where the shopkeeper caught a glimpse of us. We hurriedly walked as fast as we could without worrying about him and passed through a cornfield.

The night was quiet, the bags were heavy, and the cornfield seemed never-ending, making it the longest walk of my life. Thankfully, it was a full moon night, providing us with some visibility. Our hearts were pounding as we walked, jogged, and ran toward the bus stop at the University entrance, which was about a kilometer away from the village.

Suddenly, two men came sprinting toward us. Despite our efforts to outrun them, our luggage slowed us down, and they quickly caught up and started attacking us. They yanked our bags away from us, ripped our watches off our wrists, and punched us. It was a situation that I had never been in before. Being a skinny person, I had never learned how to fight, and the same went for Venkateswaran's brother and Sathish. Although there were only two local men and three of us, we were unable to defend ourselves against them. They kept landing blows on us, and it was extremely painful. I was scared out of my wits.

Now, let us pause for a moment and discuss the significance of learning a new language.

When I started working as a lecturer in Bangalore, I began to learn the language of the state of Karnataka, Kannada, which was similar to my native language, Tamil, and my second language, Telugu. I listened carefully to the locals and tried to speak with them in their language without fear of making mistakes. In doing so, I made a few friends, including Rajendra, a mechanic who worked at a nearby shop. Although he had completed high school, he could not afford to attend college due to financial constraints. Whenever I bumped into him at the canteen or on the street, I would converse with him in Kannada and ask about his job.

On the terrifying night when two locals beat up three of us, I unexpectedly realized that one of the attackers was none other than Rajendra. I shouted out his name, and he immediately stopped attacking and asked his friend to do the same. Rajendra apologized, and they even escorted us to the bus stop and waited until we boarded the bus safely.

After arriving at the transit bus station, Sathish found a bus to take him to his destination while I accompanied Venkat's brother and traveled 50 kilometers to the city of Hosur. I visited Sebastian, who was working at Hosur at the time. He was surprised to see us arrive so late at night and shocked by what happened. He took us out for a late dinner and provided us with a place to sleep at his apartment.

The next morning, I ensured that Venkat's brother boarded a bus back home before I departed on a bus to Pondy.

When I met my friends later that evening, the storm had passed, and I felt safe and relaxed. However, I was unaware that Giri, the lecturer from Kancheepuram who had also been attempting to leave Mallathahalli that night, had not been as fortunate. Giri was an intelligent and hardworking guy. He was an introvert and unable to look people in the eye, so sometimes, he would just walk away quietly. Some people took it as a sign of arrogance, but he was super nice and was just socially awkward.

Giri packed his belongings into a suitcase and headed to a bus stop in the middle of the village, hoping to blend in with the other passengers. He managed to board the bus, but before it departed, a small group of locals got on and immediately identified Giri as their target. They assaulted him, tearing his clothes and stealing his suitcase, which they pried open and burned its contents. As a result, Giri lost his money, clothes, and other personal items, including his college degree credentials and transcripts. Sadly, I have never heard anything about him after that. I hope he is doing well.

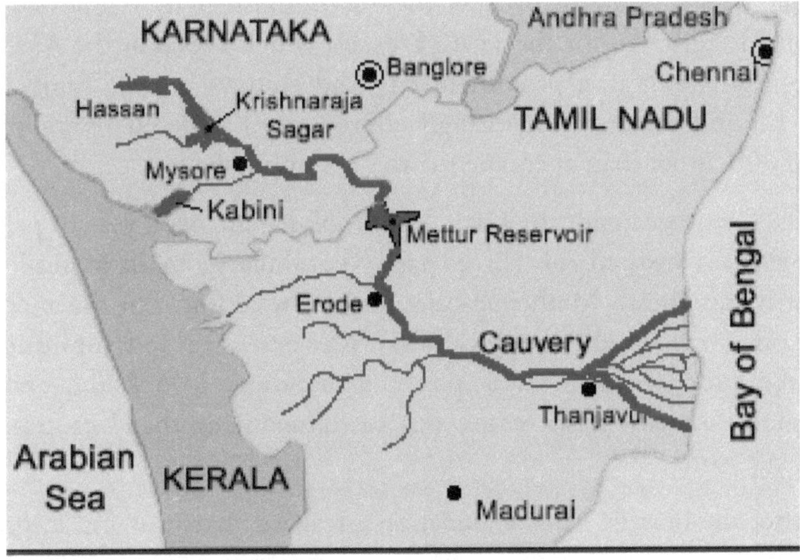

Figure 32 Cauvery River (picture from internet)

Chapter 19:
Wake-up Call

During my time at Dr. Ambedkar Institute of Technology, I noticed that many of the associate lecturers there were preparing for TOEFL and GRE to apply to US universities for graduate studies. TOEFL, the most widely recognized English language test for studying, working, and immigrating, was mandatory for anyone applying to high schools and universities in English-speaking countries such as the US. Similarly, GRE was essential for admission to most graduate schools in the US, Canada, and a few other countries. Its aim was to evaluate a student's logical, mathematical, critical and analytical thinking, and writing abilities.

I also observed that the associate lecturers who scored well in the exams tended to vanish. Upon inquiry, I discovered that they had all received admission offers from universities in the US and had left. Though I was unaware of how they accomplished it, I followed suit. Initially, I registered for the TOEFL exam, which I took at the American College in Madurai, a prominent city and cultural hub of Tamil Nadu state. I found the exam surprisingly effortless and achieved a score of 563 out of 600, more than adequate for any US university.

On the other hand, the GRE exam took me almost a year to prepare. The exam consisted of three parts: vocabulary, mathematical, and analytical questions. Mathematical questions were fine, but the analytical questions were tough, the vocabulary was extensive and sophisticated, and the time constraint was pretty demanding. I took the exam in Bangalore, but my performance was so traumatizing that I cannot even recall my score now.

After the horrific GRE experience, I realized that studying in the US was not for me. I forgot about the exams and returned to my old routine of going to work during the day, playing cricket in the evening, and watching English movies on the weekends. I lacked motivation and was merely whiling away my life.

The rude awakening came one day when DR, the friend I had referred to Ambedkar College because he could not find a job after graduation, returned to Bangalore from Pondy after being missing for a week. I asked where he had been when he walked in with his luggage. He replied that he went to Pondy to see his aunt for sponsoring his trip to the US. That was when I discovered that he was going to the US to pursue a master's degree in Computer Science.

I was completely caught off guard. I was so engrossed in my routine that I had no idea what he had been up to in the past few months. While he embarked on a new adventure and pushed himself to the next level, I was still stuck in a dead-end job, feeling directionless. With shaken confidence, I asked DR how he managed to pull off such an impressive feat. He told me he had applied for the master's degree at several universities in the US and received admission.

It was then that I made a decision about my future: I would pursue a master's degree in the US and start my career there. However, the significant issue that remained was how to pay for my studies. Over the weekend, I went to Pondy and discussed the possibility of a loan with my brother-in-law, Ramasamy. He asked if I would be able to secure admission. I assured him that my grades and TOEFL score were excellent, so getting admission should not be a problem.

Upon my return to Bangalore, I initiated the application process, selecting schools that did not require a GRE score. I applied to four midwestern schools whose application fees were within my budget with my modest salary. Regrettably, three of the schools rejected my application. However, The University of Central Oklahoma in Oklahoma City accepted me into their Applied Mathematics and Computer Science program, and I was overjoyed to receive the I-20, which confirmed my admission. Nonetheless, the challenging part lay ahead: acquiring a visa to travel to the United States.

After receiving my admission, I visited Pondy and consulted Ramasamy about the funds I needed for my first semester, which amounted to at least 4,000 US dollars (100,000 rupees that time) for tuition and living expenses, not to mention the airfare, which was a lot back then. Compared with my monthly income of a meager 750 rupees, living expenses of 500 rupees, and my family's monthly expenses of roughly 2000 rupees, 100,000 rupees is a considerable amount to raise. I knew my family would have to borrow money at a high-interest rate, but I had no other option. I was determined to make it happen and pay off the debt once I established a career in the US.

Ramasamy agreed to help, but with one condition: I had to resign from my lecturer job and return to Pondy to work on the visa and loan preparation. I explained that resigning would only add to our financial troubles, but he refused to budge. Ultimately, I had no choice but to quit my job.

Returning to Bangalore, I packed up my belongings, bid farewell to friends, and left with mixed emotions. Leaving behind a familiar place, a daily routine, and many friends was not easy. However, deep down, I knew it was the right decision. I had a unique opportunity to turn my life around. If I worked hard and put in effort, my worst nightmare could turn into my greatest memory.

I returned to Pondy in February 1992 and had to leave for the US by the end of May to start school. During those three months, we managed to get everything in order except for the visa interview. The interview was the ultimate test of my preparation. If I could persuade the consular officer, both verbally and through the paperwork, that I was qualified to study in the US with good intentions, I would be able to have a new life. However, there was no backup plan if I failed. I would be stuck in the same cycle again, with no other options, not even a low-paying job.

Despite my research and advice from friends who had already gone through the process, Ramasamy insisted on getting help from his "experts" in Chennai. As always, he got his way. We dropped everything and headed to Chennai.

To prepare for our visa application, we rented a large house and visited various people to gather information. One of these individuals was Nithi, a family friend who had successfully sent his son to the US a few years prior. Some of the advice he gave us was already familiar to me. I later discovered that Ramasamy had actually paid him for "the advice."

During this period, Ramasamy and I frequently argued, and as the interview day approached, I grew increasingly anxious and stressed. The possibility of failure weighed heavily on my mind—I had already resigned from my job in Bangalore and disappeared from college without formally quitting, forfeiting my withheld salary. With no way to return to my previous employment, I worried that I would again face the painful job-hunting process. These concerns frequently kept me awake at night.

Nonetheless, the interview day finally arrived.

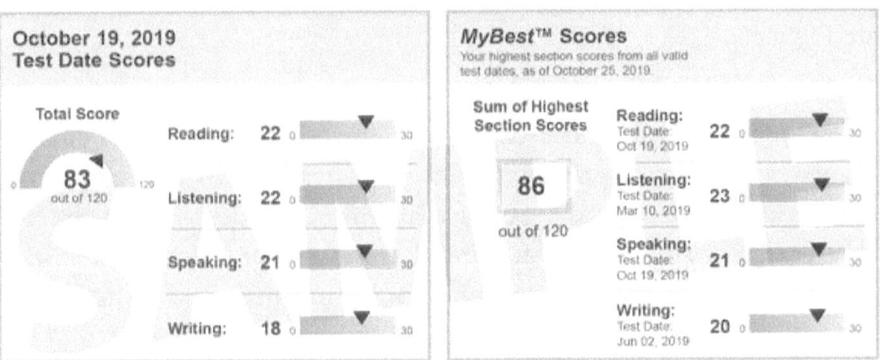

Figure 33 Sample TOEFL score cards. The scoring system has changed since my time and the total score is 120 now for computer-based tests (picture from internet)

Chapter 20:

F-1 Visa

The U.S. Consulate in Chennai is situated in an upscale area in the southern part of the city, away from the noisy downtown. The consulate compound includes an office building, a warehouse, a garage, two guardhouses, a bike parking shelter, a covered waiting area for consular applicants, and several small utility structures surrounded by a gated fence.

On the day of my interview, the consulate had just reopened after a three-day weekend, and I expected a long line. Applicants would be assigned a number, and arriving late meant waiting for a longer time to be interviewed. There was a rumor that consulate officers might be more likely to reject applications toward the end of the day when they got tired. Therefore, Ramasamy arranged for his brother, my cousin Guru, to queue from 12 am until 6 am to avoid this situation. I went to bed at 10 pm and woke up at 5 am, then hired an autorickshaw, a motorized three-wheeled vehicle with a tent, to take me to the consulate, which was 5 kilometers away. As I approached the consulate, the dawn was just breaking for a beautiful day. I hoped that the outcome of the interview would turn out to be beautiful for me, too.

My heart sank when I saw a line even longer than expected at the gates. However, to my delight, I found Guru standing second in line. I thanked him, and he left to rest. I stood in line for an additional two hours before the gates opened at 8 am, rehearsing my lines in my head.

The type of visa I was applying for was F-1, which was intended for foreign students seeking education in the United States. The applicants were required to demonstrate their academic and financial capabilities through the paperwork. It is of paramount importance that, as F-1 was a non-immigration visa, within a few minutes during the interview, the applicants must convince the interviewer that they had no intention of staying in the US after graduation. This step was often difficult as it was challenging to prove "the intention" and thus remained purely subjective to the interviewer. My plan was to inform the officer that I would return to India and start an industry. I had no idea whether the interviewer would accept my explanation.

Upon opening the gates, everyone was assigned a number and permitted to enter. I joined hundreds of individuals in a vast hall, each with the purpose of traveling to the US. Witnessing several people receiving rejections, I became increasingly anxious. I was perplexed as to why I had not been called yet, considering my position in the queue. Unbeknownst to me at the time, the consulate had categorized applications by visa type, such as non-immigration family visit visa, work visa, business visitor visa, student visa, tourism visa, and many others. Despite my early arrival, the vast number of student visa applications meant a prolonged wait. As time passed, my anxiety intensified, and I prayed that my interview would succeed.

Finally, my number was approaching. I observed the consulate officer in front of me put away some documents and pick up a number. My heart began pounding in my chest, and my face turned red. Just as I was about to stand up, another official arrived and announced a three-hour lunch break, instructing everyone to return later.

I re-composed myself and discovered a nice restaurant in the vicinity where I ordered a traditional South Indian meal consisting of rice, sambar, rasam, poriyal, and yogurt. While eating, I observed the people bustling around, which helped me unwind. Afterward, I found a phone booth and called my family to tell them about the delay. When it was time, I returned to the consulate, where I waited in line for another hour before gaining entry. Fortunately, our prior numbering system allowed us to be called in the order our applications were processed, regardless of the length of the queue.

While waiting in the hall, I struck up a conversation with a family comprising parents and their daughter who were standing behind me. The parents were hoping to send their daughter to the US on an H-1B work visa, a program that had only recently been initiated two years before. They were understandably anxious about the prospects of securing the visa, especially given the difficulties of sponsoring someone to work abroad, let alone a female. The parents told me that they came from a village and had to sell off their land and other assets to finance their daughter's college education. As a result, they had to face numerous obstacles to accumulate the funds required for their daughter to obtain a work visa in the US. Although I did not know whether they had to resort to high-interest loans like me, I understood that the stakes were similarly high for them.

Their number was called. The daughter was visibly nervous when she approached the window. The officer asked her some questions, and she answered in a soft monotone voice. After stamping her passport, the officer asked her to wait aside, and she gave a big thumbs up to her family, beaming a big smile. Her family was thrilled, and I congratulated them.

Time went by, but my number was still not called. My nerves started loosening up around 4 pm when suddenly I heard someone calling my number from the speaker. I was startled. It took me a few moments to return to reality and confirm that it was indeed my number. I rushed to the window, where I saw a middle-aged Caucasian consulate officer with a stern look. This made me even more nervous. He looked at me and then looked at my papers. I could see his brain working but had no idea what was going on in there. He did not ask me any questions, and I did not dare to say anything. He then put down my documents and instructed me to pay my fees at window 3.

Pay my fees at window 3? What happened to my interview? What happened to all the grilling questions I had prepared answers for? I was in a way disappointed that I was not interviewed. But I got my visa. I was on cloud 9. At window 3, I joined a short line of visa applicants and paid my fees and then returned to my seat. Thirty minutes later, I was called over to collect my passport, which now had a US visa stamp.

It was the most exhilarating feeling I had ever had in my life. I was on top of the world and finally felt that I had a plan for my future. On my way back, I had the urge to jump up and down with excitement and hug everyone I encountered. I had just obtained a visa to go to the USA, and there was nothing more I desired. With a mere stamp on my passport, everything was going to change: the way I ate, the way I moved around, and the way others treated me. I was still the same person—five foot five inches, scrawny and soft-spoken, but the world was a whole new place. I had elevated my future to an entirely different level, and from this point on, it was up to me to decide what I wanted to do with my life and realize my potential.

After acquiring my visa, I hired an autorickshaw, bought some chocolates, and headed back home. I shared the news of my visa with the driver, but he neither understood nor cared about it. Nonetheless, he was happy to accept chocolates from me. Upon arriving home, I distributed chocolates to everyone, as it was customary in India to celebrate the good news with something sweet. The news could not have been any sweeter.

My mother was both happy and deeply concerned when I received my visa. She must have secretly hoped that I would not get it, but now that it was a done deal, I was bound to go to a foreign land where I knew no one. Reality hit her hard, and she started crying. She was uncertain about how I would manage my life and what I would eat in a foreign country. However, I reassured her that I would take care of myself.

Meanwhile, I had to hurry because school was starting in just a week. We bought new clothes, cooking utensils, and snacks. I asked Alphonse to help me with my airfare while Ramasamy was working on a $4,000 loan for tuition and living expenses. Although we applied for a loan from a bank for my living expenses, it was rejected due to my lack of regular income. The airfare was an immediate and relatively smaller amount. So, I turned to Alphonse for help. After giving him the loan documents, he helped me secure a loan of 30,000 rupees.

I purchased a new suitcase for the trip and a ticket with Air India and TWA. The day of my departure was set, and I was thrilled to finally have a way out of our financial troubles, at least temporarily. I could now carve out a future for myself and help my family out of their financial pit. There was a long way to go, and my journey was about to start.

Chapter 21:
Departure to the USA

I traveled to Pondy to bid farewell to all my relatives and friends. Leaving them behind was a bittersweet moment, but I was also thrilled to start a new life in the promised land. In the evening, my family accompanied me to the airport, but to my surprise, out of all my close friends, only Sebastian showed up. I checked in my luggage and said goodbye to my mother, sisters, and relatives. As I was about to enter the security check gates, I spotted my other friends approaching, and they were all drunk–Whenever they gathered, they felt compelled to party and drink excessively. This time was no different, except they went too far and lost track of time. Feeling embarrassed by their behavior, I tried to distance myself from them, but I was unsuccessful.

As I proceeded through the checkpoint with the crowd, I turned back and saw my sisters and mother in tears, but I remained composed. The past few months had been stressful dealing with Ramasamy, but now, I felt both relieved and excited. I passed through security swiftly and without any issues. It was 1992, which was way before 9/11, and security checks were effortless. I boarded the plane and settled into my seat. Looking out the window, it felt like I was observing my previous life through a glass pane.

After a day of physical and emotional exertion, I closed my eyes to rest as the plane was about to take off. It was well past midnight, and I felt exhausted. Suddenly, an announcement blared across the cabin. The air hostess was seeking someone who could speak Telugu, a language predominantly spoken in Andhra Pradesh. Despite my limited knowledge of the language, I raised my hand as I knew some Telugu mixed with Tamil words. The air hostess led me to an elderly Indian woman a few rows ahead of me in economy class.

The old lady appeared scared and on the verge of tears. She spoke only Telugu, and no one else on the plane could communicate with her. I conversed with her to the best of my abilities, which, thankfully, helped her calm down. She was traveling alone to see her son in the USA, and the thought of being unable to communicate with anyone had caused her to panic. I comforted her and promised to keep her company throughout the journey, ensuring she reached her son safely in New York. I sat next to her throughout the flight.

After the brief delay, the flight was finally ready to take off. As I strapped in, I felt mixed emotions of anxiety, joy, and terror all at the same time. As the plane began its ascent, a shiver ran down my spine. Outside, the lights quickly receded behind us, and the buildings transformed into tiny boxes. Soon, there was nothing but miles and miles of water below us, and we were up in the sky.

After finishing my dinner, I found myself too excited to sleep. When my relatives asked me why I chose to study in a foreign country despite having responsibilities back home, I explained that I did not want to be confined to my village and was eager to explore the world.

Our flight from Delhi arrived within two hours, but our layover turned into a five-hour delay before we boarded our plane to London. Throughout the journey, I conversed with the Telugu woman and kept her up to date about everything on the flight. When we were switching terminals in London, my nature break took a little longer. The lady feared that I had left her and yelled out for me from outside the restroom. I had to finish my business early and hurry out.

We continued our journey and arrived at New York La Guardia airport at 8 pm. I made sure the Telugu lady met her son at the airport before I went my separate ways. She and her son thanked me profusely. Unfortunately, due to the delay in Delhi, I missed my connecting flight to Oklahoma City, and I had to spend the night in a hotel. Once I had settled in, I reached out to DR, the friend who woke me up from my mundane routine by coming to study in the US. He was surprised to learn that I was in New York, and we talked for a long time.

The following morning, I stepped into the bathtub to take a shower. I turned the knob and found only cold water. After contacting the front desk, they provided instructions that I could not understand. A bellboy arrived at my room and turned the shower knob all the way to the left. Hot water spurted out. I felt foolish.

The bathtub was not the only thing that functioned differently here. The switches' on/off positions were opposite to those in India. In India, the on position was at the top, while in the US, it was at the bottom. In this country, cars drove on the right side of the road, and the steering wheel was on the left, while in India, it was the opposite. In the US, people used miles, whereas, in India, they used kilometers. Everything was strange to me.

DR came to visit me before I took the shuttle to the airport. When checking out of the hotel, I was charged $25. I realized that it was for the phone call to DR that I made the night before and was astonished at the sum. Another lesson for me. I had not yet reached my destination, and I was already facing the harsh realities of life. As an Indian student with loans, I had to survive the initial months with only $4,000 for college tuition, apartment rent, and food expenses. I had no idea where the money would come from after it was gone, so I had to be very cautious with my spending. I said goodbye to DR, headed to the airport, and boarded a TWA airline to the Midwest, which is no longer in operation now.

I reached Oklahoma City in the afternoon. It had just rained, and it was wet everywhere. Before my journey, I had contacted Ravi Prakash, my sole contact from Bangalore. Ravi was also a Dr. Ambedkar Institute of Technology lecturer and guided me through the university application process. Although he agreed to pick me up, I did not inform him that I had missed my flight out of fear that the phone call would be too costly. I had not considered the trouble it might cause Ravi or how I would reach the apartment. As a result, Ravi drove to the airport with his roommate Bala, waited, and drove back, wondering what happened to me. Once I arrived in Oklahoma, I had to take a shuttle and pay $25 to reach Edmond, a suburb of Oklahoma City.

Upon reaching Ravi's apartment, I struggled to climb the stairs with my luggage, only to find out that everyone was out for their classes. After waiting for a few minutes, some passing Indian students told me that I had better complete my registration before the offices closed for the day. In a rush, I went to the International Student Office to finish my paperwork and then headed to the admissions office to pay my fees. I had to select my courses on the spot, and the students there advised me to register for Logic, Cobol programming, Basic programming, and a couple of other courses. Although I had no idea what I was doing, I registered for all of them.

I noticed there were quite a few Indian students. When I returned to the apartment, I encountered Ravi Prakash, who had just returned from his classes, and Rudra Prasad, his roommate whom I had previously met at Dr. Ambedkar Institute in Bangalore. Also present was Bala Talkad, Ravi's roommate from Bangalore, who had accompanied him to the airport. They asked why I had not called after missing my flight, and I explained the situation truthfully, feeling foolish. They laughed and, fortunately, did not make a big fuss about it. Eventually, I grew closer to Bala, and we became good friends.

I used the apartment's landline phone to call my family back home. During this time, cell phones were not yet available, and each apartment had its own landline. I spoke briefly with my mother and Ramasamy, who were eager to know about everything, including my living arrangements, the food I was eating, and the people I was interacting with. However, I had to end the conversation quickly due to the cost of phone calls at 85 cents per minute. They were disappointed that I could not talk for longer. Suffering from jet lag, I went to bed early that night.

The following morning, I had cereal with milk for breakfast, which was my first-ever cold breakfast in 28 years. This took place in 1992, marking the beginning of a new chapter in my life.

Figure 34 My very first flight, Trans World Airlines (TWA).
A major American airline which operated from 1930 to 1995 before it
went bankrupt (picture from internet)

Interlude 7: A Foreign Place

The school year in the US typically starts in the fall, similar to India. However, I was one of the few students who started in the summer because I wanted to complete my education as soon as possible and find employment so I could support my family back in India. The apartment where I stayed was conveniently located, just a five-minute walk from school, and Walmart and other grocery stores were within easy walking distance.

The supermarkets in the US fascinated me, especially the huge stores with rows and rows of groceries. Unlike in India, here we could see and touch whatever we wanted without the assistance of a store clerk. We simply selected the items we wanted and paid for them at the checkout counter. I was amazed by the wide selection of products and the concept of purchasing my own goods. In India, we had to ask the grocery clerk for what we needed usually by providing a list, and customers were not allowed inside the store due to the small size and theft concerns.

As I left the store, I noticed a tall red machine with a Coca-Cola sign on it. I was unfamiliar with the vending machine, but it looked tempting. My friend encouraged me to buy it. A can only cost 25 cents, but I had to think twice. I dropped a quarter into the slot, and a red can emerged. It was cold and heavy, with an opening for drinking. My friend helped me open it, and the can hissed and fizzed, which was thrilling. The feeling of the cold, sweet, carbonated liquid flowing over my lips, tongue, and down my throat was enthralling. I took another big sip and burped, feeling a sensation I had never experienced before in my life.

The milk packaging was different in the United States compared to that in India. Here, it was sold in a gallon plastic carton, whereas in India, it was sold in plastic bags that were more accessible and cheaper. After finishing the milk, I washed the empty carton and put it on the shelf. When Bala asked me why I did that, I explained that I could take the empty cartons to India when I returned home. Everyone in the apartment burst into laughter, but I did not understand why it was funny. In India, nothing went to waste, and everything was reused in some way, even though recycling was not a common concept. Recycling only occurred when there was an abundance of things.

For example, in India, if a shirt is worn out at the elbow, you remove the sleeves, turn them inside out, sew the sleeves back on, and it becomes a new shirt. If a dress went out of style, you either added new buttons or sent it back to the dressmaker to create a trendier frock. Eventually, when the fabric became too old and worn out, it would be used as a filling for quilts or rags. Even today, I still recycle whenever possible, not because I want to bring things back to India but to preserve our planet.

California, the state I live in now when writing this memoir, is the leader in recycling and composting. It is heartening to witness every house having three bins—one for trash, one for recycling, and one for compost. Californians possess a strong awareness of the environment, global warming, and its impact on our planet. I had a neighbor named Mark who refused to fly unless it was absolutely necessary because he despised leaving a carbon footprint by flying. Air travel contributes significantly to a person's carbon footprint throughout their life. Although I love to travel and cannot stop flying, I am compensating for it by planting trees, recycling, and composting. Each of us must play a part in saving the world in whatever way we can.

The differences between the United States and India are vast, encompassing tangible items and, more importantly, values and perspectives. As I began my new life in Oklahoma, I gradually transformed into a new person, evolving a little each day.

Chapter 22:
Edmond, Oklahoma

Initially, life in Edmond was a struggle for me. In the first month alone, my funds went down from $4,000 to roughly $1,500 after paying for school fees and living expenses. I started panicking and desperately needed a job.

International students were restricted to working only 20 hours per week on-campus, and securing an on-campus job proved arduous. The school had a significant number of international students that year, including 30 Indian students and a substantial number of students from Bangladesh, Pakistan, Nepal, and other countries. All of us were in search of employment. The available job openings were primarily in the custodial department, library, or Computer Science lab, and all the international students competed for the same jobs.

Every day after my classes, I made it a routine to walk to the custodial supervisor's office on the other side of the campus and exchange greetings with him. After that, I would return to my apartment, have lunch, and venture outside the campus to explore the stores and restaurants within a mile-long stretch. These included fast food chains like Grandy's, Long John Silver, Arby's, and Wendy's. I would talk to the managers, complete application forms, and move on to the next establishment in my search for employment.

On one occasion, I entered Albertsons, a large grocery store chain, and noticed a young employee restocking the shelves. He offered his assistance, but I declined. I said I needed to speak to the manager and that only managers could provide the information I was seeking. Later, I encountered an older employee and asked if I could speak to the manager. He directed me to the same young man I had previously encountered. I was taken aback and felt compelled to apologize to him.

Unfortunately, he did not receive my apology kindly and responded curtly. Needless to say, I was not able to secure a job at Albertsons.

I used to come home daily feeling frustrated and desperate, which went on for a month. One day, it was particularly bad. I went to all the restaurants, grocery stores, and even hardware stores and spoke with the hiring managers, but they all turned me down. When I got home, I was feeling really sad. Sunil, one of my roommates who was also from Dr. Ambedkar Institute in Bangalore, India, was living with us. Whenever I came home, he asked me if I had found a job. Then, he would criticize me, saying that I was not trying hard enough and that I was not using the right approach or saying the right things. He did not offer any constructive advice and just put me down, especially that day. I went to bed feeling upset and could not sleep.

Lying in bed, I worried about what would happen in a few months. One thousand dollars would barely cover my two-month rent and living expenses. How would I be able to pay my fees for the next semester? I felt like I was suffocating under the weight of my own dreams. I started crying, something I had not done since my grandmother passed away a few years ago. The next morning, I woke up with a resolve that I would find a job no matter what.

During that time period, I developed a coping mechanism to pass the time and alleviate stress by indulging in TV shows, particularly sitcoms. We owned a bulky TV set with vibrant colors that we acquired from a garage sale for just one dollar. One day, all my friends left for Texas to scout out potential schools for transfer, and I found myself alone in the apartment. I browsed through the basic channels such as NBC, ABC, CBS, and PBS and stumbled upon a show called "Married with Children" featuring Christina Applegate, a popular Hollywood actress at the time. The show revolved around a family of four, with a father who sold shoes and had a fondness for football and women, a mother who enjoyed shopping and dressing up but disliked cooking, a beautiful yet unintelligent blonde daughter, and an intelligent but short son who had a penchant for women and kept a mannequin in his bedroom. The sitcom was uproariously funny, with amusing characters and witty dialogue. Subsequently, I started watching other sitcoms like Saved by the Bell,

Fresh Prince of Bel Air, Full House, and Who's the Boss? And Bill Cosby. Later on, after completing college, I enjoyed Friends, Seinfeld, and Big Bang Theory. The laughter from these shows lifted me out of the dark depths of despair.

A few days later, I resumed my routine of job search, pestering restaurant and store managers. When I was at Grandy's, the manager, who had previously turned me down numerous times, surprisingly did not refuse me this time. Instead, he asked me to wait and went inside to speak with his supervisor. After a few minutes, he returned and instructed me to come to his office. He asked me to fill out some paperwork and hired me on the spot. I could not believe it. Finally, I secured my first job in the US, even though it was a menial labor job of cleaning tables, coolers, and other items. Nevertheless, I would be able to temporarily support myself and continue my studies. I was too thrilled to comprehend what had occurred that day, but in retrospect, the manager and his supervisor at Grandy's probably created a job opening for me.

Grandy's job paid $4.25 per hour, and although it was not enough to cover my expenses, it was a start. I knew that the work experience would be crucial for my future, but I also had to continue my job search. Every Tuesday at 1:30 pm, the human resources department on-campus would release job listings. Interested students would rush to the other side of the campus to find the supervisors from each department for an interview. The supervisor from the custodial department would sometimes conduct the interview on the spot and, if in a good mood, offer a position. At times, he would even hire a student whom he knew by first name. So, I made sure to meet him every day after school and say hello.

After struggling for two months, I went to the human resources department, as usual. One Tuesday afternoon, I picked up the job posting for a cleaner and hurried to the other side of the campus to meet the supervisor. I greeted him and handed him the post. This time, he took a look at it and asked me to fill out some forms in his office. Then he said, "You've got the job!" I was overjoyed. All my struggles had finally come to an end, and I did not have to worry about my finances anymore.

The following day, I met with the custodial service supervisor, who gave me a rundown of my job duties and instructed me to report to work at 10 pm. Upon arrival, I was greeted by a friendly, chubby African American woman who gave me a tour of the building. My tasks included vacuuming the classrooms and hallways and cleaning the writing boards, as well as the bathrooms. By 2 am, exhaustion had set in, but I pushed through and completed my tasks by 3 am.

I was earning around $170 per week from my two jobs, resulting in a total monthly income of $680. My rent was $200, and my additional monthly expenses amounted to about $300. Not only was I able to cover my living expenses, but I could also save a little for future semesters' tuition. Although it was challenging to balance over 20 hours of work per week with my studies (approximately 20 hours at the custodial department and 6 hours at Grandy's), I was grateful to be able to support myself without relying on anyone else. However, a tragedy struck just when I thought my life in the US was starting to look peachy.

A group of four Indian students traveled to Texas to visit one of their cousins. Three of them had been living in the US for some time, while the other had only arrived ten days prior. One of the three students insisted on driving as he had recently obtained his license and wanted to experience the thrill of driving. They visited their cousin and began their journey back home. However, just three hours into their return journey, they had an accident on the freeway. Their car crossed over the median and collided with an oncoming truck on the opposite side of the freeway. Two of the students on the right side of the car died instantly, including the newly arrived student. The driver and the passenger sitting behind him both sustained fractures.

Upon hearing the news of the incident, we were all deeply shocked. A service was held at one of the churches to mourn their loss. Although I had only met them once on-campus, I was overwhelmed with sadness and depression. I could not imagine their parents' grief after losing their son just ten days after sending him away to begin a new chapter of his life. The incident's shadow lingered for a long time, serving as an alert for me. Life is unpredictable, and accidents can happen anywhere. Life is short, and I am determined to work hard and live it to the fullest.

Figure 35 Grandy's in Edmond, Oklahoma (picture from internet)

Chapter 23:
Transfer to SDSU

Ravi Prakash, my colleague at Dr. Ambedkar Institute, shared an apartment with us and was one of the kindest souls I had ever met. He had arrived in the United States before me and reassured me that everything would turn out well during the stressful college application process in India. Once we became roommates, he frequently checked on me to ensure that I was comfortable and settling in nicely.

A few weeks after I resolved my financial conundrum, Ravi gave me an application form for the master's program in Computer Science at South Dakota State University. At the time, I had never heard of the school, nor did I know where South Dakota was located. While Central State University was easy to get into, it lacked a reputable faculty and programs, and most students transferred out within a year. Bala and I decided to apply for South Dakota State University and Indiana State University. Within a month, we heard back from both schools requesting supporting documents.

After reaching out to South Dakota State's International Student Office, I was informed that I needed to provide several documents, including a financial statement demonstrating my ability to support myself during the two-year program. Unfortunately, this was impossible for me as I had no funds available. However, there was a solution: find someone who could provide a financial statement with the required amount and indicate their willingness to sponsor my studies. The sponsor would not have to fork out a penny, as I planned to support myself through work, but there was a risk that he would be held accountable if I did not fulfill my end of the agreement.

I recalled a distant family friend my third brother-in-law, Vijayaraghavan, had mentioned. His name was Ramanujam, and he lived in Sacramento, California. So I called him around 7 am Central Time and introduced myself. Ramanujam answered groggily, said that it was still 5 am in California, and asked me to call back later. This was my first experience with time zones, as there were none in India. I was baffled by how a country could function with people living in different time zones. I worried that I had already burned a bridge with Ramanujam because I was not aware of the time difference. It seemed unlikely that anyone would want to sponsor a stranger who had not shown basic courtesy by waiting until they were awake.

After fidgeting for two hours, I called him again and stammered out a request for help with my financial statement, explaining that I would not be able to get admission without it. He asked how much money I needed, and I answered 25,000 US dollars. My heart was pounding as I said the amount, knowing it was a lot for Ramanujam, who was just an engineer and might not be able to pledge such a large sum. Surprisingly, Ramanujam promised to get the statement to me within a week. I was at a loss for words but thanked him anyway.

Within two weeks, Bala and I received our I-20s from South Dakota State University and Indiana State University. Bala suggested that we choose Computer Engineering at Indiana State University in Terre Haute. I trusted Bala's experience and instincts, so I agreed to do it. I said goodbye to all my friends, and we handed our apartment lease over to three new students from India. I remember giving them advice on job searching, grocery shopping, and adjusting to life in the US, feeling like a mentor even though I had only been there for three months.

Leaving my job at the custodial department of the school was the toughest part of my departure. When I was hired, I expressed my gratitude to the supervisor repeatedly. He smiled at me and made a request, "Babu, please don't leave in the middle of the semester. It would be challenging for me to make alternate arrangements, and it would add extra work for me to hire someone again." I promised him that I would not. However, it had only been a month, and I had to move on. I felt bad, but I had no choice. When I went to quit, the supervisor was not there, so I apologized to his assistant and left a note for him. Then I saw Grandy's manager in person and told him I was leaving for South Dakota for a better school. He wished me good luck.

After clearing out the apartment, we were all set to leave. Bala needed to visit his brother in California and his uncle in Las Vegas first, so I had to travel to Indiana by bus on my own. Whenever I felt low, I used to visit a church in Edmond and met a pastor named Chris, who was very kind to me. I asked him if he could drop me at the Greyhound bus station. It may sound strange to the locals, but for someone like me, saving money was crucial. I would do it if I could avoid calling a cab and save a few bucks. Chris agreed to give me a ride.

I was looking forward to going to Indiana. However, the day before my departure, Bala called me and told me that the Computer Engineering program in Indiana focused more on hardware than software, which could limit our career prospects after graduation. He suggested we go to South Dakota instead. After considering the situation, I realized I did not want to travel to Indiana alone. I immediately contacted Greyhound Bus Service to book a ticket to Brookings, South Dakota, instead, and they informed me that a bus would leave the following evening. I promptly called Chris about my new plan, and he agreed to give me a ride and adjusted his schedule accordingly.

The bus trip remains vivid in my memory. Seated next to me was a 15-year-old young man who was traveling alone. He had no interest in the typical school life and was heading to Missouri to live with a friend. I was impressed by his free spirit and willingness to take risks. At the Wichita, Kansas, stop, he bid goodbye to me and left. The driver tried to stop him, but he ignored the driver and walked away. The driver later told me that the young man was supposed to get off in St. Louis and report to a social worker. To this day, I often wonder what happened to him.

Bus rides in the United States are different from those in India. In India, a bus typically has working personnel on board, such as a driver and a conductor who collects fares from passengers. In the US, passengers pay for their fares before boarding the bus. Additionally, long-distance buses in India did not have restrooms at the time, unlike Greyhound buses in the US. In India, buses would stop at restaurants for a thirty-minute break, during which the driver and conductor would receive free food while passengers could buy food and use restrooms. Nowadays, Indian buses have been upgraded with sleeper seats, television screens for movies, and other amenities, including restrooms.

Finally, after a 14-hour bumpy ride, I arrived in Brookings feeling tired and hungry. I found a payphone and called the International Student Office. They directed me to an Indian student who picked me up. We had a brief drive to his apartment, where I spent a couple of hours. Soon after, Bala arrived.

After spending a few days with some Indian students, Bala suggested that we move to the University dormitory. Despite being more expensive, the dormitory offered a range of amenities such as VHS player rentals with free movies, ping pong and pool tables, and even cross-country skiing equipment that could be rented for free. Cross-country skiing involves using one's own locomotion to move across snowy terrain rather than relying on ski lifts or other forms of assistance.

Although I enjoyed the dormitory and the convenience it provided, there was one aspect that I could not adjust to—the showers. The college dormitory showers were communal, which meant that there were at least four showers next to each other with no screens in between, and everyone showered naked. In India, men would always wear their underwear or a piece of cloth around their waist while bathing in public, such as in the Ganges River, and would never expose their private parts. For a while, I showered with my underwear on, and other students gave me strange looks. One day, I realized that if I wanted to fully embrace the American way of life, I had to do things the American way. I began showering naked and felt a sense of liberation.

*Figure 36 My student ID cards: University of Central Oklahoma (top)
and SDSU (bottom)*

*Figure 37 Me in front of the Computer Science Department
in SDSU (1993)*

Chapter 24:
Jobs in Brookings

When I considered going to Brookings, South Dakota, my biggest concern was income. It had taken me almost two months to find two part-time jobs to cover my living expenses in Edmond, and I was not sure if I would have the same luck in Brookings. I wondered if there were on-campus jobs available and how competitive they were. I also wondered if finding a job outside campus would be easy and if they were available to international students. So many questions raced through my mind constantly.

However, my top priority was finding the right school with the right major. My sole purpose for coming to the US was to finish my master's and carve out a better future with a stable job. This difference in priorities between education in the US and India, or between local and Indian students, is striking. For Americans, the college major is more about what the student wants to do with their life and having fun along the way, whereas for Indians, it is all about which job leads to a bigger paycheck and a prosperous career.

Initially, I was admitted to SDSU for Electrical Engineering but switched to Computer Science following Bala's advice. However, after a semester of studying Computer Science, I found out that I did not enjoy the subject and struggled with my grades. So, I switched back to Electrical Engineering.

After settling the major, I applied for a job as a beverage runner at the Student Union Cafe at SDSU and was called for an interview with a supervisor named Jason, who was also a student. He looked at my application and noticed that I had similar work experience in the US. I described my duties at Grandy's, and he was impressed and hired me right away. The pay was again $4.25 an hour, which seemed to be the standard everywhere. Later, I came to know that this was called the minimum wage. I worked 20 hours a week, which was the maximum allowed hours for any student working on-campus. Other international students were jealous that I was able to land a job so easily when they were struggling. They did not know that back in Edmond, I had spent two months walking miles, harassing people, and making a fool of myself every single day. Only those who plant seeds get to harvest.

As a beverage runner, one of my responsibilities was to refill the milk dispenser whenever it ran low. Although it may sound simple, it was actually a challenging task that required me to climb onto the counter where the dispenser was mounted, open the dispenser door, remove the nearly empty milk bag, replace it with a new one, carefully cut the opening without spilling any milk, and seal it with the knob to prevent any milk from flowing out. If not done correctly, there was a risk of spilling the milk or breaking the bag. In addition, I had to ensure that all the soda had enough carbonation and was flowing smoothly. I either had to regularly taste the soda or wait for a student to inform me if it was flat. I also had to ensure all condiments, such as ketchup, mustard, mayonnaise, and ranch, were fully stocked. Moreover, I had to wipe the counters clean whenever they got dirty and, at the end of each day, mop the floor, vacuum, and take out the trash.

Although it was manual labor, it was something I had never done before in my life. I enjoyed the hard work and felt a sense of fulfillment at the end of each back-breaking day. As an added bonus, I was able to take home leftover food from the cafeteria. They had vegetarian selections with cheese, which quickly became my favorite food after tasting it.

One month later, I applied for a job off-campus at Burger King and was called in for an interview. During the interview, the manager, Mike, asked me some basic questions and asked if I had a green card. Without hesitation, I answered yes. Although it may not have been the most honest answer, my primary concern was survival. I was offered the job, and like my previous job, the pay was $4.25 per hour. I worked 20 hours per week, resulting in a total of 40 hours of part-time work each week.

Burger King was a different experience. I had to wear a uniform consisting of a maroon-colored shirt and navy blue pants. The restaurant was located not too far from Binnewies Hall, the dorm where I resided. In order to fight the icy, frigid South Dakota cold air during my commute to work, I would wear a jacket over my Burger King shirt and conceal my hat inside my jacket. Once I arrived, I would retrieve frozen burgers from the freezer and place them on the broiler belt along with buns on the bottom belt to get them toasted. Additionally, I would submerge pork and chicken burgers in the deep fryer and remove them when the timer went off.

I worked at these two jobs, beginning in September and October 1993, respectively, until September 1995. Despite my grueling work schedule, my earnings were only enough to cover my living expenses, but not the tuition, which was considerably larger. Working forty hours a week at $4.25 an hour only earned me $170 per week. Consequently, I was eager to take on any other job that would supplement my income. One day, I came across a job posting for a snow blower position at the dormitories, so I signed up for it without any hesitation. After all, how difficult could it be?

One night, I received a call at 2 am when I was sound asleep. I fumbled for the phone, assuming it was a call from India, but it turned out to be the dormitory office asking me to clear the snow on the sidewalks. The temperature outside was about 10 degrees Fahrenheit, which was 12 degrees Celsius below zero. I donned my thickest jacket, gloves, scarf, and shoes and made my way to the front desk to check-in. The receptionist handed me a key and directed me to a shed covered in snow in the middle of a parking lot in front of the dorm building. Even though the snow had stopped, the parking lot was still covered in knee-deep snow, which I had to plow through to reach the shed.

I had to take off my gloves to open the shed with the key. My hands were already freezing by the time I retrieved the snow blower. I put my gloves back on to warm my hands up but had trouble finding the switch on the blower. So, I removed my gloves again to check if it was hidden under something. While searching, I noticed a cord that reminded me of some scenes from the movies. I realized that the motor started by pulling the cord. After a few attempts, the motor finally started with a loud "Vrrrrrrrommmmm!"

Once I took the blower outside, I began clearing the snow from the sidewalks. Watching the blower lift the snow and spray it on the sides was entertaining, but after a few minutes, I realized I was covered in snow from head to toe. I had to pause, dust myself off, and start again. After struggling for two hours, I finally cleared all the snow from the sidewalks. This experience made me realize that there were various honorable jobs in this world, but I needed to carefully choose what I wanted to do with my life. I quit the job that very night.

In early 1993, shortly after the start of the new year, a unique opportunity presented itself to me.

As I mentioned earlier, I switched back to Electrical Engineering after one semester. One day, while on my way to class, I unexpectedly crossed paths with Dr. Ellerbruch, who was the head of the Electrical Engineering department. I had only met him once before, during the orientation, where I had shared with him some details about my family background, including my father's dementia and my mother's struggle to raise our family with minimal financial resources from farming. Not certain if he would remember me, I greeted him as we passed each other. To my surprise, he asked me to stop by his office after class.

Throughout the class, I fidgeted with nerves, wondering if I had done something wrong. Once the class was over, I made my way to Dr. Ellerbruch's office and knocked on the door. To my relief, he greeted me with a warm smile on his face. He asked about my experience at Brookings and how I had adjusted to life there. As I pondered the purpose of these questions, he asked me if I would be interested in working as a teaching assistant. I could not believe my ears.

The role of a teaching assistant would involve teaching basic electrical labs to first-year students in the department, conducting simple experiments in the lab, and grading students' papers. The department would pay two-thirds of my tuition fees in exchange for my work, and the remaining third would be paid to me in cash. This meant that not only would I not have to pay for my tuition, but I would also be earning a considerable amount of money! This was an opportunity that many students would have fought to obtain. I could not believe that he had offered it to me.

From that point on, I had not had to struggle financially while in school. I balanced three jobs, working 20 hours weekly, attending classes, and completing school assignments. I needed all of these jobs to cover my personal expenses and repay some family loans. I am grateful to Dr. Ellerbruch for his timely assistance, and I continue to feel indebted to him to this day.

During the writing of my memoir, Xiaoyu, my co-writer, suggested that I reach out to those who helped me along the way and express my gratitude. I was able to locate Dr. Ellerbruch's contact information online and called him. Understandably, he did not recall me as it had been over 20 years, but he was pleased that I had contacted him.

My position as a teaching assistant ran from January 1993 to December 1994. I worked at both the student union and Burger King until September 1995, when I completed my master's program. This was one of the most challenging yet rewarding periods of my life.

Figure 38 Me (first from right) with students in SDSU Binnewies Hall (1992)

Interlude 8: Learning to Drive

After a couple of months of working at Burger King, one day, my co-worker Jason approached me and offered to sell me his car. I declined, as I did not see the need for one. Everything I needed was within walking distance on-campus, and I had never driven before, nor did I have a driver's license. I also did not want to deal with the expenses of owning a car, such as insurance, gas, and maintenance.

But Jason said, "It's only $300." So I said, "Let us go see it." All my rationale about not needing a car went out the window once I heard the price. In the 90s, a regular car would normally cost around $15,000. After work, he took me to his house nearby and showed me a 4-door light green 1978 Ford Granada that looked like a large boat. I fell in love with it right away and gave him a check for $300 on the spot, even though I did not know how to drive. Jason had to ask his brother to drive it back to campus and park it near the dormitory.

Then Bala and my tennis friend Gary taught me how to drive. It was not as easy as I expected at all. Both of them had a torrid time teaching me. Bala was frustrated, and his blood pressure went up. Gary almost had a heart attack when I slammed on the accelerator instead of the brake on a busy street. But somehow, I pulled through and was ready for the driving test.

I went to the DMV feeling nervous. The examiner was a tall Caucasian man looking like a cowboy with a thick mustache and heavy boots. He instructed me to drive through downtown Brookings, but I made a mistake during a right turn and did not look to my left, causing incoming cars to suddenly stop. The examiner's face went pale. Needless to say, I failed the test.

I had to wait for two months before I could apply again. This time, a courteous and well-mannered Caucasian lady accompanied me on the ride. As I approached a yield sign, I continued driving past it before realizing my mistake. To my surprise, the lady simply reminded me to yield the next time and passed me. I was ecstatic as I no longer had to depend on others for transportation.

I bought the car in September, and one day in late November, I ran into a problem when I needed to run an errand. After clearing the ice from the windshield, I attempted to start the engine, but all it did was a click sound, and nothing happened. Despite several attempts, the engine failed to start, forcing me to walk in the cold.

Later that evening, I contacted Jason and asked him about the engine's failure to start. He casually said, "Oh, the car doesn't run in winter. It is too cold for the engine to start." I was shocked. I could not drive the car in winter when I needed it the most. I had to wait six months until May, when the temperature rose to the 60s, to drive the car again. There was nothing I could do. You hire a full-time employee who is only available to work six months a year—that was the deal I got for going cheap.

Once I received my driver's license, I was eager to hit the freeway. A newly arrived Indian student in Brookings asked for a ride, so I took him with me on my trip to Sioux Falls, which was about 50 miles south of Brookings. As I approached the ramp to the exit of freeway 29, I noticed a huge truck coming toward me. The driver looked at me in horror and honked his horn as loudly as he could. I was frightened. The other Indian student closed his eyes and put his head down. I slammed on the brakes and narrowly avoided colliding with the truck, coming to a screeching halt on the shoulders. Only then did I notice the sign that read "Do not enter."

On another occasion, I had to drive to a nearby town with my friend Waleed. It was after 8 pm, and I turned the headlights on as it was getting dark. After approximately ten minutes of driving on the freeway, the headlights began to flicker like something out of a horror film. A couple of minutes later, the lights went off entirely. We got off at the next exit to check the car, but we could not figure out what was wrong. We had no choice but to get back on the freeway, and with the moon providing some illumination, I carefully drove at 50 miles per hour. Other cars honked at us, sending shivers down my spine. Luckily, I managed to make it back to Brookings unscathed. However, when I later looked into the cost of repairing the lights, it was $300, so I decided not to repair them and to avoid driving at night from then on.

Learning to drive, buying a car, and getting scared of my wits were all valuable experiences. They taught me to be independent and cautious and to value my life. Once I was able to drive, job opportunities opened up for me. When I left Brookings for California, I sold the car for $300. Ford Granada has been good to me.

Figure 39 Ford Granada 1978 (picture from internet)

Chapter 25: Friends

Friendships play a vital role in my life in both India and the US. I always made sure I had long-lasting friendships, which were crucial for my emotional wellbeing. During my time at SDSU, I established a close-knit group of friends with whom I engaged in activities such as playing tennis and ping pong, watching movies, going out, and studying for exams. Through their companionship, I felt at home in this foreign country.

Bala was like a Godfather to all new students and had been a constant companion throughout my student life in the US. Despite only being in the country for six months, he understood US life better than any other students who had arrived in the past year. His uncle lived in Las Vegas, and his brother lived in California, and he had visited them before coming to Oklahoma. Furthermore, he already knew how to drive.

When I first arrived in the US, I was clueless about how the school system worked. Bala played a pivotal role in helping me settle down and catch up. He guided me on which courses to choose and how to apply for on-campus jobs. When I needed to apply for my Social Security Card in Edmond, I asked him for help. He had already arranged for a rental car to drive four other new students who were also applying for a social security card to the social security office. He even assisted with the forms. Without him, I would not have made it.

However, Bala and I had a fallout during my second year. We had lived together for over a year, but one afternoon, while I was napping in my room, a student named Sridhar Pampati woke me up and informed me that he would be taking Bala's place as my roommate going forward. When I realized he was serious, I became very angry with Bala. It felt like a divorce being notified by an attorney. It took me about a week to come to terms with the new living arrangement.

Sridhar was a very bright student who was not afraid to express his opinion, but sometimes his behavior could be off-putting. We got along well as roommates but pursued our interests independently. In contrast, Bala never acknowledged that he had moved out without telling me. He had done so to save money—the dormitory rent was $150, while the trail house he moved to was only $50. I was not sure if he was too embarrassed to tell me or if there was another reason, but he never explained. Given our history, it would have been much easier if he had sat down and talked to me about it. Nonetheless, we remained great friends and ultimately moved to California together.

Gary and I became friends while working at the student union. He was a highly-strung Caucasian man who wore thick glasses and had a passion for playing tennis, which was also one of my favorite sports. After work, we would often hit the ball around, and he taught me a variety of techniques since I was still a beginner at the time. As I gradually improved, we began playing sets, and while Gary was initially better, I gradually challenged him more and more. One day, he won the first set, and I won the second set, which made him very angry. The third set was a close contest, and we ended up in a deuce. Gary served, but I easily returned it with my signature wicked spin, and he hit the ball into the net, losing his serve. His frustration got the better of him, and he threw his racket into the pine trees nearby. When he climbed the tree to retrieve it, it was getting dark, and he was unable to find it. Although he said he would come back the next day, I never found out what happened.

Gary also helped me learn how to drive using his car. He taught me the basics of driving an auto-shift car. During one lesson, he was explaining the difference between the brake and accelerator pedals. I was driving smoothly until I approached a yield sign, and Gary asked me to apply the brakes and yield to oncoming traffic. However, I stepped on the accelerator by accident, and we charged forward. Gary went into a rage and started screaming at me. I was scared and decided to stop taking lessons with him after that. Once I moved to California, we lost touch. I often wonder where Gary is and how he is doing now.

The friend I mentioned earlier, whom I played tennis with in frigid temperatures, Bob, was a tall Caucasian man who had a deep voice and also wore thick glasses. Although he had registered for classes on-campus, he never attended them; instead, he played tennis and went fishing. He relied on food stamps for his living expenses, which was shocking to me. I was surprised to learn about the food stamp program, as I could not believe that people could live without working yet claim poverty as a reason to receive aid. As someone who had come from a poor country where people struggled to survive, I could not understand why individuals in America could not find a job, even if it meant working at a place like Burger King for $4.25 an hour. I found it difficult to comprehend why the government would encourage laziness, given that America is a wealthy nation with an abundance of jobs and resources. I lost touch with Bob as well after I left Brookings.

Khun Za, who was from Burma, lived in Binnewies Hall with Joshua Doohan while I shared a room with Bala. I became friends with Khun immediately. Like many other students who did not score well on their TOEFL exams, Khun had to take English classes. Writing essays was a requirement for the class, and Khun struggled with them. He came to me for assistance, and I wrote the essays for him every time. Even today, he remains grateful for my help.

After graduation, Khun moved to Chicago in search of a job, but he was unsuccessful after a year. I invited him to come to California and stay with me while he looked for work. He took me up on the offer, stayed with me, and eventually found a job. Later on, he was able to apply for asylum and become a US citizen. Burma, also known as Myanmar, has experienced intermittent military rule for the past three decades, prompting many individuals to leave the country in order to survive.

Akbar, who hailed from Bangladesh, invited me to join him in visiting his friends at University of Southwestern Louisiana during the summer. He owned a sports car with a manual transmission, while I was only familiar with automatic cars. As a result, Akbar was the sole driver for our trip. While we were driving through Texas, we encountered an empty freeway, but Akbar drove at a cautious speed of only 60 miles per hour. I suggested he increase the speed to 75 miles per hour, which he reluctantly did. However, our joy came to a halt when a Texas highway patrol car with flashing red and blue lights pulled us over. After Akbar presented the officer with the necessary documents, the officer requested that he step out of the car. Shortly, he came back, and it was my turn to face the music. The officer asked me where we came from and where we were headed, and then, to my surprise, he let us go with just a warning.

Still in disbelief over our luck, I asked Akbar what the officer had said during their conversation. His response was both amusing and truthful: Akbar had confessed to speeding because I had urged him to do so. I was taken aback by his response, but we were both thrilled that we had escaped with just a warning. We spent a few days at the university before heading back to South Dakota. During the return trip, Akbar grew tired while we were driving north through Oklahoma, Kansas, and Nebraska, so he asked me to take over. However, I was unfamiliar with driving a manual car, so together, we came up with an ingenious plan. I would be behind the wheels and apply the clutch while he shifted gears. Although it worked flawlessly at first, things became more challenging when it began to snow as we drove through Nebraska. Despite the slippery conditions, I remained in third gear throughout the journey because I was too afraid to stop and switch places with Akbar. Thankfully, after a few anxious hours, we arrived in Brookings without a scratch.

Raj and I became friends during our school days, bonding over movies and pool games in the dormitory. One day, Raj approached me with a request for financial help to pay for his school fees. He explained that his family was going through a difficult time, and he was unable to arrange the funds required to cover his educational expenses. As someone who also hailed from a family struggling with financial difficulties, I found it hard to refuse his plea for assistance. Raj promised to return the money in a few months, and I agreed to lend him approximately $2,000 by charging his school fees to my credit card.

Two months later, I asked Raj to repay the amount he borrowed, but he requested two more months to settle his dues. This continued for a year, and eventually, I moved to California, completely forgetting about the loan. Ten years later, I decided to catch up with an old SDSU friend named Sai, who told me that Raj was in Minneapolis and still in touch with him. I mentioned in passing that Raj still owed me money.

One day, out of the blue, I received a call from Raj, who apologized for not repaying the loan and promised to return the money he owed me. However, I had completely forgotten how much he owed me at that point. Within a week, I received a check for $1,000 in the mail as repayment.

Vijay from Malaysia and I connected over our shared Tamil language and stories about our homes. Vijay was a smart and hardworking person with a great sense of humor. Tamilians in Malaysia have a rich cultural history, and the majority of Malaysian Indians trace their origins back to Tamil Nadu and Sri Lanka.

Jacob, from Kansas City, also originally came from Malaysia. I was impressed by his beautiful handwriting, which was meticulous and thoughtful, just like Jacob himself. He worked very hard and always looked out for me. After graduation, Jacob and another student named Nataraj from South Dakota moved with me to the Bay Area. At one point, we all lived together in a two-bedroom apartment with Madhu and Pandey. I am still in touch with Jacob, who now lives in Gilroy, about an hour away from me. Nataraj later moved back to India and tragically committed suicide because of his failed marriage and ailing parents.

Although this chapter may seem tedious to read, this lengthy list of names played a vital role in one of my most difficult yet fulfilling years. As a young, inexperienced, and anxious foreigner with limited resources, my friends provided me with a source of comfort during times of both joy and sadness. They also offered guidance and motivation when I needed it the most. I would like to express my gratitude to each of them in this chapter.

Figure 40 Bala (second from left, top row), Zabar (2nd from right, top row), Madhu (first from right, top row), me, (first from left, bottom row), Jacob (second from left, bottom row), Vijay (third from left, bottom row) and Arul (Extreme right) in 1996

Chapter 26:
Valley Fair

Working at Valley Fair, an amusement park, taught me how to be a leader and find solutions to problems. It was a huge boost of confidence for me to know that I can achieve a lot by working hard.

Valley Fair is a 125-acre amusement park in Shakopee, Minnesota. Owned by Cedar Fair Entertainment Company which now owns almost 20 other amusement parks such as California's Great America, Canada's Wonderland, etc. Valley Fair opened in 1976 featuring over 75 rides and attractions including eight roller coasters, and it also had a water park called Soak City.

Legally, international students were allowed to work only on-campus for 20 hours during their coursework, but the international student advisor, Margot Jenkins, was kind enough to let us work for 40 hours a week at Valley Fair in the summer. I did not go in my first summer because I was helping Dr. Galipeau in the Electrical Engineering department. In the second year, I applied in the spring and was offered a position to operate the rides. Normally, Indian students prefer to work in the food industry for two reasons: one, there would be more hours involved in cleaning after the park closed; two, the workers stayed indoors. Ride workers would always have to stand in the sun, and it was not fun in summer. But I had no choice.

I learned how to operate a variety of rides, including the monster, Ferris wheel, and some other little rides for children. The Ferris wheel was particularly interesting, as I had to ensure the wheel was balanced by adding people to the gondolas based on a chart. For instance, if there were 20 people, we added them to alternate gondolas. The children's rides were straightforward to operate. The monster ride was a real challenge, not only for the riders but also for operators like myself. It had eight tentacles revolving around the center, and riders sat in bucket chambers at the end of each arm. Once the riders boarded the bucket, I had to lift its bottom, which weighed around 30 pounds, and lock it. When I completed this process for all 12 tentacles, my back would already start aching. At the end of the ride, I had to walk around and unlock the buckets to allow riders to disembark. I worked on this ride for three or four hours before moving on to the Ferris wheel or the children's rides for the day. Within a month, I had gotten a tan from standing in the sun all day, particularly given that my complexion was already dark. I tried to sit down whenever there were no customers, but the lead would come and remind me that employees were not allowed to sit while working according to the company policy.

After working on the rides for two months, I became weary of them and approached the manager to ask about the possibility of transferring to food service. However, he told me that a mutual exchange was required for such a transfer. Despite my efforts to find someone willing to switch, I was unsuccessful. Ultimately, I spent roughly 40 days in the rides department.

Many European students, including those from Sweden, the Czech Republic, France, Spain, England, and Germany, were employed at the park. I learned that European and American students enjoyed working on the rides as they could enjoy the sun and leave right after the park closed. Conversely, Asian students preferred indoor jobs and longer hours to earn enough money to pay for school. One day, while chatting with an English student from London who worked in food service, I mentioned my desire to leave the rides department. The English student from food service told me that he had been seeking someone to switch with from the rides department. We discussed this with the manager, and I was transferred to the corn dog stand. I was so happy when they made the switch. Working at the corn dog became my dream job.

At the stand, everything we served was on a stick. During the morning preparation, we placed a hotdog on a stick, dipped it in batter, and then fried it. The result was a delicious, crispy, brown exterior with a soft and savory interior. My personal favorite was Cheese on a Stick. We sliced a large block of cheese into small rectangular pieces and followed the same process as we did with the hotdogs. The easiest item to prepare was a Pickle on a Stick. We opened countless buckets of dill pickles, placed a stick in each one, and left them in the water. Teenagers were fond of the pickles and would purchase them in scores.

I worked with a group of high school students at a stand during the peak season. While most of them disliked working at the cash register, I enjoyed it and appreciated the opportunity to interact with customers. Our work hours were from 8 am to 12 am, totaling 16 hours per day. We had one day off each week, during which we caught up on laundry and rest. Since I was the only one in our group with a car, I often gave rides to my coworkers.

Occasionally, we were asked to cover shifts at other stands. I had worked at several other stands in the past, including the pizza stand, Mexican food stand, pretzel stand, and a few others. Among them, the pretzel stand was one of the most challenging. Only a few employees who received training were allowed to work there, but I was unsure if they received the same pay as others. The German stand was also noteworthy, selling beer, ready-made pretzels, sauerkraut, and potato salad.

Once a month, the employees had a special night out after work. During this time, three rides were open, and there were stands offering ice cream, funnel cake, and pizza. Corkscrew, a famous rollercoaster ride that spun riders 360 degrees, was a popular choice among us. We would ride the coaster repeatedly until we became tired or bored, then turned our attention to the food stands.

In late summer, Jaldu, a fellow student from SDSU, was reassigned to our corn dog stand from a different food stand. He was also studying Electrical Engineering at SDSU, and we took some classes and worked on some projects together. Within a few weeks, he was promoted to become the leader of the corn dog stand. I was very upset since I had been working at the stand for a longer time than him. How did he become my boss just weeks after arriving here? I expressed my concern to the manager, who listened and requested that I be patient. He assured me that there would be promotions and that I would be considered for them.

Shortly after that, I was promoted to lead the German stand. However, I was not too enthusiastic about it since the German stand did not attract many customers and was not an exciting place to work. Nevertheless, I accepted the promotion. One of my strengths was cleaning and closing the stand quickly, which led to resentment from the German stand employees.

They were unhappy because it meant fewer hours and harder work. One employee would take long breaks and ignore instructions, which made matters worse. Later, I heard that he had been fired for stealing money while working as a cashier. There were dramas like this every day.

One busy day, I was working in the kitchen while a high school student named Megan was manning the cash register. Suddenly, I heard a commotion coming from outside. I stepped to the front and saw a long line of customers, with an elderly man at the front arguing with Megan. The man claimed he had given her a $100 bill, but Megan was certain she had only received a $20 bill. Without hesitation, I told Megan to give him the change for $100, despite her reluctance. As a senior employee, I made the decision to save the customers in line from further delay, even though it went against the usual protocol that required recording the customer's information and verifying the claim at the end of the day. Fortunately, my actions did not result in any repercussions.

Working at Valley Fair taught me valuable life lessons such as discipline, hard work, and persistence. As a lead employee, I effectively managed and motivated my team to achieve our goals. Additionally, I formed meaningful friendships with my colleagues. Most importantly, my job allowed me to pay for my college tuition without taking on a student loan.

Figure 41 Me working on the rides (1995)

Interlude 9: Cholesterol Problem

In South India, dairy plays a significant role in the local cuisine. Milk products such as plain milk, yogurt, butter, and ghee (refined butter) are all common staples. However, it is interesting to note that cheese is not a prevalent ingredient in the daily diet. In fact, I had never tasted cheese while growing up. When I came to the United States, I was surprised to find cheese widely used in many dishes. I was particularly impressed by the delicious taste of melted cheese on pizza, which I had never experienced before. I ended up eating pizza almost every day during my early days in the US.

While living in Brookings, I discovered a pizza chain called Godfather's Pizza. The restaurant offered a lunch buffet for only $3, which I frequented three to four times a week. In addition to pizza, I also enjoyed Mozzarella sticks, a deep-fried dish made with bread crumbs and Mozzarella cheese. They were so delicious that I took some home with me every day after working at the cafeteria. Despite being a vegetarian, my love for cheese knew no bounds.

When I moved to California and started working at KLA Instruments, I received health benefits for the first time in my life. The first thing my doctor asked me to do was to undergo a full physical checkup, which included a blood test. I went to the hospital and had my blood tested. A week later, I met with the doctor to discuss the results.

Upon entering the doctor's office, I was greeted by a smiling doctor who handed me a copy of my blood test results. As I scanned through the report, I noticed that Good Cholesterol, Bad Cholesterol, and Overall Cholesterol were all marked in red. The doctor went on to explain that these readings indicated that my cholesterol levels were excessively high. I was taken aback by this revelation as I had believed that being a vegetarian would prevent me from such health concerns. However, it seemed that the modern American diet, consisting of an abundance of cheese and fried food, was causing cholesterol issues. This was the first time I had become aware of dietary problems. The doctor advised me to reduce my intake of cheese, fried food, and other foods high in saturated fats. Sadly, this marked the end of my love affair with cheese. Nowadays, I eat cheese sparingly.

A few years later, while working as a consultant at Wells Fargo, I became friends with one of the mainframe developers named Pardha. We often took long walks after lunch and discussed various aspects of life. During one of our conversations, I mentioned my own cholesterol issues and the importance of getting annual checkups. Taking my advice, Pardha went for his own checkup and discovered that he had diabetes. Although I was saddened by this news, I was glad that I had helped him identify his health condition at an early stage, allowing him to take the necessary steps to manage his health.

Chapter 27:
MS Project with Dr. Ali Salehnia

During the second year of my master's program, each student was required to choose a research topic and submit a paper at the end of the year with the guidance of a professor. At first, I worked with Dr. Galipeau, who assigned me mini-projects that involved collecting data. However, without access to the internet at the time, it was a challenge to gather sufficient information since the library had limited resources. In the end, Dr. Galipeau was not satisfied with my progress and dropped me from his advising list, saying he already had too many students to mentor.

I then sought guidance from Dr. Madeline Andrawis. I took her courses and was all set to work on my thesis under her. She expected me to work on some of the latest technology in semiconductors, but I had no idea how. I tried my best, but she was not satisfied with my work and announced that she could not assist me anymore. Unable to write a thesis without proper guidance, I felt frustrated and hopeless. I went into a church and prayed to God for help.

The dejection lasted for a week until my friend Bala noticed my changed demeanor. I shared my situation with him, and he suggested that I approach Dr. Ali Salehnia from the Computer Science Department for help. Although I was skeptical that he would guide a student from another department, I decided to follow Bala's advice since I had no other options available.

I timidly knocked on Dr. Ali Salehnia's office door the next day. He was a 40-year-old man from the Middle East with curly hair. I explained my situation and asked if he could be my guide, fully expecting him to decline since I was not from his department. To my surprise, he agreed to mentor me, but only if I chose a Computer Science topic for my thesis.

Upon receiving approval from Dr. Ali Salehnia, I started my research immediately and spent several hours every day in the library sifting through books until I found a topic that piqued my interest: "Ethics in Computer Science and Engineering." I was thrilled to begin working on it and delved deeper into related material from the library. However, my time in graduate school was limited since I had already turned 30 and could not afford to spend any more time switching between majors, unlike most second-year graduate students who were typically 23 years old.

After relocating to California, I searched for material in all the libraries in the Bay Area, which had more abundant resources than the Brookings Library. I began writing a few chapters and sent them to Dr. Ali Salehnia via postal mail. He reviewed and corrected my drafts and sent them back, and this process continued for a couple of years.

My thesis focused on some of the most significant disasters in history caused by human error resulting from carelessness or irresponsibility. One of these disasters was the infamous Chornobyl disaster on 26 April 1986, at the No. 4 reactor in the Chornobyl Nuclear Power Plant, located north of Ukraine in the Soviet Union. It is considered the most catastrophic nuclear disaster in history in terms of both cost and casualties and is one of only two nuclear energy accidents rated at the maximum severity of seven on the International Nuclear Event Scale, the other being the 2011 Fukushima Daiichi nuclear disaster in Japan. The initial emergency response to the Chornobyl disaster involved more than 500,000 personnel and an estimated cost of 18 billion Soviet rubles.

The disaster resulted from a combination of operator negligence and critical design flaws. During a safety test, operators accidentally lowered power output to near zero during a planned decrease in reactor power. While attempting to stabilize the reactor, the operators removed several control rods that exceeded the limits established by operating procedures. When the test concluded, the operators initiated a reactor shutdown. However, due to the design flaw and previously removed control rods, this action caused localized increases in reactivity, resulting in steam explosions and a meltdown of the reactor core. Airborne radioactive contamination was released for approximately nine days and settled onto regions of the USSR and Western Europe, finally ending on 4 May 1986.

Initially, the Soviets downplayed the accident as a minor incident, but the evacuation of over 100,000 individuals led to the realization of the full extent of the situation by the global community. In my thesis, I discussed ethical concerns, such as the lack of adherence to proper guidelines and the Soviet Union's failure to promptly disclose the disaster to the world despite the airborne radioactive contamination that impacted neighboring countries for years.

Another example I cited in my thesis was the Bhopal Disaster, also known as the Bhopal Gas Tragedy. A gas leak incident occurred on the night of December 2nd or 3rd, 1984, at the Union Carbide India Limited (UCIL) pesticide plant in Bhopal, Madhya Pradesh, India, and is considered one of the world's worst industrial disasters. Over 500,000 people were exposed to methyl isocyanate (MIC) gas.

The Indian government and local activists asserted that poor management and neglect of maintenance led to a situation where ordinary pipe maintenance caused water to flow back into a tank containing MIC, triggering the disaster. However, Union Carbide Corporation (UCC) disputed this by alleging that water entered the tank as an act of rescuing the situation.

Following the disaster, the healthcare system was quickly overwhelmed. Medical personnel were unprepared for the thousands of casualties, and doctors and hospitals were unaware of proper treatment methods for the inhalation of MIC gas. Mass burials and cremations were conducted, and within days, trees in the area had withered due to exposure to the chemicals. Bloated animal carcasses were visible everywhere.

In relation to this issue, my focus of discussion is on the question of who was to blame and how the disaster could have been averted. After the disaster, there was a sense of panic among the management, with each party blaming the other. The Indian management blamed the US corporation for not providing appropriate safety measures and overseeing the company's operations, while the US corporation blamed the local management of the company for failing to adhere to established regulations, thereby allowing the disaster to occur.

After completing my thesis, Dr. Ali Salehnia approved my work and signed off on the paper. However, I still had a significant challenge to face, which was defending the thesis. I scheduled the defense for August 1997 and arranged to fly back to SDSU for the occasion.

At that time, I had a colleague named Alpa Kohli who had just joined KLA Tencor, the company I worked for at the time. Alpa had graduated from one of India's prestigious universities, the Indian Institute of Technology. We bonded well, and she assisted me greatly in my final preparations for my defense, including creating a PowerPoint presentation.

To receive valuable feedback before the actual defense, I presented a trial run of my defense to my entire Customer Acceptance Team at KLA Tencor. It was very useful to present to an audience beforehand.

On the day of my defense, I was overcome with nerves as it felt like the outcome would determine the course of my entire life. Nevertheless, I tried to reassure myself by reminding myself that I already had a job, and while the defense was important, it was not the end-all-be-all. However, I knew it was crucial to obtain my official degree after working hard to come to the USA and persevering through numerous struggles.

As I entered the room for the defense, I was greeted by four professors, including Dr. Ellerbruch, the head of the department and a strong supporter of mine; Dr. Ali Salehnia, my mentor; Dr. Finch, another EE professor, and a fourth professor from mechanical engineering to ensure objectivity. I presented my paper and went through my slides. Dr. Finch posed several challenging questions, but I was able to answer most of them. Dr. Ellerbruch also offered assistance, while Dr. Ali Salehnia remained mostly quiet.

At the end of my presentation, I was asked to leave the room so the professors could deliberate on the outcome. Feeling unsure of how I did during the defense, I waited nervously outside the room for 15 minutes until Dr. Ellerbruch emerged and extended his arm to congratulate me. I was ecstatic! Finally, I accomplished what I had set out to do in America: obtain my master's degree. Adding "M.S." to my name and being recognized as an engineer felt amazing.

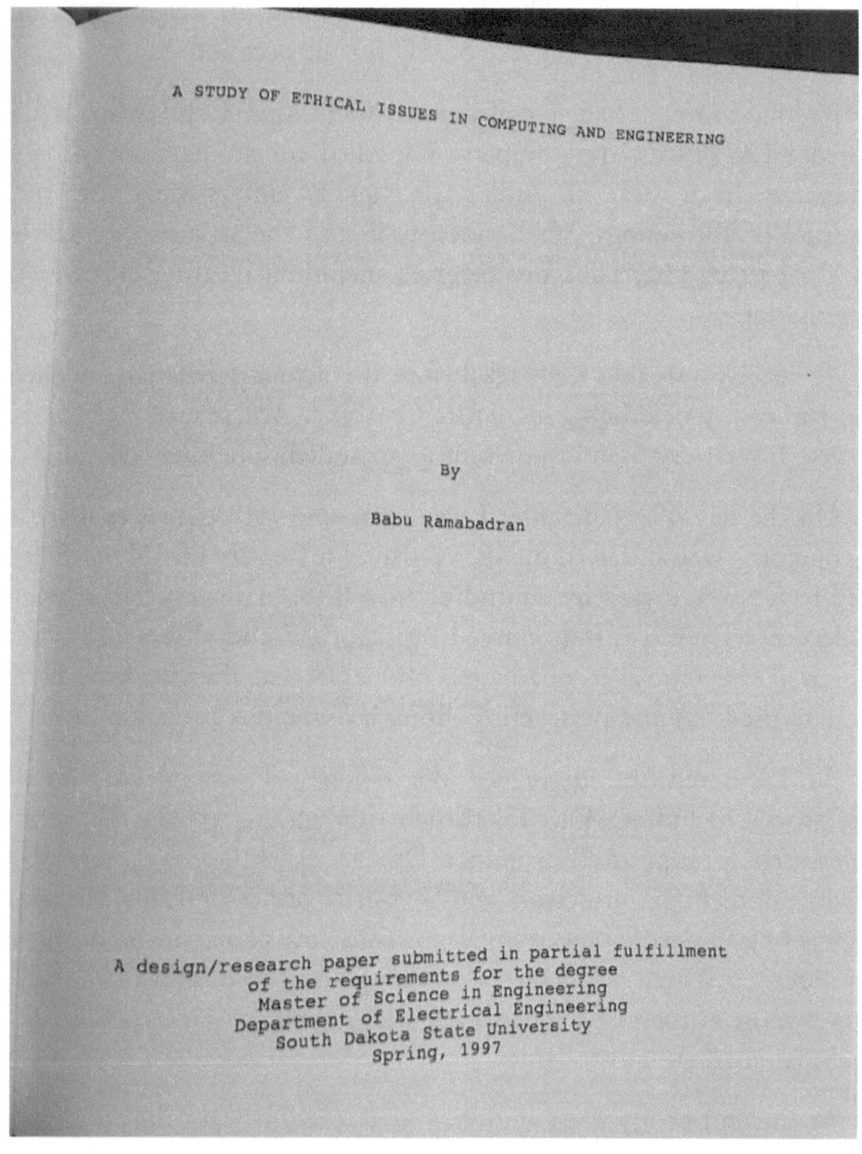

Figure 42 Cover page of my thesis book

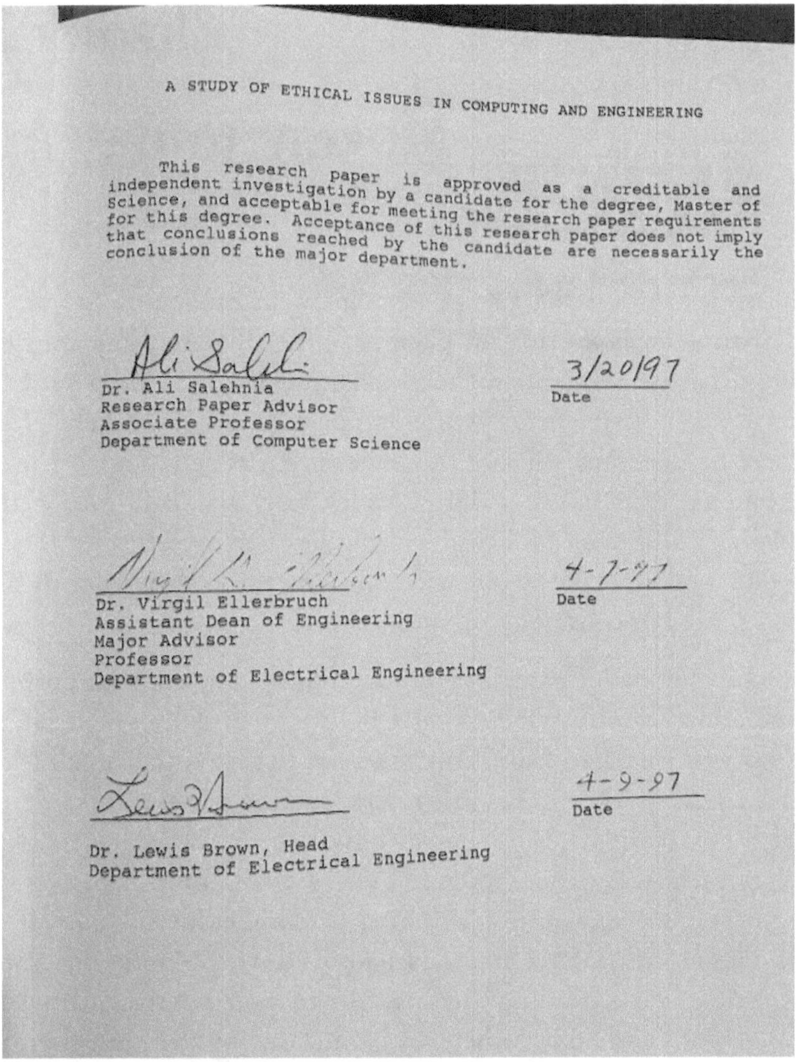

A STUDY OF ETHICAL ISSUES IN COMPUTING AND ENGINEERING

This research paper is approved as a creditable and independent investigation by a candidate for the degree, Master of Science, and acceptable for meeting the research paper requirements for this degree. Acceptance of this research paper does not imply that conclusions reached by the candidate are necessarily the conclusion of the major department.

Dr. Ali Salehnia
Research Paper Advisor
Associate Professor
Department of Computer Science

3/20/97
Date

Dr. Virgil Ellerbruch
Assistant Dean of Engineering
Major Advisor
Professor
Department of Electrical Engineering

4-7-97
Date

4-9-97
Date

Dr. Lewis Brown, Head
Department of Electrical Engineering

Figure 43 Approval from the professors

Chapter 28:
Moving to Bay Area

In September 1995, I had already been living in Brookings, SD, for three years, a year longer than I had planned. When I started my coursework in 1992, I needed to take some additional prerequisite Computer Science courses for a semester before switching back to my main field of study, Electrical Engineering. During this time, my friends Jaldu (the one who got promoted earlier than I did at Valley Fair) and Bala were planning to move to California. I initially had my heart set on New York because my friend DR lived there, but when they mentioned moving to Silicon Valley, I started to consider it an option.

Silicon Valley offered numerous highly paid job opportunities and the added bonus of being near friends. I casually asked Jaldu if I could go with them to California, and he suggested that I call Madhu, another friend from our Electrical Engineering class, to ask if I could stay at his apartment. Madhu had moved to the Bay Area six months earlier, which was where Silicon Valley was, after completing his coursework, and had found a job as a semiconductor chip designer within two months of his arrival. I had lived with Madhu one summer in his trailer house in Brookings and in an apartment in Minneapolis when we both worked at Valley Fair. After getting the green light from Madhu, I called DR and let him know that I would be moving to California.

Three of us began our journey from Brookings, South Dakota, to Sunnyvale, California. I had sold my Ford Granada for $300 and switched to a used Pontiac Grand AM, which I was confident would be able to handle the trip of almost 1,820 miles. We faced the challenge of traveling without cell phones or GPS and relied on paper maps for directions. During the mid-September hot weather, Bala's car would overheat, and he had to stop every hour to pour water into the radiator to cool the engine down. Although it was frustrating to stop so frequently, we stuck together and continued on our journey.

Around 7 pm, we arrived at a small town where we stayed in a motel room for the night. The next morning, we hit the road early to avoid the heat and drove through several states, including South Dakota, Wyoming, Utah, Nevada, and finally, California. Along the way, we were treated to a stunning array of landscapes, including mountains, deserts, rocks, forests, and lakes. We also had the chance to immerse ourselves in Western American culture, meet locals, and experience life on the road. It was a thrilling adventure that exceeded my expectations.

As we approached the California border, we suddenly realized that we had lost track of Bala's car. Jaldu suggested that we pull over and discuss our options. Fortunately, Jaldu had Pandey's phone number, so we decided to head straight to his apartment. We suspected that Bala had grown tired of keeping tabs on us and had decided to go his own way, and he was heading to his brother's house anyway.

The road through the Sierra Hills presented a formidable challenge, with countless bends, slopes, and hills. Nevertheless, we managed to navigate it safely and eventually arrived in Sacramento and then the Bay Area. When we reached Sunnyvale in the South Bay Area around 11 pm, we stopped at a gas station and used a public phone to call Pandey. Within minutes, he arrived and took us to his comfortable apartment, which boasted two bedrooms, two bathrooms, and a fully equipped kitchen. We ended up sleeping in the living room, snuggled up in our sleeping bags.

I woke up to the noise from the kitchen. Madhu was busy getting ready for work, and we engaged in a friendly conversation before he departed for the day. That evening, Pandey treated Jaldu and me to an Indian restaurant called Swagat in Milpitas, which was about 20 minutes away. Pandey introduced us to the owner, and to our surprise, he inquired if any job vacancies were available. Even more surprisingly, the owner offered us jobs on the spot. We had already secured employment within just two days of arriving in the area. It was a relief to resolve my problems before they began.

At the restaurant, I took on multiple roles: customer service, order taking, table busing, cleaning, and kitchen assistance. One night, I catered to an Indian classical dance performance, serving appetizers and drinks during the break. I spoke to a college student who asked about my occupation during the event. I told him that I had recently relocated to the Bay Area and was seeking full-time employment in the semiconductor industry. The student revealed that his uncle ran a semiconductor company and encouraged me to speak with him. The following day, I contacted the uncle, Shyam Das, and arranged a meeting at his office.

In Mr. Das's office, he described the job requirements to me. His chemical processing unit involved running experiments on chips within a chamber, utilizing acids and pressure settings. After determining the salary and start date, I thanked the owner of Swagat and promptly resigned from my position. It was essential to begin my professional career as soon as possible.

The following Monday, I began my first full-time job at Das Devices. There, I encountered a recent Indian college graduate who was exceptionally intelligent. He provided me with extensive guidance on the processing tool, including how to manage pressure, handle chips, and avoid mistakes. Although it felt overwhelming initially, I gradually adapted to the tasks at hand. After several months of work, I began applying for other jobs by attending job fairs.

In the past, job fairs held significant importance. Many were hosted at the Santa Clara Convention Center, a large meeting and convention facility in Silicon Valley's heart. During these events, I strolled around the booths, conversed with recruiters, and handed them printed resumes. Occasionally, they even conducted interviews on the spot. In late October of 1995, a recruiter from a semiconductor company called KLA Instruments contacted me about a position. The company produced huge wafer inspection equipment for chip companies like Intel, Samsung, and Hitachi.

I interviewed with the manager of the team, along with two other engineers, and they were impressed with my background and communication skills. They contacted me within a couple of weeks to offer me a position. I was ecstatic to receive a professional job at a big company and began working as a contractor with a title as Customer Acceptance Engineer on Boxing Day.

The manufacturing team put in extensive effort day and night to ready the equipment for the customer acceptance engineers. Upon handover, we conducted rigorous tests to identify any defects. To enter the cleanroom where the machines were produced, we were required to wear full protective gear from head to toe, including garb, gloves, and goggles. Unsurprisingly, it was called a space suit.

The machine I worked on was called 21XX, which featured two containers on each side referred to as "boats" that transported silicon wafers. Wafers were substrates for microelectronic devices built inside and upon the wafer. A robotic arm retrieved the wafer from either boat and inserted it into the machine. A microscope-equipped camera scanned the wafer for defects, displaying a magnified image on the monitor positioned overhead. Our objective was to identify any abnormalities, such as dust particles or small droplets of moisture, that could lead to a short circuit. Defective chips were subsequently removed. I found the work to be fascinating, though it took me about a week to properly don the garb and acclimate to the pace of the manufacturing aspects of large equipment.

We had customers from various regions, such as Japan, Taiwan, South Korea, and Europe. After work, we entertained them by taking them out for dinner and drinks. One of our customers from Japan finished testing a day ahead of schedule, so I suggested going sightseeing on an extra day. He was pleased with the idea as he did not know where to go. I took him to Monterey Beach, Carmel-by-the-sea, and the 17-mile drive, which were all famous and beautiful scenic spots in the Bay Area. He enjoyed the beaches and nature; the whole experience made him extremely happy. As a result, he promptly signed off on the machine, and my manager was impressed with how quickly and smoothly the transaction went through.

During my time at KLA Instruments, I enjoyed my job and made many friends. Our group was like a close-knit family. We bonded over lunch every day in the cafe as a team, which was instrumental in our team building. We also went out after work and engaged in various activities together. Our manager, David Moezidis, was jovial, kind, and helpful. He was one of the best managers I have ever encountered in my professional career.

Figure 44 Mr. Jayaram, owner of Swagat Indian Cuisine (middle), Ratnendra Pandey (right), my college mate from SDSU and me outside the restaurant when getting pictures for this book (2023)

Interlude 10: Personal Hygiene

During my time at KLA Instruments, I developed a friendship with Andrew Carino, a Filipino American colleague whose parents immigrated to the United States when he was very young. He shared stories about his childhood in Manila, where he spent his days visiting beaches and living a carefree life before moving to the US to escape poverty.

On one occasion, Andrew was driving us to a restaurant for lunch when he appeared uneasy and kept glancing at me. Eventually, he opened his car window and asked me to do the same despite the chilly January weather. Confused, I asked him why he wanted the cold wind blowing at us. After hesitating for a moment, he asked if I used deodorant. Surprised, I asked him to repeat his question. He then explained that the smell emanating from my armpits was so strong that he had to open the windows to get some fresh air.

Although I was initially shocked by my ignorance and lack of awareness about basic hygiene, I was grateful for Andrew's honesty. In India, using deodorant was not a common practice at that time, especially in rural areas where people were more concerned with basic necessities like food, water, and shelter. Deodorant was not readily available in stores, and while some people used cologne, it happened sparingly.

Andrew's comments inspired me to start paying attention to body hygiene, and I have been taking care of myself ever since. Moreover, I began to notice other Indian immigrants who were not using deodorant, and if I knew them well enough, I would politely explain the importance of personal hygiene. Some people were appreciative and started taking care of themselves, while others were offended. However, I remained undeterred and continued to help those who were receptive to my advice.

Chapter 29:
Roommates

After moving to California, I lived in an apartment in Sunnyvale where I resided for several years until my marriage. Initially, I shared the apartment with Madhu and Pandey, Jacob and Nataraj joined us after a semester. All of them were students from SDSU. Jacob shared the larger room with Madhu and me, while Nataraj shared the other room with Pandey.

Jacob was originally from Malaysia and studied Electrical Engineering. As mentioned in an earlier chapter, his father was an engineer, and his family belonged to the middle-class in Malaysia. Jacob was a diligent and hardworking student with excellent handwriting and tennis skills. He always stood up for me when my other friends were unkind. When Madhu got married and moved out, another SDSU student named Gautam took his place. Gautam had come to the Bay Area after completing his research in Chemistry and securing a job here. He was very conscientious with finances and lived with us for a short period. When he left, he was unhappy because I asked him to pay for some expenses he owed. Jacob defended me and ensured that Gautam paid his dues.

Nataraj was an introverted and quiet individual with a big mustache, a muscular build, and a polite disposition. He worked out frequently, and everyone liked him. When he came to the apartment with Jacob from South Dakota, we were pleased to welcome him as a roommate despite our already crowded room, which included Madhu, Pandey, Jaldu, and me. After Jacob and Nataraj joined us, six of us lived in the two-bedroom apartment. Although it was a bit cramped, we were content living together and enjoyed our bachelor lifestyles while paying only $150 per head in rent.

Pandey and I have been close since he arrived at SDSU. He was always straightforward and a no-nonsense guy, which often got him into trouble. When I first arrived in California with Jaldu, Pandey picked us up late at night and took me to Swagat, an Indian restaurant, the very next day. He helped me secure a job that provided the income I desperately needed and led to my break in my career with Das Devices and later KLA Tencor. Pandey is an excellent example of a true friend who always positively impacts others' lives. We are still in touch and fondly reminisce about our SDSU days.

Jaldu and I worked together at the corn dog stand at Valley Fair. His work was methodical, thoughtful, and disciplined, which was the opposite of my bubbly, emotional, and outgoing personality. As mentioned in the previous chapter, he became the leader of the stand even though he joined after me. However, I was disappointed with the Valley Fair management, not Jaldu.

I remember one time when we were driving back to Brookings from Minneapolis after a weekend at work in Valley Fair. I was driving, and Jaldu was asleep in the passenger seat. We were on a one-lane road in each direction, and I was driving fast as usual when a slow driver in front of us annoyed me. I waited for an opportunity to pass him, and when it came, I quickly switched to the opposite lane. Jaldu woke up just in time to see a car dashing toward us, honking like crazy. In a fraction of a second, I spun the steering wheel and made it back to our lane. Jaldu did not sleep for the rest of the night.

I shared a room with Madhu, and Jaldu stayed in the other room with Pandey. We established a routine of working, cooking, and having fun on weekends. Madhu and I bonded over sports, and we often played tennis and jogged together. Jaldu and Pandey also became good friends, while Bala dropped in occasionally. To this day, all of us remain close friends.

Madhu noticed how frugal I was with money. Every morning, I would wake up early, take a shower, and apply moisturizer to my body before getting dressed. When the moisturizer container was almost empty, I would squeeze it hard, making a noise and trying to get the last bit. Madhu noticed this and made fun of me, but he also appreciated frugality, unlike many Americans who waste resources.

Madhu's father was an office clerk from humble beginnings. He was wise enough to save money and eventually bought a large house in Bangalore, where they lived comfortably. Many years later, the house required renovations, so Madhu began sending money back from his salary every month. Since I shared a room with him, his rent was cut in half, allowing him to save even more money. He renovated the house by building shops downstairs and adding more rooms and bathrooms, of which he was very proud. His father managed Madhu's money wisely and even earned interest on it.

I wish my family knew how to handle money effectively and utilize the money I sent them in a constructive way. They borrowed money with high-interest rates, and I ultimately ended up paying for the entire expense. This has been a recurring issue in my life. For instance, I once borrowed money from a credit card and sent $10,000 to my cousin Guru (the guy who stood in line for me for my US visa interview) when he wanted to open a restaurant in Pondicherry. However, I never received any updates, and the restaurant ultimately failed due to poor management, resulting in the loss of all the money invested.

While Madhu and I shared common interests, we also had our fair share of disagreements. One weekend, while Madhu was working diligently cleaning the kitchen, washing dishes, and cooking, I was sitting on the couch watching television. I commented that he did not add enough salt when dinner was served. Madhu flew into a rage and chased me with a knife. Luckily, Bala was present and managed to diffuse the situation. At the time, I did not have the emotional intelligence to understand why he was so upset just because I gave him my honest opinion, but chasing me down with a knife did not seem like the best way to enlighten me either.

Another issue we frequently fought about was television. Madhu owned the television set, but I took it over after moving in and watched all the sitcoms airing during primetime. Madhu preferred national geographic shows about animals, particularly hyenas. One time, when I was watching a sitcom, Madhu wanted to watch something else. We had an argument that quickly escalated. Madhu became upset and threw a beer bottle at the television, fortunately missing it but hitting the wall instead, causing a dent that we had to pay for.

Another TV-related incident occurred one night, though it did not involve me. One night, Madhu watched his favorite snake show and went to bed. At that time, Jacob and Madhu were sleeping on one side of the room while I was on the other. We were abruptly awakened by a loud noise in the middle of the night. I turned on the light to see Madhu standing by his bed, shouting at the top of his lungs. He was pointing at a corner of the room, yelling, "Snake! Snake!" I instantly realized what was going on— he had a nightmare about snakes after watching the show. Jacob was up against the wall, holding his hands to his chest in fear, without knowing what the heck had happened to Madhu. I consoled Madhu and assured him that everything was alright. He calmed down and fell asleep within a few minutes, but I had trouble sleeping for the rest of the night.

The following day, our neighbor asked us what had caused all the commotion and whether there had been any police involved. After that, we were always careful about what shows Madhu watched and his sleeping habits. We referred to this caution using the idiom "once bitten, twice shy," which originated from Madhu's favorite animal.

Living with roommates at the beginning of our careers was a fascinating experience. It was distinct from college life, where everyone was focused on grades and finances. Now, it was a time of establishing our careers, enjoying life, and being anxious about the future while also learning to adjust to each other's quirks and habits. Nonetheless, we enjoyed living together as a community and were happy for each other's successes.

Figure 45 Revisiting the apartment in 2023 for this book

Chapter 30:
Skiing Accident and Las Vegas

I always seem to have some sort of mystical power or personality trait that attracts dramatic experiences during my travels.

For instance, I had a long-standing desire to learn how to ski, particularly after moving to California, where the ski resorts in the Lake Tahoe area were a mere four hours away in the north. Madhu also expressed interest in donning snow gear and hitting the slopes, as did Ajay and his wife Leena, who were my high school juniors in Pondicherry. We set off on a trip to Lake Tahoe, and Madhu and I enrolled in our first-ever ski lessons.

Upon stepping onto the vast expanses of thick, untouched snow, Madhu and I were filled with excitement. Growing up in a tropical country like India, snow was not something we were familiar with. Our group was divided into smaller teams of six individuals, each equipped with ski shoes, skis, and poles. I felt awkward walking around in the shoes and carrying the equipment, as it all felt foreign and cumbersome.

Our instructor led us to the bunny slopes, where we were taught how to use the poles and skis and the fundamental techniques for stopping, turning, falling without getting stuck between the skis, and getting up again. Then, we all began to practice, and it was amusing to watch people tumble awkwardly and attempt to get back up like fat ducks—Madhu and myself included.

Eventually, we started to get the hang of it. Skiing is all about utilizing your core and the muscles surrounding your hips to maintain balance. Practicing beforehand is undoubtedly beneficial for building muscle strength in the quadriceps, glutes, hamstrings, and hips—the areas that get the most exercise. Having good balance can also help stabilize injury-prone parts, such as the knees, which can be seriously damaged and even require replacement surgery for some.

Endurance was crucial in skiing, requiring more cardiovascular activity than many people realize. Prior to our skiing class, we did not engage in exercises such as running, biking, or interval training, which partially contributed to our miserable performance.

Madhu and I cautiously rode the conveyor to the top of the bunny slope and successfully skied down without any problems. We repeated the process and gained more confidence. However, during our third attempt, Madhu began wobbling and swinging his arms around with his pole in hand. Although I had limited knowledge about skiing at the time, it seemed apparent that this was not the correct technique for descending the slope. While contemplating what to do in that situation, something flashed before my eyes and hit me in the mouth. I felt a sharp pain in my mouth, and blood started coming out—it turned out that Madhu's pole had chipped my front tooth, and my lips started bleeding.

We immediately went to the first aid station, a small room with only one nurse. The nurse attended to me, cleaned the blood from my lips, but was unable to do anything about my chipped tooth. Despite having stretchers, medicines, masks, and a first aid kit, they lacked the necessary dental tools or expertise. I needed to see a dentist and an orthodontist for further treatment.

We had to abandon our lessons and spend the rest of the day riding on the ski lift, enjoying the scenic view. I felt self-conscious whenever I talked, chewed, or laughed. I was frustrated with Madhu for being accident-prone, but we could not do much about it. Accidents happen.

Upon returning home, I visited an orthodontist and received a temporary crown while they took my measurements. Two weeks later, I returned for the custom crown fitting, which the orthodontist did an excellent job on. I still have it to this day, and it feels almost like a natural tooth. Unless I deliberately examine it beneath my tooth, it is barely noticeable.

Regarding skiing, I have a love-hate relationship with it. I attempt to ski every decade, detest it, and then give up. I even tried snowboarding a few times, which seemed a bit easier as I only had to handle one piece of equipment instead of two plus the poles, but still no success. However, I do not believe I missed out much. I have no knee issues, and my remaining teeth are still intact.

On another occasion, my roommates and I took some enjoyable trips during long weekends. Once, Bala suggested we visit Las Vegas and stay at his aunt's house. Bala, his nephew Achutha, Madhu, Nataraj, and I took a ten-hour road trip to Las Vegas, which left us feeling exhausted by the time we arrived at Bala's aunt's house. We stayed in the basement, which surprisingly had ample space and amenities, including beds, a couch, a television, and a bathroom.

There was a restroom in the basement, and after Madhu used it, I went next. Unfortunately, when I flushed the toilet, it did not go properly but started overflowing instead, which caused me to panic. I asked Madhu to tell Bala, but he was too embarrassed to do it. So I had to go and tell Bala myself, and he rushed downstairs to turn off the valve. He then told his aunt of the issue, who was cool about it and called a plumber to promptly fix the toilet.

The following morning, I woke up at 6 am, as I am a morning person. Everyone else was still asleep. I walked outside near the porch and saw the newspaper lying on the floor through the window. When I opened the door to retrieve it, an alarm immediately blasted, startling everyone in the house. I was frightened and looked like a thief caught in the act. Bala's aunt rushed over and found me outside the front door with the newspaper. She turned off the alarm and called the police to inform them that it was an accident. I felt awful for causing two incidents in two days, but Bala's aunt was kind and told me not to worry about it.

Apart from the hell I raised in Bala's aunt's house, we had an excellent time in Las Vegas. We watched shows, visited casinos, and ate buffets. True, my adventures are always a mix of trouble and fun, but isn't that what life is about?

Figure 46 Snowboarding in Lake Tahoe

Interlude 11: On Off Vegetarian

My intermittent vegetarianism began at age six, as my family has always adhered to a meat-free diet and never cooked or consumed meat at home. While at school in Pondicherry, I stayed with Saro and her family and was introduced to meat dishes prepared by Saro's mom and aunt—both skilled chefs. Despite having no prior experience with meat, I relished their signature dishes, including prawn curry, shark minced meat curry, goat curry, fish curry in sauce, and chicken curry. Even a simple dish such as egg curry tasted delightful with their encouragement.

Later, upon moving to my sister's house, I reverted to vegetarianism, given that they too did not prepare any meat dishes. I maintained a meat-free diet throughout my high school and college years, and although I occasionally indulged in eggs, it was a rarity and only upon the insistence of my college friends. However, I found that I lacked energy and quickly became tired even after short walks due to my slender build.

Upon arriving in the US, I maintained a vegetarian diet throughout graduate school and for two years thereafter. One day, Viji and Kishen invited Madhu and me over for dinner. Viji and Kishen were both former SDSU students who had relocated to the Bay Area approximately a year before we did. Kishen was a bright, witty, and lively person, while Viji possessed an exceptional intuition for reading people and achieving her goals in life. Despite being polar opposites in nature, they had fallen in love and started a family in the Bay Area.

For dinner, Viji prepared a tantalizing chicken curry for everyone and a vegetarian dish for me, as she knew I was a vegetarian. Before the meal, Viji asked why I abstained from meat. I responded that I had given it up as a teenager and had not discovered a compelling reason to resume eating it.

Viji said she would give me a reason to resume eating chicken that day. She told me that the primary component of the Indian diet was rice, which provided starch but insufficient protein, a crucial nutrient for the body. Although lentils and beans provided some protein, they only constituted a small proportion of the food. Moreover, much of the food was deep-fried and fatty, with high cholesterol content. The combination of starch and fat would lead to weight gain but not increased strength. Viji's perspective enlightened me: If I desired to maintain an Indian vegetarian diet while obtaining sufficient protein, I would have to consume an implausible number of lentils and beans, as tofu was not yet a popular protein-rich food.

Then Viji asked me, "Babu, would you like to try the chicken?" Without hesitation, I said yes. I indulged in the scrumptious chicken curry she had prepared. Since that moment, I have expanded my palate to include a variety of meats, such as beef, pork, fish, turkey, and lamb. In fact, I now regularly consume chicken and fish.

Presently, vegetarianism has evolved to encompass various dietary preferences. For instance, there are vegans who abstain from consuming dairy and pescatarians who only consume fish and no other meats. Although I cannot predict whether I may transition to any of these categories in the future, I am content with my current dietary habits now.

Chapter 31:
Milwaukee Girl

I was always timid and inexperienced in terms of relationships and interacting with girls. Indian culture was strict about boys and girls socializing with one another during adolescence and even adulthood, which applied to me in particular. As a result, I mostly kept my distance from girls and was intimidated to converse with them as though they were from another planet. I attended a high school for boys only and a college exclusively for men, except for Tagore Arts College, where girls were present while I pursued my Bachelor of Science degree in Mathematics for a year.

Prior to my marriage, I had never been in a relationship. Firstly, it was not supported by my parents, and secondly, I was not confident to ask a girl out. The only person I had a crush on was Saro, one of the girls I lived with in Pondy. My friends knew about my feelings for her and encouraged me to approach her, but I never dared to do so.

When I arrived in the United States to pursue my master's degree, there were girls everywhere on-campus, but I continued to spend time with only male friends as I had done before, even though we were all in our late twenties. After starting my career in the Bay Area, my friends Madhu, Bala, and I began discussing the possibility of getting married in the near future. Madhu already had a steady girlfriend in India whom he planned to marry soon, while Bala had recently proposed to Shailaja, our college mate in Oklahoma. This left me with a lot of pressure to start from scratch. I was not particularly interested in an arranged marriage, and I was not sure whether Indian girls would be able to adapt to life in the US.

In the mid-90s, with the advent of the internet era, Madhu suggested placing an advertisement online. Though hesitant at first, I agreed to place an ad on matrimony.com, an Indian website. The advertisement stated that I was a successful engineer living in California seeking a bride. After placing the ad, we all moved on with our lives and forgot about it. However, a few weeks later, I received an email from a man in India. He told me that one of his daughters, Uma, was pursuing her master's degree in biochemistry at the University of Wisconsin in Milwaukee. At 25 years old, she was seven years younger than me. He also provided me with her phone number.

The University of Wisconsin, Milwaukee, was a public urban research university and the largest university in the Milwaukee metropolitan area in Wisconsin. However, the distance between us concerned me as Wisconsin was in the Midwest, and I was on the West Coast. And all else aside, my primary fear was calling an unknown girl for romantic reasons. It was like venturing into the dragon's den without knowing what a dragon was. I worried about what I would say and how she would react.

Several weeks passed before I gathered the courage to call Uma. The conversation was initially awkward as I stammered and asked her about her studies. She shared that she was pursuing her master's in biochemistry, emphasizing animal cells and how they regenerated and healed after an injury, which I found fascinating. I also asked her about her future plans, and she told me that she had another year left in school as she was in her third semester. During the conversation, I shared that I worked as a Customer Acceptance Engineer in San Jose, California, for a major semiconductor company named KLA Tencor. Overall, it was a good introductory call, and it was not as scary as I had thought. Girls were humans, after all. I was pleased with how things were progressing.

I called Uma's sister, a doctor in the US, and asked about Uma. During our conversation, I shared more details about my job and family, and she gave me some insights into her family. Based on our chat, Uma's family seemed middle-class and close-knit. Later, I contacted Uma again and requested that she visit her in Milwaukee. She agreed, and things looked promising.

One weekend, I took a 5-hour direct flight to Chicago. From there, I rented a car at the airport and drove to Milwaukee, which was less than two hours away. However, by the time I arrived, it was already late evening, so I opted to stay at a motel. The following day, I drove to the University of Wisconsin, Milwaukee, and contacted Uma at her dormitory. She was dark, petite, and initially quite reserved. We decided to have lunch at a nearby restaurant.

After ordering our food, we found out that we were both vegetarians, which was a good sign. Uma shared with me her thesis work on animal cells, which I found to be fascinating. In return, I explained the semiconductor industry to her and my job as a wafer inspection Customer Acceptance Engineer. I told her about how I needed to work in a cleanroom environment every day, wearing full garb with a mask and goggles. She found this equally interesting.

I asked about Uma's upbringing. She shared that she grew up in Chennai and attended a reputable private university where she pursued a degree in Science. Her area of interest was animal cells; however, she struggled to find any schools in India offering specialization in this field. Consequently, she expanded her search to include universities in the US and discovered a program at the University of Wisconsin, Milwaukee, that appealed to her. After applying, she was granted a full assistantship.

Uma admitted that relocating to the US was the most challenging experience she had encountered so far, as she was living half a world away from home. She missed the food from her homeland, a sentiment that I could relate to. However, once she began her studies, she was engrossed in her coursework and stopped dwelling on thoughts of home. I could identify with her struggles, having gone through a similar experience myself when I first arrived in the US. Although I missed home deeply in the initial month, I was able to overcome it quickly once I became immersed in my studies and began job-hunting.

After finishing our meal, we strolled along the shores of Lake Michigan on a lovely summer day. The breeze from the lake was gentle and refreshing. I asked Uma if there were any other nearby tourist attractions, and she suggested a zoo in town. I asked if she would like to visit it, hoping to spend more time with her and get to know her better. However, she politely declined, stating that she had to work in a computer lab that evening.

Things took a sharp turn from that point on. I was eager to move quickly and believed I was ready for marriage, thinking I had everything figured out. Without hesitation, I suggested to her that we plan a wedding in India during late summer or fall, and she could return to finish her studies before moving to California. However, she seemed taken aback and did not comment on my proposal, simply stating that she needed to go to work.

I felt frustrated and disappointed that she could not take the evening off, especially since I had flown all the way from California, spent money on a rental car and hotel, and made such an effort to see her. We finished our walk quickly, and I dropped her off at her dormitory. Then, I checked out of the hotel and headed straight to the airport for a flight back to California. On the plane, I replayed the lunch and our walk over and over in my head, wondering where it had gone wrong. Had I been too hasty in proposing? Looking back now, I understand that I rushed things, especially considering that she had only met me once and was focused on pursuing her dream of finishing her studies.

At the time, however, I believed I was right. Given the effort and money I had put in, I felt entitled to more of her time and attention. I sent an email to her father after returning to California, informing him that I had visited his daughter and leaving it up to them to decide what to do next. He responded a week later, thanking me for visiting his daughter and explaining that Uma was focused on finishing her studies and not planning on getting married immediately. I thanked him in return, and that was the end of my courtship with Uma—the first and only time I had ever pursued a girl.

After living in the United States for several years, my perspective changed significantly. For instance, I aimed to become more self-sufficient instead of depending on my relatives constantly. I yearned for solitude rather than being surrounded by family members. Additionally, I desired to eat healthier instead of consuming rice and fried foods every day. Consequently, when I searched for a partner, I hoped for someone who shared a similar mindset, which is why I wanted an Indian woman who had undergone similar changes.

However, when I proposed to Uma abruptly, my traditional Indian values and beliefs emerged, repelling her and leaving me perplexed and ashamed. After the ensuing drama, I grew exhausted and gave up on my previous approach. Instead, I called my mother and requested her to find a bride for me. She was elated and promptly began the search. I had my wedding in India four months later. More on that in the following chapter.

Chapter 32:
The Wedding

After being left with a bitter taste from my trip to Milwaukee, I made the decision to hand everything over to my mother. She proceeded to make copies of my Indian horoscope and sent them to our relatives. It's important to note that Indian horoscopes differ from their Western counterparts. Vedic astrology, also known as Jyotisha or Jyotishya, is the traditional Hindu astrology based on the sidereal zodiac. Western astrology, on the other hand, uses the tropical zodiac. These two terms refer to different systems of ecliptic coordinates used to divide the ecliptic into twelve "signs."

An Indian horoscope is typically composed by a priest specializing in the zodiac after a child's birth, based on the zodiac signs present at the time of birth. This horoscope is meant to provide information about the present and make predictions about the future, particularly in regard to events such as marriage.

My mother decided to hire a marriage broker to assist with finding a suitable match for me. The broker could be either full-time or part-time. His or her job is to compare horoscopes for matchmaking and coordinate potential marriages. However, this profession is slowly dying due to the popularity of online matrimonial sites and dating apps. Nevertheless, through the broker, my mother and brother-in-law, Ramasamy, received five profiles of prospective brides. They discussed these options with a priest and ultimately narrowed it down to two candidates.

After considering both options, my mother eliminated one girl due to her young age, leaving only the other girl named Meera as a potential match. Meera hailed from the metropolitan city of Chennai, where her father was a Chemistry professor at Madras Christian College. She had a brother named Aravind. My mother believed Meera would make a good match for me and sent me her picture via postal mail. I anxiously waited for two weeks before finally receiving the picture. Upon seeing it, I immediately liked Meera. In the letter, my mother included Meera's phone number.

Upon dialing her number, a rough male voice answered, but upon introducing myself, the person on the other end enthusiastically greeted me. It was Meera's father, Sivasubramaniam, who was a professor. At that time, it cost 85 cents per minute to make a phone call to India. I was mindful of the time and consciously tried to keep my conversations brief. We talked for around five minutes before he handed the phone over to Meera. Knowing it had already been 4 dollars and 25 cents, I quickly introduced myself again. Then I asked her if she liked computers. She replied with a "yes." I asked if she wanted to work in the US, to which she also replied with a "yes." Finally, I asked her if she wanted to marry me, and again, she said "Yes." Then I hung up. That was probably by far the fastest proposal on the planet.

Following the call, things moved rather rapidly, even by my standards. I informed my mother that I was interested in Meera and was ready for marriage. My mother began to make all the necessary arrangements, and a date was set. I flew to Chennai and was surprised to see a group of over twenty individuals waiting for me with flowers upon my arrival at the airport—My family, along with several nephews, aunts, and uncles, had been waiting for more than three hours since the early hours of the morning, and Meera's brother, father, and mother were also in attendance. Although I felt somewhat flustered, I was happy to see everyone. I accepted the flowers, hugged each person, and then got into the car.

The following morning, I went to Meera's house to meet her for the first time. Accompanying me were my mother, sisters, brothers-in-law, and nephews. Once we all sat down in the living room, Meera came out with coffee and snacks, placed them on the table, and greeted us with folded hands before returning to her room. Unfortunately, I barely had the opportunity to glance at her as the men began to discuss the schedule and events.

Most of the wedding events focused on logistical arrangements, such as menu selection, sarees, and jewelry for the bride, temple visits, and other similar details. These details required a great deal of expertise, ranging from hiring musicians, purchasing banana trees to place in front of the wedding hall, buying fruits and sweets to be carried in front of the bride's car on the way to the wedding hall, hiring priests and chefs for the wedding meals, and so on. Fortunately, my mother was an expert in this area, having been a part of numerous weddings in the past. Meera's uncle and aunt were experienced as well, and so the planning went smoothly.

For my part, I was primarily focused on getting to know Meera. I finally mustered the courage to walk into the kitchen, where she was located. After some initial shyness, we began talking and getting to know one another. We planned which temples to visit, and I offered advice on how she could prepare for her visa.

We had our official engagement ceremony at Meera's house on the same evening. Upon entering the driveway, I was blown away by the lit-up lamps that led up to the house as if they were welcoming me. As I entered the house, I saw women dressed in beautiful silk sarees, children running around, and elders trying to create a perfect setting. It felt like a real wedding was already taking place, with more than 200 people in a festive mood. A priest conducted the beautiful ceremony, which was followed by a sumptuous dinner served on banana leaves.

After the ceremony, I went to Pondicherry to prepare for the wedding. I handed out invitations to all of my relatives and friends. Meera and I visited a few temples, including Tirupati, the most popular temple in South India, which was six hours away by train, and Guruvayur, a very traditional temple in the state of Kerala, which was ten hours away. Meera and I sat together on the train and bus and ate with our families. Being so intimate with someone I barely knew felt strange, but the temple visits were refreshing.

The wedding was scheduled to take place at Anandha Thirumana Nilayam, one of the most prestigious halls. Wedding halls play a crucial role in Indian weddings, as they reflect the status and image of the families involved. I had asked my third brother-in-law to reserve Anandha well in advance, and the rental cost was 25,000 rupees or $1,042 in US Dollars, which was a significant amount at the time.

The day before the official wedding, we had a reception, during which I wore a suit, and Meera wore a traditional saree. Meera was seated in a tent-down convertible with women walking in front of her, carrying flowers, fruits, sarees, coconuts, and other auspicious things on plates. When Meera arrived at the wedding hall, I greeted her, and we were both taken to the stage, where we were greeted by friends and relatives who showered us with gifts and blessings. It was a long evening, and I crashed into the bed, exhausted. The next morning, we had to wake up early to prepare for the big day.

The wedding day finally arrived. At 4 am, I woke up, showered, dressed in a traditional dhoti, and arrived at the wedding hall. The priest was already there, and Meera arrived in a white silk saree, with jewelry sparkling on her body, looking absolutely stunning. The ceremony began promptly at 6:30 am, with rain pouring outside as if the rain gods were showering us with blessings. The priest started the fire pit on the stage and added ghee to fuel the fire, resulting in a lot of smoke. Our eyes were burning from the smoke, and we were tired from lack of sleep. Cameras were flashing, and the crowd continued to grow. Around 1000 guests gathered, most of whom we did not know. They were relatives and friends of both families and people from our villages. The ceremony lasted for about two hours, during which I tied a yellow thread around Meera's neck with three knots, symbolizing the consummation of the Hindu wedding ceremony and our marriage. The first knot represented accepting Meera's family as my own, the second one represented Meera accepting my family, and the third one represented our future family together.

We were escorted to the dining hall, where we found that most of the guests had already finished their meals, leaving only a limited amount of food remaining. Despite this, our primary concern was ensuring that everything proceeded smoothly and without any hitches. Fortunately, the wedding was a great success, with everyone enjoying the ceremony, food, and festivities.

Following the wedding, we proceeded to register our marriage with the state of Pondicherry. This step was crucial as it allowed us to apply for Meera's dependent visa. Then, we also had to register in Chennai because we were unsure whether the embassy would accept documents solely from Pondicherry, which is a Union Territory. In India, certain regions have this designation, which means that they only accept documents from the respective level of government. For instance, Pondicherry obtained independence from France a year after India broke free from Britain, and as a result, it has a unique status with tax benefits, a separate government, and its own governor. In the end, our marriage was recognized three times due to the multiple registrations, and we had all the necessary paperwork in hand for the visa application process.

Figure 47 Meera (left), me, and my mother (right) in the wedding hall (1997)

Figure 48 Meera and me at the wedding (1997)

Chapter 33:
Meera's New Journey

Meera and I took a cab from Chennai to the U.S. Consulate early in the morning with all the necessary documents. I dropped her off at the entrance, and then the driver parked in a back alley so we could wait for her. Feeling tired and sleepy, I decided to rest in the backseat while the driver remained in the front. Suddenly, I was awoken by loud thudding noises and saw a policeman outside knocking on the window with his cane. The driver was also startled and jumped out of the car.

The policeman inquired about our presence, to which I explained that I was waiting for my wife, who was applying for a visa at the US Consulate. The policeman's expression changed, and he smiled, asking if I was an engineer living in the US, to which I confirmed. He returned to his motorcycle and returned with a receipt for a fine of 300 rupees, which was about 10 US dollars back then. I handed him the money without any dissent. Unexpectedly, the policeman seemed uneasy and returned 150 rupees, explaining that there were three cops and each of them would be satisfied with 50 rupees. The driver was shocked by the proceedings. Once the policeman left, he started shouting at me for giving away so much money.

Reflecting on the incident, I realized how much I had changed in the last five years. I genuinely believed that the money was fine and would go to the state government rather than as a bribe.

After a few nerve-racking hours of waiting, Meera emerged from the consulate with a happy expression and handed me the passport with the visa page. The page indicated an H-1B work visa instead of an H-4 visa for dependents. We had to return the next day to have it corrected; entering the US with the incorrect visa would have resulted in trouble.

Packing was a mix of agony and excitement. We went wild and bought numerous souvenirs, including cookware, kitchen utensils, spices, snacks, and clothing. Both families and friends put in the effort to finish packing and we ended up with nine pieces of luggage. Unfortunately, I fell ill on the day of departure to the USA and was unable to help. I lay in bed and watched everyone pack. Later I took a lot of medication in order to board the plane.

Traveling with nine pieces of luggage, including a bulky 2-foot-wide and 1-foot-high bull statue made of mesh paper, was a grueling journey. Why the statue? Well, in Pondy, we came across a boutique that sold handcrafted goods and instantly fell in love with the bull statue for no reason. Although it was not heavy, it was quite bulky, and we had to carry it in a large cloth bag on top of our other luggage. It caused considerable unnecessary stress and, in the end, was utterly useless.

We had a layover in Los Angeles before flying to San Francisco, our final destination. Upon entering the country, all the luggage had to go through US customs, which means checking out all nine pieces of luggage in LA, going through customs, and checking them in again. The cost of transporting the luggage from LA to SF was $150. Additionally, we had to carry all the suitcases from one side of the airport to the other, up and down stairs. When we finally boarded the flight, I breathed a sigh of relief and collapsed onto the seat.

Jacob and Khun picked us up at the airport. Jacob brought my car, and Khun brought his own as the luggage would not fit in a single car. Meera was amazed by the number of cars speeding on multi-lane highways.

After nearly 20 hours of flying and layovers, we finally arrived home. I cooked a simple meal of lentil sambar and string beans curry, which Meera found delicious. After a six-week trip to India, I had to start work the next day. My office was just ten minutes away, so I came home for lunch. Meera had cooked, and I enjoyed returning home for lunch and seeing her.

At work, my colleagues pooled their money and bought me a complete set of CorningWare, including plates, bowls, coffee cups, and smaller plates. Meera loved them and suggested that we invite them over for dinner.

It was our first party, and with the help of Shailaja, Bala's wife, we worked hard to make it a success. All my friends showed up, but only one of my colleagues came. I was very disappointed. When I asked them why they could not make it to the party the following Monday at work, everyone gave a feeble excuse that they had other engagements to attend to.

As Meera and I shared the same living space, I gradually grew to know her better and appreciate her qualities. She was kind and nurturing, with an innate desire to receive affection and respect. Meera listened to my counsel and demonstrated exceptional execution. Her acumen was evident in her sharp, intelligent, and smart disposition. Meera took pride and responsibility in managing our household, exhibiting impeccable decorating skills. Although selective with her friendships, it lasted a lifetime when she forged a bond. Moreover, Meera had a green thumb, which was evident when we later purchased a home in San Ramon with a barren garden. She transformed it into a picturesque paradise, attracting various animals such as birds, bees, and insects for honey and fruits.

In contrast, after a week of adjusting to our daily routine, my life had returned to normal. However, it was different for Meera. In India, she was surrounded by her family and friends, who lavished her with love and affection. Now, she had only me. Unfortunately, I was unaware of how to show her love. I believed that tending to her needs was enough to demonstrate affection, but I lacked emotional empathy, which was what she needed the most at that moment. I often left her alone at home after work to play tennis with my friends. When I returned home, I would find her crying, and although I asked what was wrong, she would reply with "Nothing." I would move on, avoiding the situation altogether. Regrettably, I never took the time to analyze the situation and rectify my behavior. I did not treat her as a wife but as a roommate.

Due in part to my personality and the Indian culture's separation of males and females, I was insensitive to Meera's needs. With no dating experience and no understanding of what went on in a woman's mind,

I regret not having dated more in college to better understand how to treat Meera during her time of need.

I lived in a two-bedroom apartment in Sunnyvale with Jacob and Khun during that period. While Meera and I shared the larger room, Jacob and Khun shared the smaller one. Meera suggested that we rent a separate apartment, but I was hesitant about paying for an apartment on my own. To be honest, looking back now, I am not sure why. I was making a decent salary, and my wedding expenses were covered with a loan from my 401k, which was my employer-sponsored personal pension account. I would still have to repay the loan, but in retrospect, it was manageable, and I should not have worried too much about the finances at that moment. My biggest regret was not providing Meera with a sense of home when she needed it the most.

While Meera struggled with homesickness and occasional bouts of crying, Jacob and Khun were kind to her. Meera took on the responsibilities of cooking, cleaning, and caring for the house. After hosting a party for our friends and their families, Meera became fast friends with Shailaja, Bala's wife. She later connected with Sreelatha, Madhu's wife, and Viji, Kishen's wife.

Madhu and Sreelatha began to visit us frequently. Madhu and I played tennis during their visits while Meera and Sreelatha went on long walks. Meera and Sreelatha even took Java courses together as they pursued their careers simultaneously in the same field. This shared interest became their talking point, bringing them closer.

Occasionally, Kishen would join me for a game of tennis while Viji accompanied Meera on her walks. Both Kishen and Viji were very supportive of Meera and encouraged her to chase her dreams. Kishen was a brilliant individual working in the semiconductor industry, while Viji was a career-driven woman who knew how to get things done. We were impressed by their level of organization and efficiency when they planned their meals for the day and shopped accordingly. Eventually, they moved back to India and built their dream home in Bangalore. Viji played a crucial role in helping Meera assimilate into American life and provided the emotional support that Meera needed the most.

Meera and Shailaja, Bala's wife, did not connect right away, but now they have a strong bond and would do anything for each other. Unlike Kishen, Madhu, Viji, and Sreelatha, we did not start spending time together with Bala and Shailaja until much later. We often visited each other's homes, cooked dinner, and engaged in pleasant conversations when we hung out.

Whenever Meera and Shailaja entered a conversation, they became so engrossed that they forgot everything around them. We would tease them by saying, "Would you like to get a room?" Their discussions ranged from work, kids, cooking, parents, husbands, friends, and everything in between. While Meera and Shailaja cooked and chatted, Bala and I watched a basketball game. In Meera's early years in the US, Shailaja was a constant source of support, and my marriage would not have survived this long without her. In return, Meera helped Shailaja transition from a biotech career to a software career at her bank.

We all enjoyed playing board games together, with taboo being our favorite game, followed by Pictionary. We would sometimes stay up until 3 am to play, eat, have a good laugh, and enjoy each other's company.

Once Meera had settled down, my priority was for her to find a job. However, she felt unprepared, so she enrolled in Java programming and Oracle database courses, which also helped her cope with homesickness. Meera was a bright student who quickly grasped the concepts and performed exceptionally well in her courses. Nevertheless, securing a job was still a considerable distance away.

Our financial situation was not ideal at the time, as only one of us was employed. Therefore, instead of buying a house, we had to rent an apartment. We had a wedding loan of twenty-five thousand dollars, and both our families were facing financial difficulties. Meera's family suffered significant financial losses due to poor inventory management and sales in their garment store, which eventually led to its closure. They later opened a sweet and savory shop that initially performed well but eventually shut down.

In Indian culture, it is customary for children to financially support their parents once they have started their careers. However, Meera faced several hurdles before she could fulfill this obligation. She had previously managed a leather garment company providing jobs for underprivileged women but had no experience in the software industry. To obtain an H-1B visa, she needed a job offer from a company that could sponsor her. Additionally, she needed to learn how to drive so she could go to work.

Interlude 12: Learning to Drive

From the outset, my goal for Meera was to cultivate her independence, enable her to establish her own career, and empower her to handle challenges on her own. I hoped to instill in her the American cultural values of self-reliance and autonomy, in contrast to the overprotective Indian upbringing that she experienced, where everything was handed to her. I recall her brother Aravind sharing with me that someone in the family would always refuel her scooter whenever she ran out of petrol. In India, it was frowned upon for women to engage in activities that were considered exclusively for men.

However, when Meera arrived in the United States, she was exposed to a completely different lifestyle. I encouraged her to find a job, and the first step was learning to drive. Initially, I taught her how to use the steering wheel in a parking lot, and after she became comfortable with that, I took her to drive on local roads with minimal traffic and numerous stop signs. She easily passed those tests.

The real challenge began when she had to drive on larger, more congested roads with heavy traffic. She became increasingly nervous as the speed exceeded 30 miles per hour, particularly when she had to accelerate to keep up with other vehicles. She was uncomfortable changing lanes and would abruptly hit the brakes, which often caused me to yell at her for stopping suddenly in the middle of traffic. Her resulting frustration and hysteria made the situation even more stressful for both of us.

My approach to teaching Meera was simple: practice makes perfect. I believed that she just needed more time behind the wheel, so I forced her to drive more and even took a leap of faith by having her drive on the freeway. I failed to realize that she was not yet ready, and her fear was hindering her learning ability.

One day, I asked Meera to drive on freeway Interstate 101 South. She drove for around 10 miles and made it to San Jose without any issues. I suggested we keep going without mentioning that I wanted her to drive all the way to Monterey Bay, a beautiful scenic attraction approximately 75 miles away that she would love to see. Meera became curious about our destination, but I reassured her that she had nothing to worry about and even joked that if we kept driving long enough, we would reach Mexico in the south. Unfortunately, she did not find it amusing.

Although Meera was comfortable driving straight in a single lane on the freeway, changing lanes, exiting the freeway, and driving on local roads made her extremely anxious. She would start slowing down, reducing her speed from 65 miles per hour to 40 miles per hour, causing other drivers to honk in frustration. I would become angry and insist that she speed up, which only escalated the situation and led to arguments. Eventually, we had to stop, both feeling stressed and overwhelmed, and needless to say, we never made it to Monterey Bay.

Together, we agreed that it would be better if Meera enrolled in formal driving lessons. As a frugal person, I was unwilling to spend any money unless it was absolutely necessary. In this case, however, the stress and anxiety of teaching Meera to drive felt like a death sentence, and I would rather pay than die. Fortunately, after completing the driving lessons, she felt confident enough to take the driving test. Although she failed a few times, she eventually passed and obtained her driver's license.

Despite her success, the traumatic experience of learning to drive with me left her with a lingering fear of driving on the freeways, and she avoided driving. Later, she was presented with an opportunity to work on a project in Detroit, Michigan, where she spent six months. Upon returning to California for a new job, I was surprised to see that she could easily zip through traffic on freeways like the wind.

Chapter 34:
Whitewater Rafting

After all of my closest friends got married, we decided to embark on a fun trip together. I organized our first adventure as married couples with Madhu, Bala and their wives, which involved whitewater rafting in the Russian River, a Northern California city.

We drove for three hours to get to the site, and once there, we changed into appropriate clothing and were equipped with life jackets. The guide provided instructions on what to do and what not to do if we were stranded in the water. When he pointed to the raft and asked us to select one, I was taken aback to discover that they were much smaller than I had anticipated. Instead of a larger raft that could accommodate six to eight people, those rafts could only fit two individuals. There was no guide to assist us, so we would be solely responsible for ourselves, and I was uncertain whether I could handle it. Panic had already set in even before the trip began, and I could see the same fear in Madhu and Bala's eyes.

Riding a raft on rapids is akin to a rollercoaster ride with unpredictability coming at you from all angles at all times. Every time the raft hits a rapid, you get a surge of adrenaline. You must steer the raft left and right, stop it, or sometimes simply crouch down on the raft. It may sound easy, but it can be daunting for the faint-hearted when you have to react within a split second with no one to rely on.

With a surge of courage, we reassured ourselves that we were capable of the task at hand. It was comforting to know that a guide in a raft would follow us in case of any issues. Meera and I got into the raft and began moving through the water. We started off well, with small and easy movements to the left and right, seeming simple enough. However, I noticed Madhu and Bala were getting ahead of us, and every time we hit a small rapid, we fell further behind. Despite trying to paddle faster, we ended up going in circles.

Being in the front of the raft, I was responsible for steering it while Meera followed my instructions and paddled. As we tried to catch up with the others, we began moving at a speed that none of us was comfortable with. I did my best to keep my hands steady on the steer, and somehow, we managed to pull through. But before I could get a moment of relief, I saw a big pile of bushes coming straight toward us. I had no time to react and just froze. Meera panicked and screamed at me, "Are you trying to kill me?"

With a loud "boom!!" our raft hit the bushes like a runaway wild horse. I closed my eyes and tensed every muscle in my body expecting bone-crushing pain, but did not feel any. I opened my eyes in surprise and found ourselves still on the raft which was stuck in the bushes. We managed to push the raft away with our oars and got away with only a few scratches.

Spring was the perfect time for whitewater rafting, as the melting snow from the higher mountains created huge rapids in the rivers. Late summer, however, was not as ideal because the underflowing river could cause problems for the rafters. We quickly discovered this when we encountered rocks sticking out of the river everywhere, causing our raft to get stuck several times. Luckily, we had already been given instructions on what to do in such situations. I put one foot on the rocks and pushed the raft away with the oar, and surprisingly enough, I was actually pretty good at it.

After a period of calm waters, we suddenly saw a violent sea of whitewater rushing toward us. I then recalled what people said about how it was always calm before a storm. Despite my attempts to steer the raft, my exhausted hands could not move the steer an inch. The rapid had hit us and thrown us into the air in no time. We soon found ourselves under cold water with the raft overturned above us. Fortunately, we were wearing life jackets, and the water was not too deep. We managed to flip the raft, retrieve the oars, and climb back in. We were in shock for a while, and Meera was clearly angry. However, she did not say anything until we stopped for a much-needed lunch break.

During lunch, we recounted what happened to Bala and his wife, Shailaja, and discovered that their raft had also capsized. I was relieved to have some company. Also, Bala was supposed to be more skilled than I was. Meera and Shailaja decided they had had enough and skipped the rest of the adventure. The van that provided us lunch took them downstream to meet us later.

This time, I teamed up with Bala, with him at the front steering and me at the back paddling. There were some minor rapids, which we navigated easily. Then, out of nowhere, a huge wave pounced at us in a menacing manner. Bala screamed at me at the top of his lungs, "Babu, paddle harder, paddle harder!" I did not know why, but whenever we approached a big rapid, my hands would tire. This time was no different. My hands were too sore to move. Despite Bala's efforts, the rapid hit us hard.

Different partner, same outcome: we were underwater in no time when the raft capsized. We managed to extricate ourselves from the water, but Bala was upset with me for not paddling properly. I explained that my hands were fatigued. After regaining our composure, we retrieved our oars and got back on the raft. Although we encountered some minor rapids after that, nothing disastrous happened.

Eventually, we arrived at the bottom of the river, where the van was waiting for us. Madhu and Sreelatha had already arrived. We were exhausted, famished, and dejected but relieved to have returned. It was a valuable lesson of counting on someone uncountable, meaning me.

History never stopped repeating itself. Even when working on this memoir, my co-writer, Xiaoyu, had to chase me down for information while he was working for free and spending hundreds of tireless hours to get this book done. I had to make up all kinds of excuses for not completing simple tasks. But I do not see any need to go into details about that...

Anyway, that excursion was an encapsulation of my life. I embarked on an adventure without any direction or preparation (basically not knowing what the heck I was doing) and failed miserably when others depended on me. Did I do my best on the job? I believe so. But was the outcome satisfactory? Unless floundering in the water was the objective, I would say no. That was my life's story. I never received adequate guidance on what to do, and most of the time, I had to figure things out on my own. On occasion, I managed to land in a big pile of bushes without a broken bone, but more often than not, I had to pick myself up from the frigid water and move forward. Reflecting on that trip now, I can laugh, but I do not find it amusing.

Figure 49 Whitewater Rafting in Russian River, California
(picture from internet)

Chapter 35:
Meera's First Job and Career

Meera had been searching for a job for over a year. I believed that she should aim for the software industry since it offered the best-paying positions and numerous opportunities in the Bay Area. However, she only possessed a one-year diploma in Operations Research from Anna University in Chennai. Operations research (OR) is an analytical approach to problem-solving and decision-making, which is valuable in organizational management. OR involves breaking down problems into fundamental components and solving them through mathematical analysis in defined steps.

Upon arriving in the US, Meera took Java and Oracle courses to update her skills. Despite her relentless preparation for interviews, it was challenging for her to secure a job due to her lack of a degree or work experience in the US. Additionally, obtaining sponsorship for her visa was even more difficult as companies preferred to hire locally.

As part of her daily routine, Meera sent out 5 to 10 resumes daily for five weeks to a variety of companies in the Bay Area. Unfortunately, she did not receive any phone calls for an interview. The few responses she received were courtesy rejections stating that the company had selected other candidates. With each passing day, Meera felt increasingly frustrated, depressed, and less confident. We even visited temples to pray for her breakthrough.

On a Friday afternoon, I returned home for lunch to find Meera in the kitchen making my favorite South Indian dish, Dosa. Just as I arrived, the phone in the living room rang. I answered the call, and it turned out to be for Meera. I handed her the phone and was extremely curious about who the caller was. Meera answered the phone, and her face lit up with excitement. She turned to me and exclaimed, "I got a job!" We were overjoyed and jumped up and down in ecstasy.

Meera's uncle had a friend who owned a consulting firm in Detroit, Michigan, which had several projects with General Motors. Meera's uncle spoke highly of her to his friend, leading to an interview for the job, in which Meera believed she performed well. She waited anxiously for a week but heard nothing. So, she assumed the opportunity had slipped away like her previous job applications. Then, all of a sudden, she received a job offer.

After the initial excitement subsided, we realized that Meera would have to move to Detroit for the job, and she was sponsored for a work visa with the condition that she must relocate. However, I had a full-time job in California and could not leave. Additionally, my green card application, sponsored by KLA Tencor, was already in progress and would take years to complete. Changing jobs would result in restarting the application process, with no assurance that another company would sponsor me.

After weighing the pros and cons, we agreed that Meera should accept the job and move temporarily to Detroit. Once she gained sufficient work experience, or if her project concluded, she could begin looking for a job back in the Bay Area in a year or so.

Making the decision to move to Detroit turned out to be the best choice we ever made. Being alone in Detroit, Meera had no choice but to be independent. She was able to find her own apartment and establish relationships with her coworkers and their families, who offered her support. During weekends, they spent time together cooking, watching movies, and shopping. Moreover, they even picked her up and dropped her off for work every day, and eventually, she learned how to drive on the freeway. Her dedication and high work standards were admired by her boss and colleagues, and as time passed, she grew more confident and discovered new qualities within herself.

Meanwhile, I was in California, missing her every day. I learned to distract myself by engaging in tennis and volunteer activities. Three months after her move, I visited her in Detroit during winter, where we spent time with her friends, enjoying good food and a movie. Seeing her thriving on her own fulfilled my dream for her.

We had initially scratched our heads, wondering how to bring her back to California, but fate intervened. Her boss, who knew about her desire to move back, found her a new project in the Bay Area. It paid twice her previous salary and had the potential for an extension. Although she missed her Detroit friends and coworkers, we were able to get our lives back on track. I found an apartment in the same complex where we had lived in Sunnyvale, and we were able to reconnect with old friends. Life was truly great.

Upon reflection, Meera's job in Detroit proved to be a turning point for us. It provided her with the independence and the foundation for an exceptional career. Credit goes to Meera, as she overcame her fears and stepped out of her comfort zone, eventually excelling in her profession. From then on, her career trajectory continued to soar. At times, we all require that extra dose of courage and encouragement to break through barriers.

Upon Meera's return, we went shopping on the weekend and I urged her to drive. She did not hesitate to take the wheel. She effortlessly navigated through local roads and merged onto the freeway with expertise. Her confidence radiated, and she easily changed lanes as though she was driving in our backyard. I was impressed.

Meera started her project in California at a startup called Done. com. Her managers were impressed with her work ethic and dedication. She worked until a week before giving birth to our son, Arjun, then took a two-and-a-half-year break to care for him. When she was ready to return to work, technology had advanced, and her programming skills were outdated. I suggested that she pursue a software test automation engineer job, but she lacked the necessary experience. She spent time preparing for interviews and landed a job at eBay, where she worked for a year. The job bolstered her confidence, and she subsequently interviewed for a consultant position at Wells Fargo, where she was hired. Seventeen years later, she is now the Vice President of her division and is well-liked by everyone.

Throughout her career at Wells Fargo, Meera has received numerous awards. When she assumed leadership of her team, they were struggling to meet deliverables, but she quickly turned the situation around, transforming them into a high-performing unit.

Despite her demanding job, Meera was also an attentive parent. She raised Arjun into a remarkable young man who excelled academically. Meera played a critical role in supporting Arjun through his struggles in middle and high school when he was bullied and abused by other students. The school provided little assistance, but Meera was always there for him when he needed it the most. Looking back, I wish I had offered Meera the same level of support when she first arrived.

Meera is an exceptional mother, a true leader, and an outstanding human being. I am proud of her.

Interlude 13: George and Tennis

George, also known as Jorge in Portuguese, was from Florianopolis, Brazil. We crossed paths on a tennis court in Sunnyvale and hit it off immediately. George held the position of a supervisor at the local Toyota manufacturing plant, overseeing the assembly line. Meanwhile, his wife Kelly managed a cleaning service company. They both put in great effort to achieve their American Dream.

George loathed losing. Whenever he lost to me, he would become angry and destroy his rackets, which were valued at $200 or more each. A week later, he would purchase another racket and return with a strong determination to beat me. However, more often than not, he would end up losing. His wife Kelly would shake her head and remind him of how expensive the rackets were.

Kelly had a teenage daughter from a previous marriage, who had a tumultuous relationship with George. She would bring boys over to the house, infuriating George. On one occasion, her daughter brought a boy she was seeing to the house and concealed him in her room. The next morning, when they were having breakfast, George discovered them. He became enraged and locked his stepdaughter in the house.

The stepdaughter called the police, and George spent a night in jail and was placed on probation for a year. Later on, his daughter got pregnant with one of her boyfriends at the age of 15 and gave birth to a son at the ripe age of 16.

Prior to this, I had never encountered the concept of teenage pregnancy in the United States. However, upon conducting research, I was taken aback by the staggering statistics on the impact of teenage pregnancy on adolescent girls in America. Giving birth during the teenage years is a significant contributor to high school dropout rates among girls. Studies have shown that only about 50% of teen mothers receive a high school diploma by the age of 22, whereas roughly 90% of their peers who do not give birth during adolescence are able to graduate from high school.

Furthermore, children born to teenage mothers are more likely to experience poor academic performance, health issues, juvenile delinquency, early parenthood, and unemployment in young adulthood. Despite these negative consequences, there is a silver lining: between 1991 and 2015, the teen birth rate decreased by 64%, which resulted in public savings of $4.4 billion in 2015 alone.

George and his family relocated to Miami, Florida. Currently, his stepdaughter resides in the Bay Area with her son, who has autism.

Chapter 36:

First House

Upon learning that Meera was returning to the Bay Area for a project from Detroit, I swiftly reserved an apartment to ensure that we had our own space. My next course of action was to search for an affordable townhome or condo. The idea was suggested by my colleague, Tuan Pham, who had purchased a one-bedroom condo for $100,000 a year earlier, which increased in value to $150,000 within a couple of years. He consistently extolled the virtues of equity buildup in California's real estate market. I realized that owning a home was a means of achieving the American Dream and accumulating equity for the future. Consequently, when Meera arrived in California, I intended to purchase a townhome or condo.

A condominium, or condo, is akin to an apartment but is owned by its occupants. A townhome is a connected residence also owned by its resident, with one or more walls shared with an adjacent townhome. Townhomes are usually more spacious and costly than condos, with fewer units in the same building.

I began searching for townhomes immediately, with a budget of $200,000 in mind. In 1999, the market was frenzied; prospective buyers had to offer $10,000 to $20,000 more to acquire a home. Most offers exceeded the asking price, and properties were sold within days. Twenty years later, the Bay Area's real estate market remains unchanged, with many people relocating to other states since they cannot afford to purchase homes here.

As a first-time home buyer, I was completely lost and had no idea where to begin. This was a time before popular real estate websites such as Zillow and Redfin came into being. The only way to purchase a home was through a real estate agent, but I did not know how to go about finding one. One day, while driving through Fremont in the East Bay, I spotted a real estate sign advertising a house for sale. Without hesitation, I called the listed phone number and spoke with an agent who proceeded to show me several homes in the Fremont area.

Once Meera and I had settled into our new apartment, I told her that we needed to buy a house immediately because prices were rising. She was hesitant to agree, as it would be a significant investment, and we had just recently moved into our new place. The agent took us to view numerous townhomes in the nearby city of Newark, but we had difficulty making a decision. The units that were less popular were undesirable, while the better ones were either sold immediately or subject to fierce competition among multiple buyers. It was a daunting task for inexperienced buyers like us with limited budgets.

One day, the agent called us and offered to show us a house that the seller was willing to sell without going through a bidding war. Though unsure of what this entailed, we agreed to give it a try but requested to see the house first. Upon entering the house with the agent, we discovered the owners still lived there. The kitchen was in disarray, with dirty dishes filling the sink and the stove coated in oil and food remnants. The living room carpet was unrecognizable due to filth, and the wallpaper looked prehistoric and unclean.

The condition of the bedrooms was equally terrible. The bathrooms were covered in hair and looked like they had cavemen for pets. The living room contained a French door that opened onto a small backyard, and when the agent opened it, a strong odor emanated from outside. We ventured into the backyard to investigate the smell and were surprised to find that it was actually coming from the neighbor's yard, which appeared to be a small zoo that housed rabbits, pigeons, and a dog.

We finished the tour in silence, and upon returning to our car, Meera began to cry. She said she did not want the house. I reassured her that we could negotiate with the agent and use the money we received to fix up the house before moving in. However, she remained unconvinced.

I spoke to Kishen and Viji, and they convinced Meera that the house could be transformed into a desirable living space. We would need to replace the entire carpet, deep clean the kitchen, and contact the homeowner's association to persuade the neighbor to clean their backyard. These minor adjustments would drastically improve the quality of the home while remaining affordable. Reluctantly, Meera agreed. We made an offer of $212,000, which was $10,000 more than the asking price, on the condition that the seller would either replace or pay for the carpet replacement. The seller agreed.

After closing escrow and taking possession of the house, we replaced the old carpet and removed the wallpaper, which was firmly adhered to the walls and required soaking before being removed. The cleaning crew did an excellent job and thoroughly cleaned the kitchen. The homeowner's association ensured that our neighbor kept his backyard tidy. We hired a professional painter to paint the house and were now ready to move in.

Meera was delighted with the house when she saw it again. She decorated it with great enthusiasm and had a natural flair for interior design. We framed a beautiful painting from India that became the living room's centerpiece. The living room floor was adorned with a stunning Persian rug. We shopped for furniture and acquired a lovely couch, dining table, and end tables. Meera purchased additional paintings to adorn the walls and some vases for the end tables. The furniture, paintings, vases, and rug transformed the look and feel of the house, making it look magnificent. We hosted a housewarming party, and everyone praised Meera's decorating skills, and we were delighted with the outcome. I was thrilled that Meera had come to terms with the house and had grown to love it. Our American Dream had finally become a reality.

Looking back now, buying the house was one of the best decisions we ever made. Seven years later, we sold the house for $400,000 and purchased a single-family home in San Ramon, one of the Bay Area's best communities, with outstanding schools.

Acquiring a house in the Bay Area can be daunting due to the significantly higher financial commitment required compared to the national average. This can be attributed to a couple of reasons. Firstly, Information Technology and the semiconductor industry, the dominant forces in Silicon Valley, offer considerably higher wages than other sectors. Secondly, the presence of top-class universities in the region means that the job market is constantly supplied with a vast workforce that requires housing and can afford it.

The proliferation of the tech industry has made the Bay Area an unaffordable location for individuals with ordinary occupations, such as teachers, office administrators, and retail workers. Even those in the high-tech industry now find purchasing a home on a single salary challenging. For instance, my close friend from the Federal Reserve Bank, Alexey Belyayev, had to relocate to Salt Lake City to find an affordable house, where he now resides with his wife Ursula and their two children.

I consider myself fortunate to own a house in the Bay Area, where the weather is superb and the sun shines all year round. There are also magnificent beaches, national parks to explore, and abundant job opportunities in various fields. The region also boasts exceptional schools like Stanford and UC Berkeley that are within a reasonable driving distance. Although I used to envision living in this region for the rest of my life, I recently began toying with the idea of spending some time in a tropical location during winter. Moreover, given that my mother is in her 80s and not in good health, I may decide to live in India for several months each year to assist her. Nonetheless, the Bay Area will always be my home, as I have lived here for almost half my life and plan to remain here for most of my remaining years.

Figure 50 Our first house in Newark, with Barbara, our neighbor during the Easter of 2002

Chapter 37:
Arjun Was Born

In the year 2001, Meera and I had been married for four years. My mom and sisters had been inquiring about when we were going to have a baby. However, despite our efforts, we were not successful. At the time, I was 37, and Meera was 33 years old. Finally, one day Meera told me that she was pregnant, which made me overjoyed. Passing on our family legacy was an opportunity not everyone had, and I felt privileged to do so.

After the initial excitement, we had work to do. Meera had to focus on her health and diet, so we began routine monthly checkups. The baby looked healthy and was growing quickly. We collectively decided not to find out the baby's sex during the sonogram because we wanted to be surprised.

We attended Lamaze classes every week to learn breathing techniques and other childbirth lessons. The Lamaze method of childbirth was new to me; it focused on labor and delivery as a natural event. This method was not present in India at that time. I believed it was essential for expecting couples to learn about pregnancy and childbirth instead of solely relying on the doctor and hospital. In the class, we met another Indian couple who were having twins. Although twins sounded exciting, it was also intimidating. Raising one child was stressful enough, but having two simultaneously sounded like double the trouble. While many had given birth to two, three, or even seven children at once, one was enough for me.

When Meera was seven months pregnant, her routine blood test revealed high sugar levels, leading to a diagnosis of gestational diabetes. Gestational diabetes is a condition that causes high blood sugar in pregnant women, and those who develop it are at a higher risk of developing type 2 diabetes later in life. Symptoms are rare and typically detected through a blood sugar test. Treatment strategies involve daily blood sugar monitoring, a healthy diet, exercise, and monitoring the baby's health. If blood sugar levels remain high, medication may be necessary.

This news came unexpectedly, and Meera had to be mindful of her food choices, particularly rice and sweets. However, a significant portion of the Indian diet includes rice, and pregnant women tend to eat more to support the baby's growth. Therefore, we had to decrease her rice and sugar intake and incorporate more beans, lentils, and vegetables. Additionally, she had to reduce her juice intake.

As part of Meera's exercise regimen, we shopped together for her maternity clothes, baby items, and household needs. Our friends planned a surprise baby shower for her as her due date approached. I entrusted Bala with the house key to ensure everything was in order.

On a Saturday morning, Meera and I attended our usual Lamaze class. The class ended later than expected, and Meera was starving, insisting on going to a restaurant. Normally, I would have agreed, but we had a potluck waiting for us at the surprise party, so I convinced her we should eat at home instead. Meera was aware of my frugality and reluctance to dine out, so she did not argue.

We arrived home around 1:30 pm, and I was carrying a large, heavy medicine ball for physical exercise, so I asked Meera to open the door. As she pushed the door, a bunch of colorful balloons appeared in the dimly lit room, causing her to freak out. Suddenly, our group of friends shouted, "Surprise!"

Meera was startled and froze for a moment, clutching her chest and shutting her eyes, thinking that our house had been occupied by robbers. It took her a while to calm down and realize that robbers did not need to verbally surprise her. She was delighted to see all of our friends, who gave her blessings and a lovely present. We ended the celebration by cutting a cake. It was crucial to bring joy to pregnant women's lives as they go through emotional ups and downs. Just make sure to check their cardiac history before surprising them.

We had all our preparations in place for our baby's arrival, which was due on December 18th. We had bought a crib, a baby seat, a stroller, bottles, baby clothes, and other essential items. As we had opted not to find out the sex of the baby, we chose gender-neutral clothing. We waited anxiously for the arrival of our bundle of joy. Finally, the day arrived, and Meera appeared to be perfectly normal. We went for a checkup, and the doctor reassured us that everything was fine, but we might have to wait a few more days. Another apprehensive week passed, and we returned to the hospital on Christmas Eve. The doctor suggested inducing labor, and we agreed. Meera was admitted for delivery.

The induction began around midnight on Christmas Day, and Meera went into labor, experiencing pain for more than four hours. The doctor administered an epidural, a form of anesthesia used during childbirth and other types of surgeries, which greatly relieved her discomfort. Finally, at around 4:20 a.m., the baby arrived. I was awestruck as I witnessed this natural wonder. The little head appeared first, followed by the chubby arms, chest, and stomach, all connected to a long umbilical cord. Within seconds, the legs emerged, and the baby had arrived in the world. The doctor lifted the baby and exclaimed, "You have a warrior!" It was a boy, weighing 7 pounds, healthy, and crying like a warrior baby.

When we were searching for a name for our baby, we had several options to consider. We particularly liked the name suggested by Meera's boss: Arjun (if it was a boy). The name originated from the Hindu Epic, Mahabharat. Arjun was a warrior and an excellent archer who received teachings on life from Lord Krishna in the Bhagavad Gita. When Arjun hesitated to fight against his relatives, teachers, and mentors, Lord Krishna enlightened him about life's principles. Arjun ultimately fought and killed many of them, including his own brothers. The name seemed fitting for our baby, who had fought his way into the world. Therefore, we named him Arjun.

Despite getting almost no sleep, we brought Arjun home with excitement and joy. He did well on the first day, but on the second day, Meera noticed that he was having trouble latching on to his mother's milk and feeding. We had to rush back to the hospital to have it checked out. Meera was provided with a pump for the milk, which she used religiously for the next nine months because Arjun never learned to latch on. Meera's dedication and insatiable love for her baby kept her going.

Meera did not return to work until Arjun was old enough for daycare. She stayed by his side, watching him closely to ensure that he was growing up properly, and never wanted to miss any of his firsts, such as his first sound, first crawl, first word, and first step. Under her meticulous care, Arjun slowly grew up.

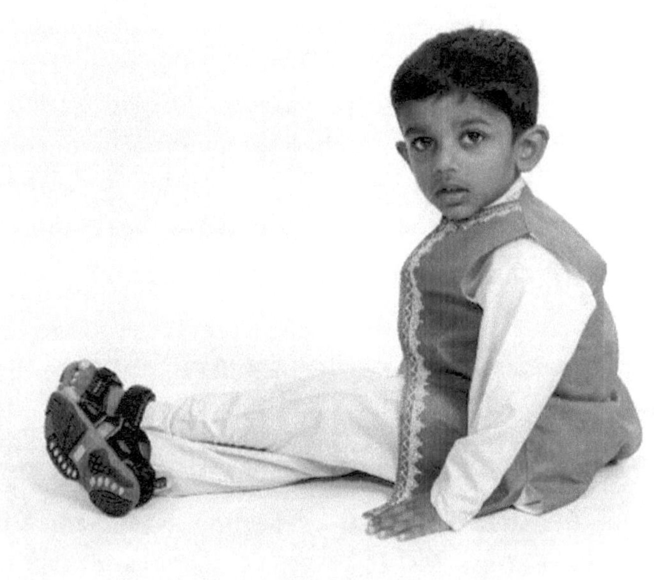

Figure 51 Arjun at two

Figure 52 Meera, Arjun, and me in Alaska (2005)

Interlude 14: Travel Bug I

In 2009, I worked part-time for an organization named World Financial Group, whose primary responsibility was to educate people on saving money for their retirement. At that time, the company was planning a trip to Taiwan and South Korea to expand its business operations and educate people on financial literacy. They offered me a chance to join the team, and since I had just finished my project with Wells Fargo and neither Taiwan nor South Korea required a visa for American citizens, I gladly joined the group.

After a 14-hour flight, we arrived in Taipei, the capital of Taiwan. Despite it being December, the moment we stepped out of the airport, a wave of humid heat hit us. The temperature was 90 degrees Fahrenheit, coupled with high humidity, making it quite sweaty. I had to remove my jacket and extra layers of clothing, leaving just a T-shirt and pants.

After attending a series of meetings, the next day, we all headed to the night market, which was a spectacular scene. The market was filled with scores of exotic street food, affordable clothing, shoes, electronics, and other miscellaneous items. We decided to start with the food court, where we could find every reptile imaginable served on a stick. I tasted a piece of snake, which had a chicken-like flavor but was rubbery. I could not bring myself to try a crunchy beetle or a cockroach, though.

A strong and unusual odor caught my attention as we were strolling around. I could not quite identify it at first. As our group got closer to the source, the scent intensified and reached its peak as we stopped by a fast food tofu establishment. Upon entering, the stench became unbearable. When the food was served, I finally discovered the source of the odor. It was called "Stinky Tofu," and it lived up to its name. I could not believe that we were expected to eat it. The tofu was repeatedly fermented until it reached the perfect level of pungency, and then it was deep-fried and served with sauce. When I was encouraged to try it, I could only manage to put a small piece in my mouth. The overpowering stink made it impossible for me to swallow, and I had to spit it out. It was definitely an acquired taste that I had no intention of acquiring. It was not for the faint of heart, or should I say, the faint of nose.

After the stinky tofu ordeal, the rest of the evening became a blur. I managed to purchase some shoes and clothing, but I found myself lying in my hotel bed before I knew it. In the next few days, we educated people about the importance of saving money. We had a great time exploring ancient temples and trying out some exquisite cuisine. Taiwan was joyful, with hardworking people who had made it an island of paradise.

Our next destination was South Korea. We arrived in the midst of extremely cold weather. Seoul was just 2.5 hours away from Taipei, but it was in the 30s Fahrenheit there. We were all bundled up in thick jackets, ear muffs, and gloves.

Upon checking into the hotel, I was surprised to discover that I had to share a room with two other women as our trip was on a budget. When we entered the room, I immediately needed to use the restroom but was unable to locate the light switch. Since it was an urgent matter, I shut the door and blindly made my way to the toilet in the darkness.

Out of consideration for my roommates, I opted to sit down to do my business rather than risk standing up and making a mess. After flushing and leaving the restroom, one of the women followed me in, found the light switch outside (how dumb was I!), and then re-entered the bathroom. Shortly thereafter, she emerged and inquired about a puddle of liquid on the floor. I was mortified having to explain the situation, and the ladies made fun of me throughout the rest of the trip.

Like Taiwan, South Korea is renowned for its food culture. During our visit, we tried Bulgogi, a succulent grilled beef dish marinated in savory seasonings. Bulgogi was one of the most popular Korean meat dishes and was even ranked 23rd on CNN Travel's reader's poll of the world's most delicious foods in 2011. Typically, the beef was grilled with garlic and sliced onions to enhance its flavor before being wrapped in lettuce. Additionally, it was traditionally consumed with Ssamjang, a thick and spicy red paste.

We also had the chance to try authentic kimchi, which is one of the oldest and most fundamental dishes in Korean cuisine. Kimchi is a spicy and sour dish that is made from fermented vegetables, typically with cabbage as the main ingredient. It can also be prepared with various other ingredients, but its popularity among foreigners stems from its high fiber content and low-calorie count. However, kimchi holds significant cultural value for Koreans, and dinner would be incomplete without it.

During our travels to the seaside, we had the opportunity to try the most exotic food of our trip. Our Korean friend ordered a collection of sea creatures, including calamari, squid, octopus, fish, and prawn. Some of the octopus and squid were still alive and kicking when served. People began picking them up with their chopsticks, dipping them in hot sauce, and swallowing them whole. Encouraged to try it myself, I also took a piece, dipped it in sauce, and put it in my mouth. I could feel the squid moving on my tongue, so I swallowed it without chewing and washed it down with water. Thinking back, I prefer the stinky tofu.

What struck us the most about our Korean experience was food's central role in their culture. South Koreans frequently come together over food, using it as a means to bond and connect with others. It was heartwarming to see family and friends gather around a table of hearty food and enjoy each other's company.

Figure 53 The financial education team visiting Taiwan (2009)

Chapter 38:
Nine Years of Consulting

The semiconductor industry experiences cyclical waves every few years, which can be likened to a roller coaster ride. In 1999, KLA Tencor underwent a downturn that led to a round of layoffs. Unfortunately, I was among those who were laid off after four years of service. However, I was fortunate that my green card application had already been initiated, and I only needed to apply for a work permit before leaving the company.

I eventually found a job at Lucent Technologies, where I was responsible for laying cables for Pacific Gas and Electric (PG&E). It was a fascinating experience that involved climbing poles, crawling into tight spaces under offices, and laying fiber optic cables all over the place. In 2001, I decided to return to the semiconductor industry and took a job at Genus Inc.

On the morning of September 11th, 2001, while driving to work, I heard something on the radio about a plane crashing into the World Trade Center. At first, I thought it was a prank, but when I changed the channel, I heard the same news. The radio reported that two passenger planes had crashed into the Twin Towers, causing them to erupt in flames and clouds of smoke.

When I arrived at work, I saw that no one was working. Everyone had gathered around a television that had been set up in the break area, watching in horror as the World Trade Center burned. We witnessed one of the buildings collapsing in real-time, hitting other buildings as it fell. It was a harrowing sight, and I could not help but think about the people who were inside the buildings. That day's events would change the world forever, affecting international relationships, immigration policies, the economy, and more. The stock market fell 7.1 percent on the first day of trading after the attacks, and New York City's economy alone lost 143,000 jobs a month and $2.8 billion in wages in the first three months.

The year 2001 left an indelible mark on history, particularly due to the 9/11 terrorist attacks that profoundly impacted American society. The road to recovery was long and arduous, and it took years for the country to regain its footing. However, amidst the turmoil, a bright spot emerged with the birth of Arjun, who came into the world in that same year.

For me, becoming a parent was a life-changing experience that I treasure to this day. Until then, I had been living solely for myself, but caring for my newborn son filled me with purpose and joy. From feeding and changing him to bathing, playing with him, and making him laugh, every moment was an expression of dedication and love, and I felt proud to be a father. Of course, I was not alone on this journey. My wife Meera poured her heart and soul into raising Arjun, and her unwavering motherly love was a source of inspiration and comfort. As we grew older, we both came to appreciate more deeply the extraordinary bond between a mother and child and how it is unlike any other force in the world.

After the 9/11 attacks, the job market took a turn for the worse, and I lost my job at Genus after only a year. For several months, I struggled to find work, but eventually, I heard about a contract position for a Software QA Engineer at Visa, the credit card company, thanks to a distant relative of my sister's, Dhamu, who was a software developer there. Although I had no prior experience in the IT industry, I decided to apply anyway, and to my surprise, I was offered an interview and eventually hired. Looking back, I realize that it was mainly due to Dhamu's influence. I was finally able to start my career in the software industry, which lasted for two decades.

Working as a contractor was a completely different experience from being a full-time employee. Contractors were regarded as low-level staff who received no benefits, no paid holidays and were rarely invited to company parties and events. I worked at Visa for ten months before being transferred to another group, where I struggled to adjust and meet my manager's expectations. One Sunday morning, while watching TV at home, I received a call from a recruiter at the contracting company informing me that my project had ended. I was devastated, but on the bright side, I had gained experience in the software industry, which would hopefully help me find a new job soon.

I applied to numerous companies in the Bay Area through third-party vendors and had several interviews. The one with Wells Fargo went particularly well, and I was offered a position. I worked in the Concord office, supporting the home equity team with their testing efforts. It was a fantastic team, and I made some great friends while maintaining a good relationship with the managers. The only thing that bothered me was my below-average income. My salary of barely $75,000 a year was insufficient for living in the Bay Area with a mortgage. However, we managed because my wife Meera was also working. After more than three years at Wells Fargo, I felt it was time to discuss the possibility of becoming a permanent employee. One of the hiring managers promised to hire me, and we discussed the hiring process, the pay grade, and the benefits. However, when it came to the salary, he hesitated to give me a number. I insisted on knowing the salary first, and he revealed that it was about $55,000 US dollars. I was disappointed and did not respond to him, so I immediately started to look for opportunities outside the bank.

I secured a consultant role at PG&E in San Francisco with a $100,000 annual salary. Departing Wells Fargo was tough, as I had formed solid friendships and was well-regarded by colleagues. However, it was time to pursue new opportunities. My focus at PG&E was on their Interactive Voice Recognition (IVR) system, which was responsible for guiding callers through phone menus once their calls were received. This technology became active once the call reached the Automatic Call Distributor's auto-attendant. For instance, if a customer reported a fallen tree, the IVR directed their call promptly to ensure that the relevant individual addressed the situation, preventing power loss for the customer. Prior to this role, I had no experience with such a system, and my time there taught me a lot.

During my tenure at PG&E, I met some wonderful individuals, including Virginia Leong, an Asian consultant with whom I developed a close friendship. Virginia was a mother of three teenagers and introduced me to Chinatown, where I purchased vegetables and fruits at discounted prices. She also acquainted me with a delicious custard dessert that seemed familiar to every Chinese person. We frequented

Chinatown restaurants, and I joked that I was half-Chinese. As time progressed, I enjoyed my time at PG&E and hoped to secure a full-time position.

Accenture, a consulting firm, primarily managed PG&E's projects. Even though I worked for a different consulting firm, I still had to report my hours and project progress to Accenture. Unfortunately, it was an unpleasant experience, as Accenture micromanaged the projects and consultants more than PG&E, particularly one of their managers. One morning, before work, I received a call from my consulting firm informing me that my project had ended. I had a hunch that the manager played a role in my project's termination.

After returning to the job market, I secured a consulting position at CAL ISO in Folsom, which is situated near Sacramento. Although it was a two-hour drive away from home, I had no other options. However, the compensation package was excellent, and I was earning $120,000 per year. CAL ISO is a non-profit Independent System Operator that provides services to California. Its primary responsibility is to oversee the operation of California's bulk electric power system, transmission lines, and electricity market that are generated and transmitted by its member utilities.

This was the furthest location I had ever worked away from home since the beginning of my career. I was working four days a week, ten hours a day. Every week, I would leave home early on Monday morning, work for ten hours, and then travel to Natomas, a suburb of Sacramento, where I stayed with a relative of Meera for the night. I would stay there from Tuesday through Thursday and return home after work on Thursday night. Maintaining this routine week after week was challenging, and I missed my family a lot. Fortunately, the project only lasted five months, the shortest period I had ever worked on.

Upon returning to the Bay Area, I had the opportunity to work with Verizon Wireless. My role involved testing their website for customer devices and accessory purchases, which helped me gain knowledge about e-commerce. However, the work environment was toxic due to the lady manager who oversaw the project. She was controlling and manipulative and micromanaged the entire team, leaving no room for anyone to voice their opinions. I was surprised to learn that this kind of work culture existed in the Bay Area, which is known for being free-spirited and innovative. Luckily, the project ended after ten months, and I returned to Wells Fargo, where I knew the culture would suit me.

While at Wells Fargo, I worked on the Store Vision Platform, their banking application. The project spanned over 18 months and was based in San Francisco. Wells Fargo had a regulation that prohibited contractors from staying beyond 18 months, after which they could return for another 18 months only if they had been away for more than six months. This policy aimed to avoid legal disputes in case the contractor sought benefits. This worked in my favor, as I had the opportunity to travel after completing my project, having worked non-stop for a long time. I worked there from 2003 to 2006 for 3.5 years and then again from 2008 to 2009 for 18 months.

After almost nine years of consulting, I landed a project at the Federal Reserve Bank of San Francisco as a contractor. I worked in the Cash Product Office for a major project that required testing efforts. My responsibilities included working on the database systems and ensuring data integrity by feeding information into the online system and verifying that the data was properly loaded into the database.

One month after commencing my work at the Federal Reserve Bank, my manager from National Cash Operations summoned me to her office and informed me that the project had been canceled. It turned out that Lockheed Martin, a third-party vendor that was hired to deliver the software, failed to meet the deadline. The Federal Reserve management had an important meeting regarding the deadline and payment for cash. Lockheed Martin demanded more money and additional time to finish the project, while the Federal Reserve pushed for the opposite. Ultimately, the entire project was scrapped, and Lockheed Martin was let go as a third-party vendor. Consequently, my services were no longer required at the Federal Reserve.

It was a very disappointing situation, but I was determined to secure a position within the bank. I asked the manager if she would be willing to refer me if a suitable role became available. Thankfully, she was happy to do so. One week later, I received a call from the Statistics Department. After going through two rounds of interviews, a written test, and a thorough background check, I was offered a full-time position.

This proved to be a life-changing moment for me. I started as a full-time employee on April 1st, 2010, and stayed with the company for 11 years until June 1st, 2021. I met some exceptional individuals, had fantastic bosses, and formed lifelong friendships during my time there. It was my most fulfilling job to date, and I was well-liked and was very popular among my colleagues. I still miss working at the bank and the people I worked with.

For nearly a decade, from 2001 until the end of 2009, I worked as a consultant in a variety of industries, including credit cards, banking, energy, and wireless communications. During this time, I gained a wealth of experience and knowledge, such as learning how to lay cables in tight spaces, like underneath or on the roof of a building. I also learned how challenging PG&E's job was as an energy provider for almost 20 million people in Northern California, where wildfires frequently occur. The company almost went bankrupt in 2019 due to its outdated power lines that caused multiple catastrophic wildfires in Northern California.

I also discovered that the energy market functioned similarly to the stock market while working at CAL ISO. Since power cannot be stored, it must be sent to power lines immediately after generation. It is difficult to predict whether demand will increase or decrease. Moreover, I learned how banks operate credit and debit cards and market these services to their customers.

Those were nine challenging yet rewarding years.

Figure 54 September 11 Attacks (picture from internet)

Chapter 39:
Federal Reserve Bank

I began working as a Test Specialist in the Statistics and Communications Department at the Federal Reserve Bank of San Francisco on April 1st, 2010. My primary task was testing the mainframe system, an old-fashioned IBM computer with specific keys for each function. Moving around the fields required the use of tabs and function keys. My duties included developing automated test scripts with Quick Test Pro, an HP application, to reduce the burden of manual testing. However, convincing the team members to embrace this idea was challenging.

In comparison to the private sector, the Federal Reserve Bank had employees with longer tenures, and the average employee age was higher. The staff members were accustomed to their usual work processes, and adapting to changes was not their strength. They were more comfortable using Excel spreadsheets and Word documents, so I had to develop the test scripts by myself.

I also participated in an ongoing project to convert the mainframe system into a web-based application, which lasted nearly eight years. Upon completion of the project, we decommissioned the mainframe and fully transitioned to web-based applications utilizing the Oracle database. It was an ambitious project, and I felt proud to have contributed to it. Even though I did not become a mainframe computing expert, I became comfortable enough to verify the behavior between the mainframe and the web-based application. After the conversion to a web-based application, everyone's work became more straightforward.

I was assigned the important task of converting production data to different quality assurance environments on a weekly basis. The testing team relied on this data for their work. I alternated this task with my colleague Johann weekly. Although Johann was intelligent, he could be abrupt at times. The conversion process was time-consuming, and I had to frequently contact the support team for passwords to transport data. If I missed a step, the data could end up in the wrong environment, rendering subsequent testing pointless. I would feel tense every Monday morning until the conversion was complete, after which I could relax for the rest of the day.

Nancy Henthorne was my first manager at the Federal Reserve Bank. She was supportive and understanding, shielding me from Susan Wong, a micromanaging director. After five years, a department-wide reorganization split our department into two, and I began reporting to a new manager, Camille Hudson. Initially, Camille was pleasant and considerate, but the workload became increasingly challenging over time, and she began expecting more from me. In addition, Susan Wong assigned me some data crunching work using spreadsheets, with very high expectations. Juggling the demands of the two became difficult for me, and I struggled for more than a year. That year, Camille gave me a below-average performance rating, and I had to undergo a performance evaluation, which I managed to pass. Eventually, the director left the company, Camille moved to another department, and Andrew Adamick became my manager. He was one of the best managers I could have asked for, polite and kind, and gave me the freedom to work outside of my comfort zone.

To repay Andrew's trust, when a new survey project came along, I eagerly leaped at it despite my lack of experience. This project, conducted every five years, involved collecting financial data from all financial institutions in the country. The collected data, including revenue, loans, and leases, was crucial in helping the Federal Reserve Bank assess the movement and scale of money. However, the survey tools were quite intricate and presented a challenge for me as a newbie. Fortunately, Xiaoyu, my friend and co-author of this book, who was also a professional in web development, provided me with the necessary assistance to get up to speed. I eventually completed the survey on time. Our work was then presented to the Federal Reserve Bank in New York and Philadelphia.

Aside from my regular job responsibilities, I also participated in various bank activities that brought me great satisfaction. Shortly after joining, Debbie, one of the managers, asked me to attend a meeting, which turned out to be an orientation for the United Way Campaign. Towards the end of each year, toward the end of the year, the bank organized a fundraising campaign for the United Way, an international non-profit organization that distributed funds to other non-profit agencies.

During the meeting, we were tasked with brainstorming ideas to raise funds. I proposed hosting an International Food Festival where employees would prepare and donate a variety of dishes, and attendees would pay an admission fee. The proceeds from the festival would be donated to the United Way Campaign. However, the campaign leader was unsure about the idea and asked me to gauge the employees' interest. I conducted a survey, and the response was overwhelmingly positive. As a result, I was put in charge of organizing the festival and spent significant time selling tickets and convincing employees to contribute food.

On the day of the event, I felt quite nervous as I was uncertain about the food selection, the turnout, and whether people would like the food. However, as the employees began to arrive, we had an impressive spread of food items available, and the attendees seemed to love them. I had even prepared a bucket of mango lassi, which turned out to be a huge hit. Over the course of two days, we raised almost $3,000. The success of the International Food Festival led to it becoming an annual event for several years, and it was eagerly anticipated by everyone. My ideas and hard work were greatly appreciated, and I received much praise for it.

Aside from the food festival, I also served as a Fed Ambassador. As part of this role, I conducted tours for high school students, financial institution employees, and members of the public. During these tours, I showed them the Currency theater that carries paper currencies from different historical periods and the vault, that carried almost half a trillion dollars in new and used currencies and provided insights into the history of the Federal Reserve Bank and how the bank operated behind the scenes.

There were annual culture-related events at the bank, and I participated in a duo dance with Koushik, a fellow employee, and it was a hit. I also joined Indus, an organization for South Asians at the Fed, to celebrate our heritage through events such as Diwali. Additionally, I worked as a Communications Coordinator for the Bank Club and organized events for employees. I founded the Fed Green Club to promote green initiatives, raise awareness about global warming, educate people on composting, and reduce the use of plastic. I was outgoing, fearless, and highly social throughout my tenure at the Fed. People knew they could turn to me for help.

After 11 years of dedicated work, I was shocked by the video call with Andrew and Betty from HR. However, I understood that there had been a lot of transformation within the bank between 2019 and 2021, particularly within our group, where top-level management had been completely replaced. The new management was focused on transforming every project into cloud-based applications, resulting in a significant layoff. I thought I would be safe since Andrew always looked out for me. In fact, I had just completed a cloud course as instructed and was about to take the certification exam. Unfortunately, the decision was beyond his control.

At 56, I felt too young to retire but too old to start fresh. After 12 years at the Fed, I had no idea what was happening outside. The Fed was my career and life. I had made many friends and built countless relationships there, feeling deeply connected and attached to the place and its people. What is going to happen to me? What should I do now?

Figure 55 Walk to Bay Bridge with the Star Team in 2017. The first from right is my manager Andrew

Figure 56 Diwali celebration at the Fed (2018)

Interlude 15: Albert Youn

One day, while commuting to work on the Bay Area Rapid Transit (BART) train, I sat beside an Asian man reading a Bible. Upon glancing at the book, I noticed red lettering and asked him about it. He explained that those were the words of Jesus, and we struck up a conversation. Before parting ways, he kindly asked if he could pray for me, which touched me deeply since I was experiencing financial and family struggles at the time. His name was Albert Youn, and we exchanged numbers. Over the next few weeks, we met regularly at Starbucks, and he brought the Bible for me to read each time.

Eventually, Albert invited me to his church in Berkeley, where I met warm and friendly people. While I enjoyed attending the church and studying the Bible, the location was quite far from my home. One day, while shopping at Smart & Final, I saw a gentle man named Scott buying a cart full of items and commented that he must be having a big party.

He revealed that the purchases were for his church and invited me to a chili cook-off event at Valley Bible Church in Pleasanton, which was only a 20-minute drive away. I attended the event and enjoyed it so much that I started going to the church regularly. It provided me with comfort and solace during the lowest point of my life.

Throughout this time, I kept in touch with Albert. Unfortunately, he lost his job as a scheduler at the Superior Courts of San Francisco and was unsure about his next career move. He went to Las Vegas to stay with his parents and worked briefly in HR for a company but did not enjoy it, so he returned to the Bay Area. We met for coffee, and I suggested that he become a recruiter for technology companies, as it was a popular career at the time. He took my advice, prepared his resume accordingly, and began sending it out.

At our next meeting, I inquired about Albert's job search, and he told me that he had not received any responses from companies. I suggested that he be more proactive and reach out to hiring managers, even meeting them in person. Despite his initial reluctance, Albert promised to follow my advice. A week later, he called me and sounded thrilled. He had secured a job at Robert Half Technology, a well-known recruitment firm. He expressed his gratitude for my advice, which encouraged him to be more assertive and ultimately helped him turn his life around. It felt good to be able to help.

A year later, Albert baptized me at the church, which had become my second family. I frequently attended events such as picnics, charity drives, and camping trips. I would take Arjun to the Valley Bible Church summer camp for several years, which he enjoyed immensely.

I appreciated the church's emphasis on charity events and giving back. I even went on three mission trips with the church to Mexico, South Africa, and Belize. During the Tijuana, Mexico, mission trip near San Diego, we built homes for low-income people over four days.

Strangely enough, despite regularly attending church, I never felt a connection with God. Instead, I found that I connected more with the people there and gained peace and calmness through interacting with them. However, I realized I could achieve the same sense of fulfillment outside the church. I did not want to attend church just to socialize, so I eventually stopped going.

Figure 57 Me and Albert Youn (2010)

Chapter 40:
Arjun's Struggles

Throughout the years, while working non-stop in various companies, I also faced family struggles. Meera and I had constant disagreements over finances and raising our son, Arjun. I have always been financially cautious and thoughtful of my expenses, whereas Meera grew up in a well-off family and was accustomed to a higher standard of living. As a result, we often had heated arguments that seemed trivial in retrospect.

Regarding Arjun, I believe in fostering his independence. I taught him how to ride a bike when he was just five years old and took him to practice driving in a parking lot after he graduated high school. I continued to teach him on local roads before he took formal driving lessons. It was crucial for him that he gained hands-on experiences in life, while Meera placed more emphasis on his academic achievements, which were undoubtedly important for his future career. However, I wanted Arjun to be equally skilled in interpersonal relationships and to embrace life. I encouraged him to ride his bike to school, but Meera never allowed it, fearing that he might get into an accident. Consequently, he never used the bike I got him for his 10th birthday.

Arjun is a caring and affectionate individual who craves love and attention. Between the ages of 2 and 15, he was hyperactive. However, he became more subdued, shy, and self-conscious once he began high school. Although he was awkward around peers of his own age, he was very comfortable around adults.

Arjun had a difficult time with his coursework throughout high school, particularly during his eleventh-grade year. Despite taking several AP and Honors classes, he found the subjects to be dry and uninteresting. AP Biology was one of the toughest courses he ever took, and he also struggled with his history classes. However, he found the content of AP Psych to be interesting and was able to perform better in that class. I tried different strategies to help him stay focused and overcome procrastination. Arjun deserves credit for being disciplined and working hard, ultimately achieving success in high school.

Meera and I wanted Arjun to learn music as we believed it was a valuable skill that would be helpful later in life. Arjun played clarinet in a concert band and alto saxophone in a jazz band during middle school. He continued playing alto saxophone for the Tri-Valley Youth Ensemble (TYME) during his ninth and tenth grade years. Arjun also received piano lessons from a Bulgarian instructor who held exclusive summer and winter concerts for his students. Despite his early love for the instrument, Arjun eventually stopped playing piano in high school due to nerves, which was a shame since the piano is such a beautiful instrument. I wish I had the chance to learn in my younger years.

In his twelfth grade year, Arjun's friend encouraged him to learn self-defense by sparring with him so he could defend himself in challenging situations. Arjun had practiced Taekwondo throughout middle school and had achieved his black belt. However, he later chose to focus on running and stopped practicing Taekwondo in high school.

Arjun's struggle with people was different from his academic struggles. He yearned for recognition and love but had some friends who only pretended to be his friends. They would invite him to hang out at the park and then proceed to make fun of him by taking off his phone case and throwing it away. Although they would apologize, Arjun realized they were only doing it to lure him back so they could continue picking on him. Sadly, Arjun thought this was how friends should treat each other.

During middle school, Arjun had a crush on a girl named Siri and confided in his friends, hoping that they would help him. However, they only used the information to tease and make fun of him. Arjun tried hard on his own but was unaware that Siri had no interest in him. When it did not work out, his fake friends continued to make fun of him and made him feel even worse.

Sunny and Anirudh, two of Arjun's supposed friends, would taunt him daily at the park, calling him names and making fun of his dark skin color. They also pressured him into doing things he was not comfortable with, such as downloading Instagram and Snapchat on his phone and texting inappropriate messages to girls from his account. Arjun was afraid of losing the only group that accepted him, so he did not dare to stop them.

When Arjun shared with me about his so-called friends he had much later, it was like a deja vu for me. I too had friends in high school who mocked me in the same way. They called me "goat," and one person, in particular, would gesture with his fingers on the side of his head like goat horns while others laughed. At the time, I did not realize that I was being bullied and just took it in stride.

It was not until I took Arjun on a trip to Hawaii in 2021 that I noticed a change in his behavior. Arjun struggled to communicate effectively with others, and sometimes, he unintentionally said things that could offend people. He also had a tendency to dwell on things and get upset, even if the people around him were apologetic. However, as we spent more time together, he gradually opened up about his struggles, and I was able to offer him advice. Our relationship grew much closer as a result.

In high school, Arjun made the decision to cut off toxic people who did not respect or value him. He tried out different groups of friends until he found those who genuinely cared about him and wanted to see him thrive. They taught him that he needed to like himself first before anyone else could like him. Motivated by their encouragement, Arjun began taking care of himself by eating healthily and working out. Two particular friends were instrumental in helping him shift his attitude:

Arjun met David Abdelmalek during his freshman year of high school when he was trying out for the cross-country team. David was a sophomore. He was popular among his peers and was known for his genuine care for others. Arjun found him to be a role model who inspired him to become a better person. David listened to Arjun's problems and offered advice and support. Arjun even joined David's Tri-Valley Youth Music Ensemble club, where they played music for seniors in various living centers. Arjun enjoyed the opportunity to positively impact the seniors and brighten their day.

Arjun's best friend for the past six years has been Anish, whom he met through cross-country and track running. Anish was always willing to listen to Arjun's problems and help him find solutions. Arjun saw Anish as a role model and tried to emulate his work ethic, ability to make friends, and prioritization skills, but he struggled to adopt the same discipline and work ethic until college.

In college, Arjun learned to keep toxic people out of his life and formed meaningful friendships with genuine people. He enjoyed spending time with his friends and relied on them for support. Arjun was a good listener when his friends needed someone to talk to, and he appreciated the opportunity to be open and honest about his own struggles. His experiences in middle and high school helped him to identify true friends from fake ones and taught him to be responsible and prioritize his time effectively.

Arjun's current objective is to complete his undergraduate degree in Economics at Arizona State University and pursue graduate studies in the same field. Additionally, he has a keen interest in data analytics, as he has demonstrated proficiency in Excel, SQL, and Tableau. After completing his education, Arjun hopes to enter the field of investment banking. I am pleased to see that he has a well-defined plan for his future, with a clear roadmap laid out before him.

During Arjun's sophomore year at Arizona State University, I visited him to help move his possessions from his dorm room to storage. I observed a significant transformation in him and was impressed with his ability to manage his academic workload and social life. At his age, Arjun is far more accomplished than I was. This bodes well for his future, and I am confident that he will excel in his career and lead a fulfilling life.

Arjun has since graduated from college and will be joining a masters program in Supply Chain management at ASU(Arizona State University) in the Fall of 2024.

Figure 58 Me and Arjun at a Hindu function in our house in San Ramon (2017)

Chapter 41:
Father's Passing Away

In 2011, Nearly 20 years after arriving in California, my mother finally visited me. Before arriving in San Francisco, she first stopped in Chicago with my sister Vijaya and brother-in-law Ramasamy. Upon her arrival, I picked her up from the airport, and my wife Meera prepared some delicious Indian food. Even though there was some tension between my mother and Meera due to a past incident, Meera was extremely nice to my mother. Meera's family had given my mother some silver vessels as wedding gifts, which she had sold without informing Meera during a financial crisis. Meera and her mother were understandably upset, but they did not mention this during my mother's visit and treated her very well nonetheless.

During my mother's stay, I took her to several places, including San Francisco, a historic gold rush city from the 1800s. Monterey is a scenic beach city on the Pacific coast with a world-famous golf course, and Redwoods is home to the rarest and tallest trees in the world, which can live for 2000 years. Although my mother did not fully comprehend the significance of these places, she enjoyed the time together nonetheless.

At the time of my mother's visit, my son Arjun was only nine years old. During our visit to the Monterey Aquarium, he was more interested in eating on the deck than observing the sea creatures inside. I insisted that he focus on the aquarium's exhibits because it is important to learn about these creatures and how they lived. My mother did not fully understand the situation as we spoke in English, but she tried to ease our tension. In hindsight, I was expecting too much from Arjun and should have been more understanding of his young age.

After spending a week with us, my mother returned to Chicago to assist my nephew, Sathi, who had just become a new father. It was typical for Indian immigrants living in the United States to invite their parents to stay with them to take care of their newborns. Normally, the parents stayed for a maximum of six months; after that, the in-laws came for another six months. They alternated their visits, with the parents returning every six months, at least for the first two years. This system allowed the baby's parents to focus on their work while the grandparents developed a bond with their grandchildren.

The following day, I received a call from my nephew, Sathi. Initially, I thought my mother required assistance, but he revealed the shocking news that my father had passed away from pneumonia in India. My mind went blank for a few minutes in shock.

My father had been suffering from dementia for most of his later years, so he only existed physically. Nevertheless, I had always admired him as my father, and he had consistently been there for me. Whenever I visited home, he was there to greet me. I could confide in him whenever I was upset, and he would listen. Now, if I returned home, I would only find an empty chair or the bed he used to sleep in. It was particularly devastating that my mother was still in Chicago. After living together for 65 years, she was not with him at the moment he passed away.

I took a leave of absence and flew to India, while my mother traveled from Chicago directly to India. My father's body was preserved in ice until we arrived. Upon seeing his body, I felt like my insides were churning, but I could not cry. All of my emotions were bottled up inside without any release. I gazed at his body for a long time. He had been a mental patient for as long as I could recall, and he always looked at me with eyes that I could not understand. I could not imagine him being "normal," and I had no idea what a typical father-son relationship would have been like. I wondered how different my life would have been if my father had been well when I was growing up. I also thought about how different his life would have been if he had been well. While these thoughts raced through my mind, my mom and my sisters cried the entire time. It was customary for women to cry when there was a death in the family.

We participated in a simple cremation ceremony, where the body was cleansed with rose water and adorned with incense and flowers. Next, the body was placed on a bed with legs for transportation to the funeral site. After the final prayers, tearful women said their goodbyes, as it is customary for women not to attend the cremation site. The body was carried by six people in a procession toward the cremation ground, with me leading the way, carrying a pot of fire to be used for cremation.

For Hindus, cremation holds significant importance as they believe it allows an individual's spiritual essence to be released from their physical body, freeing it for rebirth. Failure to conduct a proper cremation can disturb the soul, hindering its path to the afterlife and causing it to haunt living relatives. Fire is considered the ideal method for disposing of the dead due to its association with purity and its power to ward off harmful entities such as ghosts, demons, and spirits. During cremation, the fire god Agni is called upon to consume the physical body and create its essence in heaven, preparing it for transmigration. Cremations are also linked to sacrifices, as the god Pushan is asked to accept the sacrifice and guide the soul to its rightful place in the afterlife.

However, not everyone is cremated. Holy men, lepers, and individuals with smallpox are traditionally buried, with holy men buried upright and preserved with salt. Children under two years old are not cremated as their souls are considered pure. Today, some infants are taken to the middle of the Ganges River or another sacred river and dropped to the bottom with a weighted stone. Those who have died by suicide, murder, or violence are also not buried, as it is believed their souls will not rest no matter what is done to the corpse.

Families who cannot afford the wood for cremation sometimes throw unburned corpses in the Ganges. In some cases, an effigy is burned to symbolize cremation. But cremation has remained the most common way, possibly because cemeteries are a waste of space. New electric crematoriums are becoming more popular. They are more efficient and cleaner and save precious fuel and forests.

Throughout the procession, drummers and dancers followed us to give the scene a lively vibe. Once we reached a creek bed, the body was laid on top of the pyre, a pile of firewood in a square shape. I lit the pyre with the fire I brought. Once the fire was lit, I turned around and walked back without looking at the body again.

The next morning, we went back to the pyre to collect the ashes. We carried milk and poured it on the pyre before collecting the ash. Then we took the ashes to a river and spread them over it. That was the end of my father's life journey.

My father gave me the name "Devandra Chakaravarthy," which translates to King of the Heavenly World. It was a mouthful and never caught on. Also, no one took it seriously because he was already a mental patient. As a result, my nickname "Babu," meaning "kid," by which my eldest sister Vijaya used to call me, became my default name.

My father had always lived in his own world, and I never went anywhere with him nor had a meaningful exchange with him. Even after I moved to the US when I visited him, he would ask about my life, and I would tell him that I was studying engineering. Sometimes, my mother would test him about my whereabouts, and he would recall that I was in America.

During my upbringing, I often wondered what having a typical father-son relationship would be like. I would also contemplate whether my father's condition would improve, even after our trip to Sholingur. However, I do not believe I ever fully accepted his condition. Perhaps deep down, I always harbored a glimmer of hope. Unfortunately, that hope has vanished, leaving me with an emptiness as I returned to the US.

Figure 59 Procession to the funeral looking from the back
(I was leading the procession at front)

Chapter 42:
Everest Base Camp Hike

Following my father's passing, I found myself in a state of depression and despair. I lacked motivation and direction in life and had no goals to pursue. The Everest Base Camp hike saved me. It was one of the most challenging missions I had ever taken on, but it taught me that I could accomplish anything if I set my mind to it. It also helped me realize that life had given me much, and now was the time to start giving back.

One day, while having lunch with my colleague Michael from PG&E, we talked about travel and my college hiking trip in the Himalayas. We soon found ourselves discussing the idea of hiking to the base camp of Mount Everest and became enthusiastic about it. We quickly got serious about planning the trip, going on hikes at Mount Diablo in the East Bay and training at the Fed gym.

Michael, his girlfriend Sarah, and I flew together to Kathmandu, Nepal, where we were picked up by our tour group, Ace Himalayas, and taken to our comfortable hotel room. The next day, we went on a city tour of Kathmandu. We started our day by visiting an orphanage, which I had specifically requested. I brought a collection of candies, clothing, and toys for the children, who were full of energy and eager to show us their painting and sports skills. We then visited the Pashupatinath temple, a Hindu temple dedicated to Pashupati, another name for Lord Shiva. After that, we explored Kathmandu Durbar Square, located in front of the old royal palace and the Tibetan Buddhist stupa of Swayambhunath. All of these sites are UNESCO World Heritage Sites. We concluded our tour at the impressive Boudhanath stupa, the largest in the Kathmandu Valley. A stupa is a mound-like or hemispherical structure containing relics used as a meditation place.

The next morning, we arrived at Kathmandu airport to catch the scariest 20-minute flight in my life to Lukla. Nepal's weather was unpredictable, and clouds and fog could gather in minutes, making flying difficult and hazardous. While waiting in the small and cramped lounge, we overheard that some people had been waiting for weeks due to the poor weather conditions in Lukla and other places. Pilots had to ensure they avoided colliding with the Himalayas when the weather became foggy at an elevation of 10,000 feet. Luckily, we boarded our flight as scheduled.

The air hostess gave me a hard candy and a piece of cotton for my ears, but the makeshift earplug was the least of my worries. It was the most terrifying flight of my life. The aircraft was so old that it shook violently in the air as if we were coins in a piggy bank that a kid was trying to get money out of. The Lukla airstrip was incredibly narrow, and the pilot had to be exceptionally skilled and experienced to fly in such conditions and land safely. Later, I discovered that Lukla was one of the most dangerous airports globally, with a long history of accidents.

Sherpa Milan and three other porters welcomed us as we stepped off the plane. Sherpas are an ethnic group in Nepal, numbering around 150,000, and Milan means union or gender in Nepali. Sherpas are known for their mountaineering abilities, exceptional strength, and endurance at high altitudes. The most famous Sherpa was Tenzing Norgay, who, along with New Zealander Edmund Hillary, were the first two men to reach the summit of Mount Everest in 1953, making history.

At the end of each day's hike, our Sherpa took us to a teahouse where we could relax, eat dinner, and share stories. Our group consisted of two other hikers: Kenny, a Canadian physio trainer who worked with professional athletes, and Jacob, a Danish hiker. We were also joined by some German and French hikers from other groups who accompanied us halfway. It was an enjoyable experience to hike with so many international hikers and learn about their experiences.

Tea houses were available up to elevations of 15,000 feet to provide hikers with a place to eat and rest. The cost of the trip covered the cost of food, and we only had to pay for drinks. Nepal relied heavily on adventure tourism as its main source of income. Popular activities included hiking, rock climbing, whitewater rafting, and bungee jumping.

On the second day, we started our hike early in the morning, making our way through dusty hills. Along the way, we encountered a young native boy who was carrying a load much heavier than himself. He appeared very frail and weighed only around 90 pounds. He stopped and unloaded his heavy pack, then started crying. Our Sherpa asked him what had happened, and we saw that his hand was bleeding. The boy explained that he hurt himself while trying to unload the heavy load for a rest. We used our first aid kit to dress his wound and provided him with water and snacks. He was very grateful.

It was disheartening to see teenagers carrying such heavy loads up the mountain, but they had no other choice if they wanted to survive. Many of them could not afford to go to school or find better employment opportunities. Sherpa was considered a good occupation, but they needed to learn some English.

The porters, who carried our heavy backpacks, were not physically impressive. They were scrawny and short, each weighing about 100 pounds. However, they managed to carry a tremendous load of 150 to 180 pounds on their backs and run up hills. It was astonishing how they did it. Along the way, we saw Nepalese people carrying heavy doors, bricks, Heineken beer, and gas cylinders. Mules and yaks were also used to carry heavy loads. The hilly terrain had no tar roads, vehicles, or vegetation. The nearest school and hospital were hours away by foot.

On May 29, 1953, Edmund Hillary, a New Zealand mountaineer, explorer, and philanthropist, and Sherpa mountaineer Tenzing Norgay became the first climbers confirmed to have reached the summit of Mount Everest. Edmund Hillary did a remarkable job of establishing hospitals and schools in the mountains of Nepal, improving the lives of the people there. When asked about his greatest achievement, he expressed more pride and satisfaction in the work he did to help the people.

Even 70 years later, the Nepalese people in these mountains are still grateful to Edmund Hillary for the work he did. He recognized the struggles of the people, with children hiking over 5 kilometers to attend school and hospitals being equally far. In response, Hillary dedicated himself to building more schools and hospitals. After his climb of Everest, he established the Himalayan Trust in 1960, which he led until his death in 2008, to assist the Sherpa people of Nepal. His efforts led to the construction of numerous schools and hospitals in this remote region of the Himalayas.

The second day of the hike was arduous and draining. As we wrapped up for the day, we decided to go to a teahouse. I felt so exhausted that I collapsed onto the table and fell asleep. When I woke up, I tried to move but almost tripped. It turned out that my fellow hikers had tied together my shoe shoelaces. Everyone burst into laughter.

On the following day, we befriended a young Polish couple. After a tiring day of hiking, the Polish man also felt exhausted and laid down on the restaurant mat. An hour later, when the food was ready, he was woken up and handed a warm towel to clean his face. However, he was so exhausted, hungry, and disoriented that he started biting the towel thinking it was food. It was an amusing incident that lightened up the mood.

The entire hike lasted for eleven days, during which we took two days off to rest and acclimatize. As the altitude exceeded 12,000 feet, the oxygen level in the air dropped drastically, making it imperative for us to take breaks and get accustomed to the conditions. Previous incidents of hikers losing their lives due to a lack of acclimatization served as a reminder of how important it was to be careful and cautious.

Finally, we reached the last teahouse before the base camp, which was located at an altitude of 19,000 feet. The last day of the hike was particularly challenging, as the terrain had changed drastically. We encountered icy lakes, towering snow peaks, and a barren landscape without vegetation. There were hardly any birds or animals in the vicinity, but surprisingly, a dog appeared out of nowhere and followed us all the way to the base camp. It was an unexpected and heartwarming sight that lifted our spirits.

The base camp was nothing but flat terrain covered with rocks, ice, and snow. The only way we could tell that it was the base camp was from the words "Mt. Everest base camp, 19,000 feet," carved on a huge rock. We could not see Mount Everest from there because it was surrounded by mountains. However, we were informed that we needed to wake up early the next morning to witness the sunrise behind Mount Everest. We took some photographs and began our hike back to the teahouse. Halfway through the hike, I became exhausted and could not continue any further. Fortunately, Kenny offered to carry my backpack, and we somehow managed to make it back to the teahouse, feeling completely drained.

The following morning, we awoke at 4:30 a.m. to prepare for the day. I went to the restroom to use the toilet. When attempting to scoop some water from the bucket, the mug hit something solid. Since the bathroom had no light, I had to feel around it with my hand, and what I touched was freezing cold. It turned out that the water in the bucket had frozen overnight, as it was in negative temperatures in Fahrenheit (below -20 degrees Celsius). We put on multiple layers of clothing, including our thickest jackets, and started our ascent. When we were halfway to Kalapathar, we caught a glimpse of Mount Everest as the sun was trying to peek through the clouds. However, despite wearing thick socks and gloves, my toes and fingers were numb and aching from the frigid temperature.

I was so cold that I did not want to finish the hike, so I asked my Sherpa to take me back. We ran back to the teahouse, and I was pleased that I had seen Mount Everest from 19,000 feet, the closest I could ever get. It was the primary reason why I decided to hike to the base camp in the first place. Climbing Mount Everest at 29,000 feet is a highly dangerous proposition, and I doubt I can ever do it. Reaching an altitude of 19,000 feet was the best I could achieve, and I am proud and grateful to this day for having accomplished it.

Kenny and Jacob continued their ice climbing while we bid them farewell and headed back to Lukla and, eventually, Kathmandu. The trek down was significantly easier than the ascent, taking us only three days to reach Lukla after nine days of climbing and two days of rest. After finally reaching Lukla exhausted, we were greeted by bad news: our flight was delayed due to poor weather conditions.

We anxiously waited for the flight, but Michael became increasingly upset and refused to pay tips to the Sherpa and porters unless we were able to board on time. Sherpa explained that the flight schedule was beyond his control. Fortunately, we were eventually able to board the flight on time. This trek was a significant accomplishment for me, requiring hard work and perseverance. Although I had moments of doubt and considered giving up, I was able to push through with my willpower. I will always remember these challenging moments and how I overcame them to motivate myself in difficult situations.

During the flight from Lukla to Kathmandu, I experienced a sharp pain in my left ear when the plane began descending. I have always been prone to ear pain during altitude changes, which has prevented me from scuba diving in the past. The pain was unbearable this time, and I sought medical attention straightaway upon arriving in Hong Kong. I found a doctor's office while walking on the street, and he was able to see me immediately. The doctor, who happened to be Tamil, prescribed drops and medication that provided immediate relief. However, the pain lingered for a day or two, so the amazing Everest trip did not fully conclude until I arrived in Beijing.

Figure 60 Part of my hiking group

Interlude 16: Travel Bug II

Hirotaka Muira was a Research Associate in the Economic Research department at the Federal Reserve Bank. We became friends while working at the Fed and decided to go on a trip together. Our itinerary involved visiting Japan first, where Hiro would show me around, and then I would return the favor in India. The best way to see a country is to travel with a person who speaks the local language.

After a long flight, we finally arrived in Tokyo and went to Hiro's aunt's house. The Japanese people were famous for their strong work ethic, and I witnessed this firsthand during our stay. Hiro's grandmother, who was 85 years old and still working as a pediatrician, woke up at 4 am every morning to harvest vegetables and greens from her garden. She then packed the produce and later distributed it to a homeless shelter. After that, she went to the hospital and spent the day seeing patients. In the evening, she returned home and tended to her garden again. Despite working long hours that resulted in a hump on her back, she did not let it deter her from working non-stop.

Hiro's grandfather was a humble World War I veteran who treated us to dinner. We also had the opportunity to meet his sister, who was a volunteer for an animal organization. She educated us about the Asian black bear, a medium-sized species native to Asia that lived primarily in Japan's Honshu and Shikoku islands. These bears were threatened by deforestation and a lack of rain. Hiro's sister was passionate about teaching people how to protect the bears from being killed.

That night, we stayed in a traditional Japanese house called Minka, featuring tatami flooring, sliding doors, and wooden verandas surrounding the home. It was a cozy and comfortable experience. The next day, we explored Tokyo, one of the world's largest cities in terms of both size and population. When we got lost, people not only gave us directions but also guided us and ensured we reached our destination. The city's architecture was a blend of modern skyscrapers and bullet trains alongside old two-story Minka houses Bud ancient Shintoism and Buddhist temples. Most of the visitors to the temples were seniors, with few younger people in attendance.

Our next destination was Kyoto, Japan's historical city of culture. Kyoto served as the country's capital and its cultural, spiritual, and imperial center from 794 to 1868. Despite the presence of Michelin-starred restaurants and designer shops, the city's ancient places of worship, Zen gardens, and teahouses still embody the "old" Japan. During my visit, I explored a 14th-century temple that was assembled like a puzzle without the use of a single nail. In those days, iron was scarce, prompting people to construct buildings using only wood, which led to the development of advanced architectural techniques. In contrast, temples in North India were constructed using marble, while those in South India were made of granite with minimal woodwork. This explains why Indian temples have endured for centuries, whereas wooden structures in Japan have been destroyed by termites or fire.

After visiting Kyoto, we traveled to Nagoya, Japan's fourth most populous city. The Toyota Museum was a must-see destination for international visitors. Kiichiro Toyoda, the founder of Toyota, invented the automatic power loom mill in the 1800s to speed up clothes production. He sold the mill later and used the proceeds to fund his son's trip to Europe to learn about automobiles. Upon his return, Sakichi Toyoda (the son) made the first "made in Japan" car, and the rest is history.

I take pictures of everything whenever I travel, and this trip was no exception. While en route to Hiro's mother's shop, I spotted some schoolchildren in pretty uniforms and requested that his mother pull over so I could take a picture of them. In India, photographing children is customary, and they enjoy it. However, it is considered impolite in Japan, and Hiro was furious with me, threatening to end our trip. I promised him that it would not happen again. The cultural gap between India and Japan was vast.

In Japan, witnessing how orderly people were at subway stations was impressive. Even during rush hour, the platforms were packed, but commuters waited patiently and moved in and out quietly. Once the train became full, employees wearing white gloves, known as shovers, pushed more passengers in with their hands to occupy every inch of space. The punctuality of the trains in Japan was astounding. The staff apologized for the delay if a train arrived a few seconds late.

Japan is one of my favorite countries due to its exceptional culture and traditions. However, the country faces negative population growth as people have fewer and fewer children. This issue is partly due to modern cultural changes where both husbands and wives work, leaving them with very little time to raise a family. Additionally, the younger generation prefers to live with their parents to avoid the high living costs and social pressures in major cities. Japanese people generally live long lives, well into their 90s and 100s, thanks to their excellent food habits. As of 2020, approximately 28.4 percent of the Japanese population is aged 65 years or older, which puts enormous pressure on the younger generation to support the aging country. Many seniors have had to delay their retirement or go back to work after retiring.

After Japan, we traveled to India, where I took Hiro to my village, and he loved the experience. We also visited Munnar, a tea estate in Kerala, with Sebastian and Ruban, my niece Parimala's husband. While we were there, we met some schoolchildren who asked to take a picture with us.

Figure 61 Hiro and me jumping for joy in a tea estate, Munnar, South India in 2010

Chapter 43:

Surprising Sundar

In the chapter titled "The Gang," I introduced two close friends from Petit Séminaire, Sebastian and Sundar. Like myself, Sebastian also grew up without a father. Sundar, on the other hand, was known for his spiritual inclinations. His grandmother, who was a French citizen, applied for French passports for all her grandchildren, including Sundar. Unfortunately, Sundar's father, who was an alcoholic, was unable to sponsor him, so I and several other friends of his pooled together enough money to send him to France. We lost touch with him for the next 20 years, though we corresponded through postal mail during the first few years.

During those 20 years, Sundar worked diligently to obtain his teaching credentials and became an English teacher at a high school in France. His mother and the rest of his family also moved to France shortly after he arrived. He led a simple life, practicing and teaching yoga and reading philosophy, and he never married. We remained in contact with him via email and postal mail, but he never revealed his location or place of work, except that he was in Caen and had no plans of returning to India.

Fast forward 21 years later, in 2011, one day Sebastian called me out of the blue from India and asked if I could meet him in Europe. Sebastian had a business meeting in London near Caen, where Sundar was living. He suggested that we surprise Sundar by showing up unannounced. With a friend's help, we could track down the name of the school where Sundar worked. I took a week off work and flew to London, where we spent a day sightseeing, including a visit to Wimbledon to catch a few matches.

That night, we boarded an overnight bus that took us across the English Channel by ferry to Paris. Unfortunately, there was no room for us to sleep on the ferry, so we arrived in Paris hungry and exhausted the next morning. We made our way to the suburbs where Sebastian's friend lived with her husband and two young children. Despite her family commitment and busy schedule, Sebastian's friend took excellent care of us. After a long nap in the afternoon, we went for a walk along the Cheyenne River, with the Eiffel Tower visible in the distance.

The following day, Sebastian and I traveled by train to Caen and then took a taxi to Sundar's school, which was not in session as it was summer. Fortunately, the administration office was open, and we introduced ourselves and explained our purpose for being there. The staff confirmed Sundar's employment and kindly provided us with his apartment address. However, when we arrived at his apartment, the security guard would not let us in. After waiting for thirty minutes, Sebastian lost his patience and started shouting, "Sundar, Sundar!" But no one came out. Frustrated and hungry, we waited an hour before deciding to have lunch.

On our way back to Sundar's apartment after lunch, Sebastian suddenly shouted, "Sundar, Sundar!" and started chasing as a brown Peugeot car raced by. The car screeched to a halt. Sebastian flung open the door and leaped inside. I was initially puzzled but soon realized it was Sundar behind the wheel. I rushed to join them in the backseat. The look on Sundar's face was priceless. It was a mixture of shock, surprise, anger, and happiness. Turning to Sebastian, I said, "I can die peacefully now," as that was the depth of our love for our friend Sundar.

Sundar took us to a nearby beach in Caen, a port town in the Normandy district of France. During World War II, it was a critical hub for the Allied forces when they landed in Normandy to fight the Germans. Afterward, we visited a museum that displayed artifacts discovered after the war. For dinner, we went to a French restaurant and relished savory crepes filled with chicken and snails.

However, after dinner, Sundar declined to take us to his room because it was untidy and disorganized. Despite his reluctance, I persuaded him to let us clean it. When we opened the door, a foul odor emanated from the room, where piles of stuff obstructed the pathways like a maze. The kitchen was overflowing with dishes, and stacks of books made the aisles narrow. The toilet and sink were stained brown and black from years of neglect, and he had not had visitors for years. Unfortunately, Sebastian was very particular about the cleanliness of the bathrooms, so we stayed in a hotel for the night. By the time we arrived, the reception had already closed, but there was a credit card payment system that allowed us to obtain the key ourselves. I had never seen such a system in the US. We had a night of peaceful and restful sleep.

On the following day, Sundar gave us a tour of the town of Caen. The town center featured the Château de Caen, a castle built circa 1060 by William the Conqueror, which stood on a hill flanked by two Romanesque abbeys of Saint-Étienne and Sainte-Trinité, both dating from the same period. Additionally, there was the multimedia Mémorial Museum, which was dedicated to World War II, the 1944 Battle of Normandy, and the Cold War.

Later that afternoon, Sundar drove us to Paris, and we stayed at Sebastian's friend's house again. Our next plan was to find the grave of Sebastian's father, who had worked as an attorney in France and passed away in the 70s. At that time, due to policy and financial reasons, Sebastian's family was unable to get a visa to go to France for the funeral. Hence, one of his father's close friends conducted the funeral and maintained the grave. All Sebastian had about his father was the address of the graveyard and a faded picture of his father's grave, which they received from a distant relative living in France.

We took a train and a bus to reach the graveyard, and Sundar was a great help as he spoke fluent French. We checked with the office and got the address of the grave. An Indian name was listed, and we deduced that it must be the caretaker. We walked several blocks, crossing castle-like graves with dragons and Chinese symbols. As we walked down further, the graves became older, with bushes and weeds growing on them. Finally, we reached the address, where we saw a sad-looking grave without a tombstone and just a small wooden cross worn out through years of sun, rain, and snow. Weeds growing around the cross added an extra touch of desolation.

Sebastian immediately broke down, bursting into tears. He sat beside the grave and called his family, speaking with his sisters in an emotional exchange. As someone who also grew up without the love and care of a father, I could empathize with Sebastian's feelings as he looked upon the grave, realizing that any hope for a renewed relationship with his father was gone and that the emptiness in his heart would never be filled. Sundar and I left him alone to grieve for a few minutes. We noticed that the maintenance of the grave site had been neglected and realized that Sebastian's father's friend, who had been kindly taking care of its upkeep, must have passed away and hence could no longer make payments. Sebastian then took over the responsibility of maintaining the site.

Like myself, Sebastian never had a genuine father-son relationship with his dad, who was absent during his childhood and passed away when he was young. In contrast, Sundar's father struggled with alcoholism, making it difficult for him to establish a healthy relationship with his son. Although we all had our own unique wounds, we were able to forge our own paths, living in different countries and staying connected.

In the following days, we had some of the best moments of our lives exploring the Eiffel Tower, the Louvre Museum, Champs De Ulyss, the Cathedral of Notre Dame, and other notable places in Paris. Senthil, who was our friend Sai's brother and a trained guide, showed us the most significant paintings and sculptures at the Louvre Museum, including the famed Mona Lisa. The coronation of Alexander the Great was truly impressive, depicted in a vast painting rich with numerous stories. I found it interesting that despite its grandeur, people paid little attention to it, opting instead to crowd around the Mona Lisa. I suppose that's the effect of fame.

After the tours, Sebastian wanted to visit his relatives in Paris, but Sundar declined due to his discomfort with meeting strangers. Meanwhile, I wanted to continue sightseeing and visiting more museums. Sebastian got upset with both of us and decided to go alone.

I accompanied Sundar to the Roland Garros Stadium to watch the French Open Tennis Stadium and explore the museum. It was a surreal experience to touch the red clay, visit the players' locker rooms, and even sit in the press chair box of the players. I had always watched the French Open with great enthusiasm, and being there physically brought me immense joy.

As the trip drew to a close, it was time to return to reality. Sundar and Senthil saw me off at the bus station in Paris, and I made my way back to London to catch my flight to the US.

Figure 62 Me and Sebastian at Sacre Coeur (Church of the Sacred Heart) in Paris (2011)

Figure 63 Me and Sundar (right) at the press conference room at Roland-Garros in 2011 (French Open Tennis Tournament)

Chapter 44:
Toastmasters

When I joined the Fed in 2010, one of the first things I did was join Money Talks, a Fed-sponsored Toastmasters club. Toastmasters was a US-headquartered nonprofit educational organization that operated clubs worldwide for the purpose of promoting communication, public speaking, and leadership. Meetings are self-run, and members work their way through Toastmasters' education program.

Joining the Toastmasters was one of the best things I had done in my life for self-improvement. It boosted my confidence in interviews, public speaking, and social interactions, and had a massive impact on my professional career as well.

Initially, I was intimidated and struggled to speak coherently in front of an audience. It was nerve-racking, and I struggled to put sentences together. I was paired with a mentor who aided me in preparing my first few speeches. We rehearsed, made changes, and polished them repeatedly. At first, I presented my speeches using slides and could only read them word-for-word. Nonetheless, as I progressed, my confidence grew.

Every year, Toastmasters hosts speech contests. Typically, there is an International Speech Contest in the fall and a humorous speech contest in the spring. I regularly participated in both contests. One year after joining Toastmasters in 2011, one of my mentors encouraged me to join the humorous speech contest. Initially, I hesitated due to my lack of experience. However, his supportive words bolstered my confidence, and I decided to give it a try.

During my speech, I discussed my decision to marry Meera over a brief phone call. As arranged marriages were foreign to my audience, the concept of agreeing to marry someone without meeting them was even more unusual. My speech received numerous laughs during the club-level competition, resulting in my victory. I repeated the same speech at the area level, where I won once again. Despite the tough competition at another level up, the division level, I miraculously achieved 2nd place.

The entire experience was surreal and dreamlike to me, and I was beside myself for making it that far. However, deep down, I was afraid that it might have been beginner's luck and that the cultural difference might have also played a role in my success. Consequently, I did not participate in the competition for the next two years until I decided to challenge myself again in 2013. This time, I chose a topic unrelated to culture and purely humorous.

The competition was held on the fourth floor of the Federal Reserve Bank of San Francisco, with four contestants and about 20 people in attendance. I prepared a speech on "My Yellowstone trip with my family," which was unique for me since I usually travel alone. In the summer of 2013, I went on a trip to Yellowstone with my family, and Bala's family joined, too.

When it was my turn, I stepped onto the stage. My heart began racing like a stampeding bull, and my palms were sweaty. I took a deep breath and closed my eyes for a moment. Upon opening them, the words flowed fluently from my mouth.

"We traveled from California and stayed at an Airbnb about two hours away from Yellowstone National Park. The following morning, we made our way to the park's entrance, where a long queue of cars was waiting. After twenty minutes, we reached the entrance and paid for admission. I noticed a sign indicating that senior citizens received free admission. Being a cheapskate, I got an idea. My father-in-law was sitting right beside me, and he was a senior citizen. Seizing the opportunity, I asked the park ranger if we could receive free entrance and parking. The ranger readily agreed and asked for my father-in-law's ID.

My father-in-law slowly unbuckled his seatbelt, placed his hand in his pocket, and began fumbling for his wallet. After taking out his social security card, Kaiser insurance card, and Contra Costa County health card, he finally found his ID card."

Despite my nervousness, the audience erupted into uncontrollable laughter at my jokes, which helped to calm my nerves and allowed me to continue.

"The ranger jotted down some information and requested my father-in-law's signature. I handed him the notepad, but he struggled to remove the pen from the clipboard. Afterward, he accidentally dropped the pen between his seat and the cup holders, and I had a tough time retrieving it. A line of cars began forming behind us, and the ranger's expression turned sour. Five minutes passed before I finally handed the clipboard back to her. She flung it angrily onto her table, causing a large glass of drink to spill and flood the entire surface. After taking another five minutes to clean up the mess, she returned the ID and papers to us."

As the audience continued to laugh, I grew increasingly comfortable on stage. Countless hours of practice had undoubtedly helped as well. The laughter was a source of motivation, spurring me on to finish strong.

"After finally entering the park, my father-in-law was still rummaging through his wallet. I asked what he was searching for, and he told me that the ranger had not returned his ID. Therefore, I had to make an illegal U-turn on a double yellow lane and drove back for a couple of minutes. Eventually, he found his ID, and I had to make another illegal U-turn to head back into the park. Needless to say, it was quite an adventure traveling with my family."

As I concluded my speech, the audience rose to their feet, applauding and cheering. The overwhelming support nearly brought me to tears. I struggled to remain focused throughout the event while my fellow contestants delivered their speeches. However, the moment of truth arrived when the ballots were tallied, and the chief judge was ready to announce the results. By then, I had relaxed, knowing I had done my best and conquered my fears.

The third-place winner was announced, and it was not me. Then the second place winner was announced, and once again, not me. My heart pounded with excitement as the winner was finally revealed. "Babu!" they exclaimed. I could not believe my ears. They called me again. It was indeed my name. I had won the humorous speech competition at my club and would be representing us at the area level contest. I was overjoyed.

The area level comprised six clubs in the San Francisco financial district. I honed my speech, sought feedback from my mentors, and practiced relentlessly. Speaking in front of over 30 strangers with unknown competitors was nerve-racking, but I realized I could only focus on what was within my control: my speech. The confidence I gained from winning the club contest helped me deliver a much-improved speech. The competition was intense, but I emerged victorious, representing our area at the division level. It was one of the proudest moments of my life.

The division level contest featured multiple areas with a large audience of over 100 people. Despite winning the area contest, I still experienced nervousness as the date approached. Fortunately, meditation helped me calm my nerves. I gave it my all on the day of the competition and delivered a speech that exceeded my expectations. Ultimately, I secured second place. The winner was exceptional, and I had no complaints. I was proud of myself and realized that I could become an accomplished speaker with hard work and dedication.

In addition to improving my public speaking skills, I mentored junior members, providing guidance on time management, gestures, tone variation, and strong openings. Each member joined Toastmasters with a different objective in mind. For instance, Srini Reddy from National Cash Automation joined to enhance his public speaking abilities. I coached him on the fundamentals of public speaking, and he delivered an excellent icebreaker speech.

In 2018, James Chiu, another new member, was assigned to me after being a part of Toastmasters for seven years. James, a soft-spoken and gentle young Asian American who taught yoga, gave a speech rich in detail and storytelling. However, it was too long, so I helped him narrow it down to two stories that he could deliver in under six minutes. This approach made his speech more focused and engaging. Oscar Wong, a tall Uruguayan-Chinese manager who excelled in ping pong, came to me seeking guidance on presentation delivery. He delivered a fantastic icebreaker speech with my help and continued to work with me on his first few speeches, making rapid progress. Furthermore, I mentored other clubs in the area, including the Federal Reserve Club and Pinterest. Seeing people improve before my eyes as a result of my guidance is truly rewarding.

After nine years in Toastmasters, during which time I had delivered over 50 speeches and served in multiple officer roles, I decided it was time to take my involvement to the next level. My goal was to earn the title of Distinguished Toastmaster (DTM).

The DTM award was the highest level of educational achievement in Toastmasters, and less than 1% of members earned it. To become a DTM, I had to fulfill several requirements. These included completing two learning paths: serving as a club officer for 12 months, serving a full one-year term as a district officer, and successfully serving as a club mentor or coach.

Essentially, this meant I had to step out of my comfort zone and become more involved in leadership outside my club. I became the Area Director for the San Francisco downtown area, which included PG&E, Blue Cross, Wells Fargo, Salesforce, and two other clubs in the area. As the Area Director, I acted as the liaison between clubs, the division, and the district, and helped clubs fulfill their mission of helping members grow.

In addition to my Area Director responsibilities, I helped Money Talks achieve the President's Distinguished Club status twice by creating a Club Success Plan and successfully running a Club Officer Training program. For my DTM project, I coordinated and supervised several clubs in the division to successfully run a division speech contest.

In the end, achieving the title of Distinguished Toastmaster was an extraordinary accomplishment, well worth the effort and substantial amount of time I had invested. At a virtual function, I was felicitated with this title, an achievement I will always remember and proudly carry.

After leaving the Federal Reserve Bank, I could no longer attend Money Talks club meetings due to time constraints. However, several members from the district level began discussing the idea of starting a Tamil-English bilingual club in the Bay Area. The club would provide Tamil-speaking individuals, who might not have had the opportunity otherwise, a chance to improve their Tamil-speaking skills. There was a significant number of Tamil natives in the Bay Area who only spoke the language at home. We were able to recruit enough members to launch the club, including my friend Sebastian, who joined virtually from India, Sathya Sai from Edmonton, Canada, and Selvan from Texas, who held my friendship in high regard. Additionally, Joseph Albert Ravi, who was close with Sebastian and me, joined from Malaysia, giving the club an international flavor. We decided to name the club "Vanga Pesalam," which translates to "Come, let's talk!"

The Tamil club experienced a surge in popularity as it provided an opportunity for those who had lost touch with the language to practice and improve their Tamil skills. The club offers a platform for learning and practicing Tamil and English. In 2022, the club participated in its first-ever humorous speech contest in English.

My Toastmasters journey has been nothing short of extraordinary over the past 12 years. I have achieved second place in the division level humorous speech contests twice, mentored and coached several new members at Money Talks and other clubs in the area, mentored numerous clubs in San Francisco downtown, served as an Area Director overseeing six clubs in the San Francisco area, achieved the Distinguished Toastmaster status, and contributed to the establishment of a bilingual club for my mother tongue. My journey has been fulfilling in terms of my achievements and discovering my strengths in public speaking, leadership, mentoring, and networking.

*Figure 64 Humorous Speech Contest on division level in 2013.
I won the second place among 20 contestants*

Figure 65 Toastmaster Money Talks club annual event in 2019

Interlude 17: Volunteering

Volunteering has played a significant role in my life. Having lived in both India and the US for years, I understand how fortunate I am to have the life I wanted. However, I have never forgotten that people worldwide suffer from poverty, mental illness, and lack of resources. Volunteering is my way of giving back, helping those in need, and fulfilling my role as a small but important part of the world.

I have volunteered at a variety of events, including soup kitchens, tennis tournaments, NCAA basketball tournaments, figure skating championships, tree-planting events, AIDS memorials, the Lighthouse for the Blind, the United Way, the International Dance Festival, dog shelters, Hindu Temples, and church mission trips, among others.

One of my most fulfilling volunteer experiences was with Friends of the Urban Forest, an organization that focuses on revitalizing San Francisco's urban forest and combating global environmental issues through tree-planting. It was purely coincidental that I discovered them while searching for volunteer opportunities in 2020, as the pandemic had left few options. I learned about Friends of the Urban Forest from a newsletter published by The Urban Garden Initiative, a non-profit that provides opportunities to build small gardens in high schools or public areas to grow vegetables for the community.

I participated in biweekly tree-planting activities with Friends of the Urban Forest from September 2021 to February 2022. The selected trees were chosen specifically for their ability to absorb carbon dioxide from the air. According to NOAA Global Monitoring Lab observations, carbon dioxide alone was responsible for about two-thirds of the total global warming impact out of all human-produced greenhouse gases in 2021. Another issue caused by carbon dioxide is that it dissolves into the ocean, reacts with water molecules, and increases the ocean's acidity, leading to ocean acidification.

I have also raised funds for numerous charitable organizations. One particular event that touched me deeply occurred during my trip to South India in 2003. While on my way to my sister's house with my third brother-in-law, Vijayaraghavan, I noticed a school where teachers were conducting classes under trees. I asked the driver to stop the car and entered the principal's office to inquire about the situation. The principal told me that there were insufficient classrooms, so the students had no choice but to study outdoors. He took me to one of the classrooms where the students sat on a concrete floor, and they had to squat and bend down to write. It was a distressing sight. I obtained the school's contact information and continued my journey.

Upon returning to the US, I organized a potluck fundraiser for the school at Elizabeth Lake Park in the city of Fremont. Many of my friends came and supported the event, which enabled me to raise over a thousand dollars. I entrusted the money to Vijayaraghavan, who was honest and trustworthy, and he delivered it to the principal. With the funds, they purchased tables and benches for the school. While a thousand dollars may not seem like a lot, I was pleased to be able to contribute to a worthy cause.

A few years later, I returned to India and found myself in the same area as last time. The first thing I wanted to do was visit that school and see how the students were doing. The principal kindly invited me to tour the classrooms. I had anticipated seeing a few additional tables and benches, but to my amazement, every single student now had a proper desk and chair. Gone were the days of sitting on the concrete floor and hunching over to write.

The principal smiled and explained to me that my donation had inspired other donors and government grants to contribute, resulting in enough tables and benches for the entire school. Upon hearing this, I was moved to tears. It was heartwarming to know that my small gesture had snowballed into something much greater. Indeed, goodwill has a way of spreading infectiously.

In 2015, I attended an event hosted by Valley Bible Church. The church had partnered with Compassion International, a Christian humanitarian aid organization headquartered in Colorado Springs, Colorado. The organization aimed to positively impact the long-term development of children living in poverty globally.

During the event, various pictures of children from around the world were displayed, including their backgrounds and reasons for needing help. I came across the profile of a 4-year-old boy from Indonesia named Putra, who had a heartwarming smile and was gazing right at me in the photograph. His family was impoverished, struggling to provide basic necessities like food and education. Putra was at risk of becoming a child laborer without access to schooling. Gazing into his innocent eyes, I felt compelled to make a difference in his life. For the past eight years, I have been sending Putra $30 every month through Compassion International, supporting his education and wellbeing.

As I write this chapter, Putra is 12 years old and has started attending middle school. Over the years, he has made significant progress in his spiritual, cognitive, physical, and socio-economic development. I receive regular updates from Compassion International and am thrilled to see how he has grown. I eagerly await the day when he will transform into a responsible and educated young man who will positively impact his community. It is truly rewarding to witness someone's growth and development as a result of the assistance they have received.

One of my life goals is to give back to society. At the end of the day, what matters most is making a difference, no matter how big or small. I have been contemplating this goal recently and aspire to establish my own volunteering/charity organization that will serve youth, combat global warming, and alleviate hunger in third-world countries. Although the road ahead is long, I am determined to reach my objective.

Figure 66 Friends of the Urban Forest planting trees in San Francisco (2021)

Chapter 45:
The Pandemic

The 2020 COVID pandemic has profoundly impacted the world, catching everyone off guard.

The last pandemic that significantly impacted the world was the Spanish flu of 1918-1919. The H1N1 virus, with genes of avian origin, caused the pandemic, infecting an estimated 500 million people worldwide, which was about one-third of the world's population. The pandemic caused at least 50 million deaths globally, with the United States alone recording about 675,000 deaths.

As of now, the 2020 Covid pandemic has caused the deaths of 6.55 million people worldwide and has affected 618 million people. Two of my engineering college mates and three distant relatives in India fell victim and passed away in 2020. Initially, India was less affected compared to the rest of the world, but due to poor decision-making by the government, India has suffered the most so far, resulting in 14 million deaths, despite the official figures being less than a million. The primary cause of these deaths was the hospitals' lack of oxygen and respirators. With a population of over a billion, imposing restrictions on social gatherings was challenging. Finally, after a year, India was able to bring COVID-19 under control, but it came at a tremendous cost.

In addition to the devastating death toll, the COVID-19 pandemic also caused a significant upheaval in people's daily lives. Individuals were mandated to remain at home for a period of time and cease traveling. When allowed to leave their homes, they were required to wear masks and maintain a safe social distance from others. The global economy suffered greatly, leading to the closure of numerous businesses. Virtual meetings and online activities became the norm, and working from home became the predominant mode of commuting. Everyone was forced to adapt to the new reality.

Personally, this period of revelation brought more changes to my life than I ever could have imagined.

First, it brought me closer to my son, Arjun, as I was able to spend more time with him than ever before. I taught him how to drive, just as I had taught him how to ride a bike. During these moments of togetherness, we discussed our futures and life in general. He opened up to me more about his high school experiences, interest in girls, and outlook on life than ever before. Being stuck in the house together all the time led to a much stronger bond between us, thanks to COVID.

Secondly, I had the opportunity to spend a month with my mother and Vijaya, my eldest sister, in Chicago. This quality time allowed me to develop a closer emotional bond with them and deepen our relationship.

Thirdly, I achieved the status of Distinguished Toastmaster, an accomplishment that fewer than 1% of Toastmasters members have attained.

Fourthly, I experienced being laid off from the Federal Reserve Bank of San Francisco, an organization that had become like family to me.

Last but not least, I completed my autobiography. The idea to write my life story had occurred to me nine years prior, and I had shared it with many friends and professional writers, but due to a combination of poor work ethic and lack of resources, nothing ever materialized. During the pandemic, I hired a professional writer for $2,000 to help me with the project. We met virtually on Zoom for almost three months, but when it was time for him to deliver the introduction and first chapter, he vanished, and I never got my money back.

After learning of my misfortune, Xiaoyu Duan, my friend, a part-time screenwriter who also worked for the Fed, came to my aid. Despite his busy schedule, he offered to co-write with me, and we spent over three years working on the project.

As the world seems to be settling into a new order, I look back and am surprised that I was able to spend more than eight months of the year at home without venturing out. It might sound easy to some readers, but as a social creature, being around people is essential for me. Nevertheless, when push came to shove, I managed to do something that I was unaccustomed to doing. I often think about those who did not survive the initial outbreak when the world was unprepared for a major disease outbreak, and I consider myself very fortunate to still have loved ones around me.

Although COVID put a stop to my travels, it also presented me an opportunity to think, contemplate, and slow down. Working on this project forced me to think about my life's choices and why I made them. I realized that I have been speeding on the fast lane without a clear destination in mind. At times, I attended networking events without knowing what I was networking for.

Xiaoyu helped me to realize that I had been searching for something. Growing up without much attention from my father and living away from home since my childhood, I never developed an emotional connection with my family like most children. Throughout my life, I have attempted to interact with people in a way that makes me feel connected and valued.

Ultimately, my connections with family and friends are what matter most to me. I have come to understand that life is a journey, not a destination. Personal achievements and financial success are merely components of the process. In life, the most crucial aspect is seeking, whether it be for wealth, relationships, career, or something else. If you are actively seeking something, life may surprise you and grant you more than you ever looked for.

Figure 67 Xiaoyu and me visiting the US Air Force base in Mountain View (2022)

Chapter 46:
Bidding Farewell to Mother

As I was immersed in the process of writing my book, a pivotal moment disrupted my routine on February 9th, 2022. A Google Chat message from Deva, my niece in Pondy, delivered distressing news—my mother had just been admitted to the hospital.

Immediately, I called my nephew Lokesh, who informed me that my mother had suffered a stroke while alone in our village house early that morning. Tragically, with both front and back doors locked, she lay helplessly on the floor, unable to seek assistance until our loyal servant, Chandra, arrived for work an hour later. Chandra knocked on the door and received no response, which alerted her that something was amiss, so she sought help from neighbors. Unfortunately, without the key, they had to wait for Sridhar, a family friend living nearby, to come and break open the door with an iron rod. Upon entering, they found my mother motionless on the floor. Without delay, they rushed her to the nearest hospital in Madagadipet, about three kilometers away.

The key factor in stroke recovery is timely medical intervention. However, in my mother's case, over two hours had elapsed before she received medical attention, rendering the damage irreversible. The stroke had left her left side paralyzed. It pained me to hear her condition, and I could not wait to run to her bedside. However, my Indian visa had expired, and it would take me weeks to get a new one.

I prepared all the required documents and submitted the visa application as soon as I could, but it was rejected by the embassy several days later because of "formatting errors." Undeterred, I resubmitted the documents but was rejected again for the same "formatting issue," but they did not say what exact formatting issue it was. Feeling exasperated, I sought clarification from the embassy via email, detailing my predicament and seeking guidance on the correct formatting protocol. They replied to me with a simple question, "If it's an urgent issue, why don't you apply for an e-visa?"

E-visa? A simple Google search revealed that India now offers certain visa categories for online processing, with a standard turnaround time of 72 hours. I followed the steps and successfully received the visa within a couple of days, enabling me to swiftly embark on my journey to India.

Upon my arrival at the hospital, I found my mom in bed with tubes and needles stuck to her frail body. Approaching her bedside, I gently clasped her hands in mine. She opened her eyes and saw me. Tears started flowing down her cheeks, but she could not say anything. A mixture of sadness, anger, and guilt came over me. The sadness of witnessing her suffering, compounded by the frustration of my delayed presence and the gnawing guilt of wondering whether her condition could have been averted in some way, engulfed me in inner turmoil.

I could barely fathom the whirlwind of emotions coursing through her mind. She may never be able to get out of bed and walk again. She may never even be able to savor a meal again. She could only take liquid substances fed through a tube. The prospect of playing with her great-grandchildren or orchestrating familial gatherings, once her favorite activities, seemed distant and unreachable.

Following a ten-day hospitalization, mom was discharged and relocated to Pillayarkuppam, a coastal village south of Pondy, where my sister Vijaya resides. There, she received diligent care, including sessions with a physiotherapist to facilitate her recovery. Although she still relied on tube feeding, her cognitive faculties and speech showed an impressive ninety percent return to normalcy. We hired a nurse to provide around-the-clock care in her room. My sister Vijaya was also there for both physical and emotional support. Mom asked me to regularly feed her drops of warm water, a responsibility I undertook with unwavering dedication.

Regrettably, after a mere two weeks, I had to return to the United States to work at E & J Gallo Winery. It was crucial as I was financially supporting both my mom's medical expenses and daily necessities. Despite my earnest request, my manager declined to extend my paid leave. I was already having a tough time at work, and this did not make it any easier. I cut my journey short and flew back to the US with a heavy heart.

During my tenure at E & J Gallo Winery, I experienced significant stress working under a manager who scrutinized every aspect of my performance. Recognizing the toll this environment was taking on me, I made the bold decision to resign from my position within a month after returning and transitioned into a full-time role in real estate with Realty Champion, where I worked under my friend Gowtham.

In December 2022, I reached out to my nephew Sathi in Chicago, and we decided to visit mom once more. Arriving within days of each other, Sathi and I found mom in good spirits, still able to recognize people and engage in coherent conversations despite her struggles. However, due to partial paralysis, she still relied on tube feeding for food. We had a new nurse named Lalitha, who provided meticulous care such as brushing her teeth, combing her hair, cutting her nails, and even bathing her. This significantly eased the burden on my family. Unfortunately, mom's recovery faced setbacks as she experienced considerable pain during physiotherapy sessions and hence resisted doing them.

Sathi and I also bought a new fridge, television, and washing machine for the family. Prior to this, they had been washing clothes by hand and lacked access to television. The old fridge was on the brink of breaking down. I remained with my family until Christmas before traveling to the Philippines with Sebastian, where I explored the vibrant cities of Manila and the serene landscapes of Palawan before returning to the United States.

In March 2023, I found myself back in India again for a wedding, reconnecting with old college friends Saravanan and Manohar from Melmaruvathur. Ruban, the husband of my niece Parimala, played a pivotal role in facilitating my travels, providing assistance with airport pickups, transportation, etc.

As mom appeared to be making progress in her recovery, a sudden seizure struck one day while I was by her side. She was convulsing with her body trembling, and foam gathered at her mouth. Following consultation with a doctor, we introduced additional medication to mitigate further seizures. After that, she struggled to speak but was still able to recognize familiar faces. Lalitha, the caregiver, had to take maternity leave, so we hired a new nurse named Ranjita, who not only provided excellent care through remarkable patience and compassion but also continued to stimulate mom's mind by talking with her constantly. Regrettably, I had to depart for the United States shortly after, saddened by the realization that my mother's clock on earth was ticking.

Meanwhile, back in the United States, my employer and friend, Gowtham, had recently acquired a children's party franchise called Pump It Up. He offered me the position of Operations Manager for the Santa Clara branch, and we launched the business in May 2023. The location's busiest periods are the weekends when birthday celebrations are at their peak. Although managing the venue posed its own share of challenges—from interacting with customers to staff coordination and logistics—it provided a much better work-life balance compared to my previous role at E & J Gallo Winery. Weekdays were mostly about website management, customer inquiries, and online training. It allows me to work remotely from home, attend to personal matters, and do things at my own pace.

Just as everything seemed to be back on track, in December 2023, I received a call from my nephew Lokesh regarding my mom's deteriorating health. Her hands had swelled, she had ceased speaking, and she could no longer recognize those around her. Lokesh was deeply concerned and urged me to return to India immediately. I promptly sought permission for leave from Gowtham, who granted it without hesitation. Wasting no time, I began searching for flight options. The ticket price was high during the holiday season, but I couldn't care less. Ultimately, I bought a 32-hour flight with two layovers for $1200 and arrived in India within a week.

The sight of mom, after nearly two years, was truly heart-wrenching. She remained unresponsive, even with her eyes open. Her once agile right hand now lay motionless and swollen, signaling a significant decline in her bodily functions. After careful deliberation, my family and I decided against hospitalization, recognizing the diminished quality of life it would offer. Ten days following my return, she began to struggle with her breathing. We administered a nebulizer to ease her discomfort, though it provided only temporary relief.

On the morning of December 29th, for some odd reason, I decided to check on my mother around 4 am. Finding her seemingly at ease, I went back to bed and later proceeded with my usual morning run to the beach. Upon my return, my sister Vijaya shouted for me from mom's room. I rushed in and found my nephews, Nithi and Lokesh, alongside Vijaya and my brother-in-law, Ramasamy, gathering around mom's bed. As I gently touched her, I realized her body had grown cold, and her breath had ceased. Vijaya wept, and we stood in disbelief, overwhelmed by grief. The attending nurse confirmed that she was gone. Mom breathed her last breath around 7 am on that fateful day.

It was a sad end to a great life. Mom went through significant challenges to raise the five of us. She commanded respect from our relatives, often being the first to be invited to any event due to her exceptional event-planning skills. Despite limited resources, she made the impossible possible for us. Reflecting back, I regret being too harsh on her when she borrowed money. I failed to empathize with her circumstances. Though her actions may have been deemed wrong, she had no alternative. With her passing, I lost not only my last immediate family member on earth but also the person who cared about me the most, leaving a void within me.

We arranged for her body to be transferred from Pillayrkuppam to Kothambakam in a private ambulance, where we conducted her funeral according to Hindu traditions. As her only son, I performed the final rites, cremating her the following morning. On the 13th day, we organized an elaborate ceremony officiated by a priest and said farewell to my beloved mom.

During those two weeks, I stayed at our village house, overwhelmed by nostalgia for the place where I grew up. Observing its fragility, I decided to hire an engineer and a contractor to undertake its restoration, a process estimated to span two years. Now, however, it was time for me to return to the US.

Figure 68 My mother and me at the Statue of Liberty (2011)

Figure 69 With mom in Kothambakam Village (2018)

Chapter 47:

Thanking People Along the Journey

While writing my book, Xiaoyu suggested that I call and thank those who helped me throughout my life. I decided to start by reaching out to Dr. Ellerbruch, the former head of the Department of Electrical Engineering at South Dakota State University, who offered me the teaching assistantship when I needed financial help the most.

Dr. Ellerbruch had unexpectedly offered me a teaching assistantship when I desperately needed financial support after transferring to SDSU. I called the administration office to obtain his number, but the administrator had to search for it and promised to call me back as Dr. Ellerbruch had retired several years ago. I was uncertain whether she would be able to locate it, and even if she did, I wondered whether the number was still valid and if Dr. Ellerbruch would remember me after so many years.

My phone rang. I was taken aback to hear from the administrator so soon. She had found Dr. Ellerbruch's number. I immediately dialed the number and a man answered the phone. It was Dr. Ellerbruch's unmistakable voice. I introduced myself and asked if he remembered me. Unfortunately, he was unable to recall, as he had interacted with thousands of students over the past 30 years. Nonetheless, I expressed my appreciation for the opportunity he had given me by offering the teaching assistant position.

I explained to him that my family was struggling financially due to high-interest loans and could not afford to pay for my college tuition in US dollars at the time. The teaching assistantship came at the perfect time and saved me from financial turmoil. With his help, I successfully completed my master's degree, relocated to California, established a career, and built a life. I cannot fathom what would have happened to my life without his timely assistance. Dr. Ellerbruch expressed his delight in having played a role in my journey and was impressed by my lengthy career at the Fed. He also congratulated me on my son's imminent high school graduation.

I inquired about his wellbeing. Despite being in his late 80s, he was in excellent health and was capable of tending to household chores such as lawn mowing. He raised three successful children while serving as the head of the department and dean of the university, holding a successful career. His life was a model for living happily and contentedly through hard work and helping others. Now, he spends most of his time with his grandchildren. I was grateful for his participation in my US journey and hoped to visit him in Brookings soon.

The second person I wish to express gratitude to is David Moezidis, my former manager at KLA Tencor. When I was fresh out of college and searching for employment, David took a chance on me by offering me a contractor job, which later turned into a full-time position. He even offered to sponsor my work visa and green card a few years later despite the considerable cost and inconvenience it entailed. This was a big favor, considering the company could have easily hired someone locally and avoided the hassle altogether.

David was a constant source of support through thick and thin. He granted me five weeks of leave when I traveled to India to get married, permitted me to work on weekends, and used compensation time to cover my vacation. He served as a mentor, a friend, and a well-wisher, always watching out for my success in both my professional and personal life. We lost touch after I left the company.

Recently, I stumbled upon David's contact details on LinkedIn and sent him a message. He responded right away. Now he is the Vice President of a major company in the Bay Area. Despite his hectic schedule, he instructed me to schedule an appointment with his administrator for a zoom meeting. And true to his word, he joined the meeting on time.

I expressed my gratitude to David for the opportunity he gave me and for taking care of me. Curious, I asked him what he saw in me. He explained that he admired how I carried myself, interacted with others, and conducted myself at work. I praised him as the best manager I had ever worked with, which elicited a laugh from him. He expressed his pleasure in my call and was glad to have been able to shape my career and be part of my journey. He also shared that he was doing well, living with his wife and two children.

During our conversation, we discussed our colleagues at the time, including Ferdinand, who was intelligent, hardworking, and loved cars. Sadly, he passed away suddenly in his early 50s due to a heart attack. I was shocked at his untimely passing. It reminded me of the importance of maintaining proper health habits. As we age, we must take care of ourselves and adopt healthy lifestyles.

Moving on to my thank-you list, another important person is Ramanujam, who had taken a risk and helped me with my sponsorship despite never having met me in person. When I left India for college, my third brother-in-law, Vijayaraghavan, gave me his name and number as a contact in case I needed assistance. Ramanujam resided in California at that time. Desperately needing a financial statement to transfer from the University of Central Oklahoma to South Dakota State University, I called him at 7 am central time, unaware that it was 5 am in California.

Nonetheless, he readily came to my aid, assuming the financial liability without any inquiries. As my sponsor, he would be accountable for any expenses incurred if I could not pay for tuition and living costs. Given that he barely knew me personally, it was a massive risk for him to take. Fortunately, I worked part-time to support myself and did not cause him any trouble. However, I never reached out to express my appreciation for his assistance.

In 2024, after a year-long search for Ramanujam's contact information, I finally got his number in my sister Samuktha's village, Vikravandi, where Ramanujam originally came from. I called him right away. Although he did not remember the encounter thirty years ago, he was delighted to receive my call. He cordially invited me to visit him.

Upon my arrival back in the States, I promptly paid a visit to Mr. Ramanujam at his residence in Santa Clara, which was about half an hour by car from where I lived. He is now 81 years old, and he lives with his wife, Shoba, and their children. He was a civil engineer before retirement and worked in various cities across the United States, including Detroit, Chicago, and Sacramento.

He welcomed me with enthusiasm, serving tea and snacks as we engaged in conversation. He presented me with a substantial journal containing receipts, checks, and correspondence from numerous educational institutions, charitable organizations, and hospitals in India. It turned out that since 1976, he had been actively contributing to these causes, displaying remarkable selflessness in his commitment to serving the community and beyond. His philanthropic efforts extended even to international disaster relief, including contributions to earthquake-stricken regions in Japan, India, and Pakistan. His dedication serves as a profound inspiration, motivating me to similarly assist others and contribute to the betterment of society.

In addition to Dr. Ellerbruch, David Moezidis, and Ramanujam, there are numerous other individuals who have helped me along the way. For example, when two professors in my department discontinued their guidance with me, Dr. Ali Salehnia graciously stepped in to guide me with my M.S. thesis, even though I was from a different department. He remained by my side for several years after I relocated to California, and we corresponded via postal mail regarding my thesis work.

Last but not least, while I am uncertain of their identities, I am also indebted to the hiring managers of the Department of Statistics at the Federal Reserve Bank. Being hired as a full-time employee at the Fed was a life-changing opportunity that paved the way for incredible experiences. Through this role, I formed lifelong friendships with individuals at the Fed and had the chance to travel the world while contributing to various organizations that supported those in need.

While I do not consider myself a successful person by any stretch of means, I acknowledge that I have reached several significant milestones that have guided my path in life. I could not have accomplished these milestones without the help and support of others. I am endlessly grateful for those who assisted me when I needed it the most, and I will strive to pay it forward by helping those who need support.

Figure 70 Dr. Ellerbruch's profile picture from SDSU Admin office when I enquired for his contact information in 2023

Figure 78 David Moezidis, my first manager at KLA Tencor (picture from internet)

Figure 71 Ramanajuam and me in his house in Santa Clara (2024)

Postlude:
Why Did I Write This Book?

As I am approaching my golden years, my childhood memories feel hazy and distant. It is almost as if I had two distinct lives on separate continents. Sometimes I wake up in bed, unsure where I am, and ponder how I became the person I am today.

A little boy from a remote village in South India dreamed of establishing a life in the best country in the world and dragging his family out of their financial whirlpool. I never thought it would be possible until I was in my late twenties. Even then, it still seemed like a pipedream. However, a fortuitous encounter while working as an associate lecturer in Bangalore changed my outlook. Seeing DR move to the US for school inspired me, and I realized that I, too, could achieve my aspirations if I dared to dream big. With perseverance, I eventually made my dream a reality.

The idea of writing my autobiography first came to me in 2014. Despite my lack of writing skills, I attempted to collaborate with various people but, unfortunately, made little progress. It was not until 2021 that my friend Xiaoyu Duan came to my rescue. Instead of focusing on chronologically recounting my life events, Xiaoyu emphasized understanding the motivation behind my desire to write this book. He asked an insightful question, "Why do you have to write this book?"

I had never given it much thought. While I knew I wanted to write a book, I did not fully comprehend its reason. Similarly, I attended networking events but lacked a clear understanding of what I hoped to achieve through them. It took me three weeks to grapple with this question, but we eventually arrived at an answer.

The truth is, I have always felt a sense of longing. Growing up without a father figure and away from my family's care, I craved emotional connection without even realizing it. I attended networking events with the intention of forging meaningful relationships with others. Volunteering activities allowed me to become a part of other people's lives. I assumed the role of a mentor at school and in Toastmasters because I enjoyed the connections that felt akin to a father-son dynamic.

Now, it all makes sense.

Over the following weeks, Xiaoyu told me to document all significant life events and inquire why they held importance to me. This exercise allowed me to delve deeper into my psyche at various stages of my life. I gained substantial insight into my personality and the qualities that molded me into the person I am today. Through this writing and exploration process, I learned a great deal about myself, and I never imagined I could generate such comprehensive reflections.

Now that I have achieved my goal of settling in the US, I aspire to make a positive impact on others. I have already seen evidence of my ability to do so, and I take pride in my accomplishments thus far. I plan to further cultivate this through mentoring young people to become responsible global citizens and helping those in need. Additionally, I intend to travel the world and learn about different cultures, their lifestyles, and how I can be of assistance. My public speaking skills honed through Toastmasters will serve as a platform to share my experiences.

Through this book, I would also like to share the significance of environmental issues with you. I am passionate about educating people on global warming and how we can all contribute to improving the world. By making small changes in our daily routine, such as replacing a regular light bulb with a compact fluorescent light bulb, we can save up to 150 pounds of carbon dioxide emissions each year. Similarly, reducing our driving also helps in lowering carbon emissions. I have been driving a hybrid car since 2003 and recently switched to an electric one. In addition, I have been able to minimize my driving by working from home.

Recycling has always been one of my top priorities. Since most of our belongings are made of plastic, recycling them can significantly contribute to environmental preservation. It is crucial to clean plastic thoroughly before recycling. Also, reducing the purchase and usage of packaged materials will help reduce plastic waste.

Composting is another crucial practice that I value deeply. California is one of the few states that promote composting and provide separate compost bins for every household. Composting enriches the soil, retains moisture, and prevents plant diseases and pests. It also reduces the need for chemical fertilizers while promoting beneficial bacteria and fungi that break down organic matter to create humus, a nutrient-rich material.

My ultimate goal in addressing environmental issues is to plant trees. Unfortunately, the current global production of tree-planting falls short. Human activity destroys around 15 billion trees annually, with only 5 billion trees being replanted. This rate equates to a net loss of 10 billion trees each year. All trees will be gone in the next 300 years if we continue at this rate. This fact is alarming and raises concerns about what kind of planet we are leaving for our great descendants. The absence of trees would lead to the extinction of numerous animal and bird species and the drying up of land. Moreover, dead wood would increase the frequency of wildfires, which would generate soot that blocks the sun, leading to failed harvests and global famine. We have already witnessed the dire consequences of such occurrences in different parts of the world.

However, it is not too late to change our destiny. I have come across inspiring stories of individuals who have single-handedly created forests in places like West Bengal, India, Indonesia, Florida, etc. By planting more trees, we can prevent the terrible fate that awaits us and mitigate other environmental problems. For instance, trees aid in absorbing carbon and reducing global warming. To achieve this, I want to start an organization called "Friends of the Rural Forest" to primarily educate and encourage people from rural areas to plant trees. I was motivated by the "Friends of the Urban Forest" organization in San Francisco, which has done an excellent job of planting trees over the past four decades with the help of sponsorship from private companies and volunteers.

Poverty is an essential issue that has affected my life since childhood. Through firsthand experience, I have witnessed the struggles and sufferings of people living in poverty. While donating is vital, I aspire to do more for underprivileged families by helping their children receive an education. Education can break the vicious cycle of poverty, as it has for my family. By providing knowledge, individuals can acquire the skills, expertise, and infrastructure necessary to meet basic and advanced needs.

With the abundance of advanced technology and information readily available today, educating individuals to become better citizens is much easier than it was when I was growing up. Effective citizens should integrate their passions, skills, and responsibilities by participating in civic engagement programs and preparing for lives as active members of their communities and professions. By setting an example through my actions, I aim to build a society that thrives, grows, and enhances people's lives, leading to a better future for our planet's generations to come. This is my ultimate goal, and writing this book has empowered me with the courage and holds me accountable to work tirelessly toward achieving it.

I am eternally grateful to all those who have helped me along the way, and I will do the same for the ones in need of help.

I want to leave you with a story of the starfish.

As a young man was strolling along the ocean, he came across a beach with numerous starfish stranded on the sand and facing an inevitable scorching death. An old man was walking along the shore, moving slowly and halting frequently to pick up the starfish, one by one, and gently toss them into the ocean. Perplexed, the young man asked the old man, "Why are you doing this? You can't possibly save all of the starfish. What you're doing doesn't make a difference at all!" The old man responded by tossing another starfish back into the water, saying, "It made a difference to that one."

My life was exactly like that starfish several times washed up on the shore. Someone always found me on the seashore and rescued me and threw me back into the seawater. Mr. Ramanujam did it when I was applying for my masters at South Dakota State University. Dr.Ellerbruch did it when I was doing my masters in Electrical Engineering by offering me assistantship which paid for my school entirely. David Moezidis did it when I was looking for my first job in the semiconductor industry by offering me a position as Customer Acceptance Engineer at KLA

Instruments. Xiaoyu did it when I set out to write this book by helping me put this book together. I am indebted to all these people in my life forever. Hopefully I can pay it forward to others and help them in their pursuit of a better life. That would be my goal in life going forward. There is no greater joy in life than serving others.